Charles Dorrance Linskill

**Travels in Lands Beyond the Sea**

Beauty and glory of western Europe, pen pictures of castles, cathedrals, and cities

Charles Dorrance Linskill

**Travels in Lands Beyond the Sea**

*Beauty and glory of western Europe, pen pictures of castles, cathedrals, and cities*

ISBN/EAN: 9783337292256

Printed in Europe, USA, Canada, Australia, Japan

Cover: Foto ©Andreas Hilbeck / pixelio.de

More available books at **www.hansebooks.com**

# TRAVELS

## IN LANDS

# BEYOND THE SEA.

BEAUTY AND GLORY OF WESTERN
EUROPE.

## ELOQUENT AND RELIABLE PEN PICTURES

— OF —

CASTLES, CATHEDRALS AND CITIES; PALACES, PRISONS AND
PEOPLE; MUSEUMS, MONUMENTS AND MOUNT-
AINS: SEAS, SHIPS AND STORMS.

CHARLES D. LINSKILL,

EDITOR WILKES-BARRÉ "TELEPHONE," AND AUTHOR OF THE "HERE
AND THERE" LETTERS.

WILKES-BARRÉ, PA.:
ROBT. BAUR & SON, PRINTERS, 3 S. MAIN ST.
1888.

TO THE

COMRADES OF MY YOUTH,

WHOSE COMPANIONSHIP CHEERED ME;

TO THE

ASSOCIATES OF MY EARLY MANHOOD,

WHOSE CONFIDENCE STRENGTHENED ME;

AND TO THE

FRIENDS OF MY MATURE YEARS,

WHOSE PATRONAGE

HAS ENABLED ME TO TRAVEL AND WRITE,

THIS VOLUME

IS RESPECTFULLY DEDICATED.

# PRESS NOTICES.

*From Editor J. C. Powell, of the Wilkes-Barré Record, and Published in the Issue of Dec. 13th, 1888 :*

I met Mr. Linskill, author and editor, the other day, and he told me his new book would soon make its appearance. I predict for the volume a large sale as soon as it is launched. Mr. Linskill is a good descriptive writer and while abroad he traveled with his eyes and ears wide open. The letters that he sent to the *Telephone* were very interesting, and they gave him ample scope for the exercise of his literary powers; but his book will be still more interesting, for he has had time since his return to scan his note-book carefully and to search for the buried treasures of his mind. I am not surprised that Judge Harding, in ordering a copy of the forthcoming book, should predict that it would prove so interesting and valuable that it would supplant in his library a place hitherto occupied by some of the rarest gems in English literature.

*From the Plymouth Star :—*

Charles D. Linskill, of the Wilkes-Barré *Telephone*, is arranging his letters from Europe, which were originally published in his paper (where they attracted a great deal of attention and were most favorably commented upon), for publication in book form. * * * The price will be two dollars, which places it within the reach of all. * * * Mr. Linskill's letters have been highly praised and their publication in book form urged by many prominent men.

Nov. 8th, 1888.

*From the Evening Leader, Wilkes-Barré, Pa. :—*

MR. LINSKILL'S BOOK SOON TO BE ISSUED.

"Travels in Lands Beyond the Sea; or, the Beauty and Glory of Western Europe," is the title under which Mr. C. D. Linskill will soon lay before the public a detailed history of his journeyings abroad. They will constitute a book of over four hundred pages, and those who have read his foreign correspondence to the *Telephone*, of which he is one of the editors, well know how to appreciate the forthcoming work. He has received flattering testimonials from clergymen, judges and other professional men of note, and indications point to a very large sale.

*From the Wilkes-Barré Telegram:—*

Mr. C. D. Linskill's new book, entitled " In Lands Beyond the Sea; or, the Beauty and Glory of Western Europe," is a most interesting book and a copy of it should be in every household. The price asked for it is extremely low. The author is well and favorably known to nearly every person in Luzerne county.

*From the Wilkes-Barré News-Dealer:—*

Mr. Charles D. Linskill, the versatile writer, is editing an interesting book which will be given to the public in a short time. Its title will be " Travels in Lands Beyond the Sea; or, the Beauty and Glory of Western Europe." We have read with much interest Mr. Linskill's recent letters from Europe, which were not only very interesting, but instructive as well. We predict a large sale for the new book.

*From the Sunday World:—*

Editor Linskill, of the *Telephone*, is writing a book entitled " Travels in Lands Beyond the Sea," which is shortly to appear. The book will be interesting and instructive, clothed in that beautiful language for which Mr. Linskill is famous.

## CONTENTS.

PRESS NOTICES . . . . . . . . . . . . . . . . . . . . v
TESTIMONIALS . . . . . . . . . . . . . . . . . . . 16

### CHAPTER I.

INTRODUCTORY. . . . . . . . . . . . . . . . . . . 25

 Why and How this Volume Was Published—The Author's Father—Came from England—Settled in Pennsylvania—Asked His Son to Make Pilgrimage—His Sudden Death—Correspondence Lasting Sixty Years—White, Roaring Billows Cannot Drown Love Letters—Bereavement, Sorrow, Labors and Cares Call for Rest and Change—A Friend Indeed—Getting Ready to Go—Passport, and Letters from Prominent Men—Governor Beaver's Letter—Congressman Osborne's Letter—Other Letters—Taking Leave—America's Shores Sink in Silver—At Liverpool—Through England, Ireland, Scotland, Wales, France; Paris and London—Relatives Helpful—Weather Most Auspicious—Things Pictured on the Spot—Good Wishes—Grasp Each Reader by the Hand.

### CHAPTER II.

FROM THE MOUNTAINS TO THE SEA . . . . . . . . . . . . 32

 Saying "Good Bye" to Relatives, Partner and Friends—Looking Down on Luzerne and Other Counties—In New Jersey—Rushing Through Cities While Long, White, Guardian Arms Rise and Fall—In New York—Central Park—Monuments and Monsters from Beyond the Sea—Carriages for Pale Babies, and Proud Millionaires—Took Baggage to Steamship—At Coney Island; its Hotels, its Flowers, its Swimmers, its Wine, its Women, its Tower, its Friends—A Sea-shell Containing Sixty-five Master Musicians—The Gardens Blossom With Fire—A Place to Learn—A Place to Fall—Sham Battle—Bay Full of

(1)

Ships at Night — The Heavens Frescoed With Colored Lights — Statue of Liberty — Brooklyn Bridge; an Artificial Midnight Rainbow — Ready to Wave a Farewell to My Native Land.

## CHAPTER III.

"Behold Also the Ships" . . . . . . . . . . . . . . . . 40

Twenty-three Hundred Miles of Billows — Passengers Variously Engaged — Look Through the Great Ship; Where Built; Her Size; One-tenth of a Mile Long; Her Weight; Her Mines of Coal — Passengers — Crew — Two Stories Under Water — The Steerage — The Gilded Saloon — Ten Thousand Horses of Steel to Conquer the Sea — The Raging Furnaces and Sweating Firemen on the Floor of the Ship — "You Are Chalked" — The Vast, Virtuous Ocean — Noon in the Deep — Time Annihilated — The Iron Tunnel — Thirty-five Boat Loads of Fuel — Man Moves All the Oceans — Queenstown — Letters — On to Liverpool.

## CHAPTER IV.

On the Great Deep . . . . . . . . . . . . . . . . . . . 47

On Board the Ship — Hot Day — An Acre of Waving Handkerchiefs, Damp With Tears and Perspiration — Band Plays "Auld Lang Syne" — Moving off Through a Labyrinth of Great Things — Other Europe-bound Steamers — Officers Vigilant — Hills Sink With the Sun at the West End of a Broad, Silver Avenue — Hot Below Deck — My Bedroom — My Comrades — The Spouting Whale — Ship Fare — Sunday on the Sea — Religious Services — Fog — Birds — Porpoises — Big Fish — Colored Fish — The Sea Tries to Mimic the Heavens — A World of Water Five Miles Deep; its Gleaming Arms Encircle the Icy North and the Spicy Groves of "Far Cathay" — Friends on Deck — What Sea Water is Like — People from all Over the United States and Canada — A Gallant Earl and His Fair Countess; Gentle Folks; They Amuse and Treat Poor Children — Names of Some Fellow-passengers — Ocean Rough — Many Ill — The Writer Keeps Well and Sways in a Hammock Worth Fifteen Hundred Thousand Dollars — Cool on the Sea in July — Ireland Seen Through Fog — Pleasant Sight — The Old "Stow-a-way" Receives a Sovereign — Off Queenstown — Sailing Under Birds on the Irish Sea.

## CHAPTER V.

THE IRISH SEA, AND LIVERPOOL.................. 60

Sunday Afternoon of Beauty and Peace — Heaven Weds Earth — Mountain Peaks in Wales — Nobility, Peasantry, Beauty and Genius Sing on Deck — Twilight Enchanting—Ladies Scream and Faint—Revolving Lights Twinkle on England's Shores — Liverpool — Our Ship Linked to 18,000 Pounds of Steel on the Floor of the Sea —Mr. Puckey Finds Me—Liverpool Docks — Cost Hundreds of Millions of Dollars — A Vast Ship-safe — The World's Merchandise Piled on Chiseled Rocks—Acres of American Pork and Lard—Handsome Ladies—Horses a "Ton Weight" — A Horse Under Seven Tons of Plate Glass—Great Buildings— Forlorn Creatures — Railway Trains Roaring Under Hundreds of Ships — A Wilkes-Barré Girl Met — Mighty Ships Cushioned in Granite Vases—The Angel of Light Places Her Jeweled Foot on the Flowing Mane of the Sea.

## CHAPTER VI.

LIVERPOOL, MANCHESTER AND LEEDS.............. 74

Liverpool Buildings Gloomy—Seemed to Show Mourning—Death on Shipboard—Pet Names—Traveling Underground—English Cars, Locomotives and Stations—Thirty-six Miles in Forty-five Minutes—Oaks Killed by Smoke— English Landscapes — Great, Busy Manchester — Ship Canal — Magnificent Hall — Forty Acres of Masterpieces in Art, Machinery, Architecture, and Flora—Crowds of Handsome, Well-dressed Women — Gardens Blooming with Colored Lights — Fountains of Gilded Water — A Sweet Voice—Riding Through Long, Dark Highways in Granite — Hedges, Stone Walls—Under Three Miles of Rock—Acres of Smoking Chimneys—The Guest of Kind People — Pleasant Walk — Extensive Buildings — Great Co-operative Concern — Street-cars — Dummies—Road Engines.

## CHAPTER VII.

YORK AND WHITBY...................... 83

Through Farms—August First, Wheat not Ripe—City of York — Its Beauty—Its Antiquity—Promenade on Its Old and Beautiful Wall — Roman Stone Coffins — Old Places—Old Church Hidden in a City — Magnificent Old York Minster; A Window Four Hundred Years Old Makes the Sun Paint Rare Pictures, "Worth a Kingdom;" Covers Two Thousand Four Hundred and Fifty-six Square Feet—A Tall Stone Ladder—Angel Tones—Choir Uniformed—History of the Cathedral—On Through Yorkshire Highlands—Grouse on Purple Heather—River Esk—Cousin John Wears Livery—Whitby—Cousin Edward—One Linskill—High Cliff—White Waves Die at the Feet of Beauty and Innocence—The Panoramic Sea—Grandparents' Graves Near Great Columns and Arches in Ruins.

## CHAPTER VIII.

WHITBY, JET, WHALING, SHIPS, ETC. . . . . . . . . . . . . 96

A Cleft Cliff—Houses Hanging on Rocks Above Ships—Red Tiles—Narrow Streets—The Market Place—Strawberries in August—Fishwomen—Tons of Fish Gasping on Granite Pavements, and Buried in Salt and Ice—Elegant West Cliff—London Visitors—Cold—Many Ships—A Walk With Edward—Ship-Building—Windmill—By the Sea—Uncle James—A Railway on Tall, Iron Stilts Above a Granite Hamlet, and Hay-Makers by the Chapel—A Walk With Friend Waddington—His Varied and Agreeable Attainments—A Walking and Free Library—Captain Cook—Hilda's Fine Ruins—Ancient Church—Humble Elliot Wrested a Title From Fate and Royalty—A Feast at a Saloon in a Cliff—Men Gone Down to the Sea to Take Whales, Fish, Gold and Kingdoms—Jaw-Bones of Whales set up for Garden and Farm Gates—Alum—Jet-Works and Jet-Workers—When the Lordly Die, Jet-Dealers Thrive.

## CHAPTER IX.

LONDON: GREAT AND BEAUTIFUL THINGS. . . . . . . . . . . . 104

Heart of England—Leamington, Warwickshire—Oxford—Wisdom Crowns Wasting Stone—On to London—Sixty-Three Miles in Seventy-Five Minutes—Suburbs of the Great City—Paddington's Great Station—House of Parliament—Chamber of Commons—Music Wedded to Time—Sir John Puleston—House of Lords—Westminster Abbey—Cousins Found—Trafalgar Square—National Art Gallery—The "Wild West"—Blanketed Indians Under the Stars and Stripes in the World's Largest City—Awful Lightning and Thunder—Buffalo Bill, While Galloping, Shatters Glittering Balls Amid Lightning and Falling Rain—"Brother Jonathan" and "Johnny Bull" Contending Amid Clashing Elements, etc.

## CONTENTS.  5

### CHAPTER X.

LONDON: THE FOG, THAMES, AND PARKS. . . . . . . . . . . 114

Smoke from a Million Chimneys—One Hundred and Fifty Square Miles of Buildings—A Modern Jonah—Plaided with Railways—Seven Thousand Miles of Streets—London Fog—Dinner by Lamp-light—Lost in the Street—Walked into the Dock—Beef Cattle Choke—Travel Blockaded—Mails Late—Crushed by Wheels Unseen—What Makes the Fog—Particles of Soot Encased in Oil and Clogged in Mist—Foggy Days Elsewhere—Moral—The Thames: a River, Sea, Sewer, Highway and Harbor—Embankment—Obelisk—Moses, Napoleon and Others—Royal Dwellings—Parks—Palaces—Black Thorns and Bright Bayonets.

### CHAPTER XI.

LONDON'S VASTNESS, ST. PAUL'S CATHEDRAL, ETC . . . . . . 129

Fifteen Miles Through Mighty Buildings—Asking for Bread on Stone Beds—St. Paul's Marvelous Cathedral; it Whispers—Marble Horses Kneel Down With Sheriffs While Saul of Tarsus Asks a Question—Angels, Women and Warriors, in Polished Marble and Bronze, Glorifying Dead Heroes—Traveling Without Loss—A Purse Thrust Into a Stranger's Bosom—A Digression—Fragments—Another Digression—Hospital Floating Through Salt Billows—The Cruel God of the Sea—Three Grand Sights—The Land of Indian Summer—Glory Undreamed of.

### CHAPTER XII.

BILLINGSGATE, TOWER OF LONDON, FIRE, GREENWICH . . . . 137

Fish, Carloads and Shiploads—Where Slang Was Born—Monument of London—A Thousand Acres of Buildings Bow Into Ashes—Wild Fire Darts its Red Tongue at the King and at the Heavens—The Tower of London—Dungeons Dark for a Thousand Years—Old Weapons of War Blossom in Bouquets and Decorate the Ceiling—Lady Jane Grey—Traitor's Gate—Fifteen Million Dollars' Worth of Jewelry—Garments Worn by Lovers and Warriors—Cannon from the Floor of the Bone-paved Sea—Riding on the Thames—Greenwich—Naval School—Forest of Fine Columns—Painted Hall—Ship Models—Nelson Painted a God—True to the Vision.

## CHAPTER XIII.

**CRYSTAL PALACE, WESTMINSTER ABBEY, QUEEN'S HORSES, ETC. . 149**

Crystal Palace; its Fountains, Statues, Paintings, and Oriental Halls—South Kensington; a City of Palaces Crowded With Beauties and Wonders—The Queen's Monument to a Loving Husband—The Museum—The First Steam Engine—Natural Science Museum—Birds Tall and Swift as Horses—Five Thousand Humming Birds—Whales, Etc.—The British Museum—Madam Toussaud's Wax Kings, Queens, Poets, Warriors, and Murderers—A Walk Under the River Thames—Spurgeon, London's Preacher—City Temple—Westminster Abbey, Where the Famous Dead Sleep for Centuries—Solemn Place, Where Stone Faces Gaze Heavenward—Stone Lace for Frescoing—Marble, Granite, Brass and Bronze Blossom Into Angels and Bouquets to Glorify the Beloved Dead—The Queen's Stables—Sixteen Princely Horses, and Two Grooms in One Bedroom—Morocco Harness, Gold-bound—Gilded Chariots.

## CHAPTER XIV.

**SOME PEOPLE AND PLACES BEYOND THE SEA . . . . . . . . . . 162**

Questions Answered—A Floating Volcano—Warhorses With White Manes—Ocean Robed in Crimson, Green and Gold—People and Clouds Smile—Places Visited—The Largest City—The Most Beautiful City—The Largest Ship—Where Cannon Shook Purple Heather—Cousins Met in Ancient and Famous Cities—A Walk on the Moors—Turf Cakes and Milk—A Popular Authoress—With Edward on His Locomotive—Uncle James's Blessing—Kind Friends Mentioned.

## CHAPTER XV.

**FROM LONDON TO PARIS, VIA DOVER AND CALAIS . . . . . . . 170**

A Highway Upheld on Polished Granite Pillars—Barbers and Their Work—Moving out of London—Hops in Kent—Nine Tunnels—Mary Anderson and Moonlight in Canterbury's Glory—Dover; Its Chalk Cliffs, Its Barracks, Its Boasting Cannon—Martin's Picture of Cut Woods—Leave England Before Midnight—"Caffa" in "Calla" Before Starting for "Parra"—He Knew the Stomach Better than the Tongue—Locomotives Black, Green, Yellow, Brown—The Engine Snorted Above a Tempest of French Words—Rushing Through Oatfields and Willows, by Flocks and Still Waters, in "Sunny

France"—The Sea Divorced England from France—Amiens—Trees Like Soldiers—In Paris—Lonesome without Dinner and Friends—Three Bottles of Wine—Cook & Son—Met a Yankee in "Place Vendome"—Obelisk of Luxor—Place de la Concorde—Arc de Triomphe—Champs Elysées, etc.

## CHAPTER XVI.

PARIS: PLACES OF BEAUTY AND PLACES OF BLOOD . . . . . 183

Place de la Concorde—The Glittering Knife—A Lake of Blood—Pranzina Beheaded—Baptism of Blood—Foreign Armies—Lions, Bears, Eagles, Dragons—Gilded Domes Tremble—A Needle Weighing Two Hundred and Forty Tons—Asking Others to Die for Us—Champs Elysées, a Street Unequalled—A Ball-room One and a Half Miles Long, Flanked by Two Kingdoms, Nature and Art, Full of Light, Music, Beauty and Wine—The Arc de Triomphe, a Glory to Uphold Glory—Cost Millions—Pictures in Marble and Bronze—Twelve Proud, Gay Avenues Bow at its Feet—It Shows Us a Wide Panorama of Magnificence—At Dinner—Linen, Silver, Crystal, Broadcloth, Silk, Lace, Silver Hands, Gold Fingers, Mirrors, Wine, Flowers and Fountains—An Hour and a Half Going from Soup and Fish to Wine, Grapes and Peaches.

## CHAPTER XVII.

PARIS: HER PAST, PRESENT; PALACES AND PRISON . . . . . 193

A City Peerless in Beauty—Buildings Bow to Winners of Glory—Eagle-mounted Banners and Numidian Lions—Cæsar in a Wolf Den—Many Palaces, Few Homes—Golden Argosies Wrecked Under Rainbows—The Strange Woman—Woe to the City—Dying Alone—Sunday in Paris—Wine Flows—Buildings Going Up, etc.—Boulevards, Columns, Arches, Fountains—An Island of Flowers Floating Through Jet to Honor the Dead and Please the Living—Place de la Bastile—Angry Men Let in the Sunlight and Behead the Keepers—On Top of a Fluted, Vibrating Column of Bronze—The Tall, Gilded Angel—Red Lines in the Pavement.

## CHAPTER XVIII.

PARIS: PLACES MAGNIFICENT AND GLORIOUS . . . . . . . . 201

Breakfast—Guided Through Palaces—Americans Met—The Madeleine—A Marble Splendor—The Decalogue

Swings in Bronze—True Art Calls for Tears—Three Hundred Communists Killed Near a Pulpit—Trocadéro Palace and Garden —Looking Down on a Canopy which Covers Seven Thousand Seats in Red Velvet—Steel Fingers Tower a Thousand Feet where Lightning Rules—Cathedrals Cut in Rock and Lighted by Rainbows, and Filled with Music of Seas, Birds, Thunder, etc. —Panorama of Rezonville—A Frozen Battle-field—America's Monument at Yosemite Smiling Among Clouds — Napoleon's Tomb, Guarded by Marble Heroes, Three Hundred and Forty Feet Below a Golden Hemisphere.

## CHAPTER XIX.

PARIS: CHURCHES, MARKET, CEMETERY . . . . . . . . . . . 208

Note-book in Hand—Palais Royal—Dine in the Famous place—Music—Red Wine—Church St. Eustache —Crowned with Beauty and Glory—Twelve Hundred Cellars Under Twenty-Two acres of Glass-Roofed Markets—Pere La Chaise—Twenty-two Thousand Attractive Homes for the Dead—Mighty men Sleeping in Marble Beds—Abelard and Heloise, Unhappy Lovers, in Marble, Side by Side, Gazing into the Heavens—Marshal Ney's Grass-Blade Monument—A Beautiful Park—The Louvre Palace—Art Gallery one-fourth of a mile in Length—Great Paintings—Brilliant Rooms.

## CHAPTER XX.

PARIS: NOTRE DAME, PANTHEON, ST. CLOUD. . . . . . . . . 216

Banks of the Seine—Gods Distilling Water—Bridges —How I asked Questions — Notre Dame — Impressive Building—A Marble Mountain with Pearls and Shells for Windows—Shrines—Relics—A Cathedral's use—Tower St. Jacques—The Pantheon—Artists on Scaffolds for Years—Monument to Heroes and Artists.—The Great Crown—Enroute to St. Cloud—Parc Monceau—Bois De Boulogne — Grand Avenue — Fine Vistas—Rothchild's Home—St. Cloud, Where the Great Napoleon Waved his Sword, and Vast Armies Shouted and Marched to Make Millions Mourn—Angels fly Heavenward—The Ruined Palace—The Zulu-slain Prince, etc.

## CHAPTER XXI.

VARSAILLES: FROM PARIS TO LONDON. . . . . . . . . . . . 227

Forest Ville D' Avray—Boulevard De La Reine—
—Versailles—A Palace a Fourth of a Mile Long—

Magnificence Brilliant with Glories—Cost One Hundred and Twenty-seven Million Francs—Kings and Queens—Pillars of Silver amid Rainbows, Bearing up Canopies of Gold—Sevres' China Palace—Shake Hands—Angelic Guides—The Wonderful Road Thirty-five Hundred Miles Long, Running Through Empires of Wealth, Lands of Milk and Honey, and Kingdoms of Beauty and Wonder—The United States Great in Cities and Railways—No Tattered Beggars—Rushing Through France By Moonlight—Rouen Sleeping—Dieppe by the Sea—The Sea Dances in Green and White—Sea Sickness—White Cliffs of England Seen Through Mist—Rushing Through Woods, Rocks, Meadows, and Towns to London.

## CHAPTER XXII.

FROM LONDON TO CARDIFF, WALES . . . . . . . . . . . . 236

Proud England by Moonlight—Shrewsbury Station—Coffee, Dogs and Babies at Midnight—Welsh Names—Hills and Vales—Water Leaping Into Green Valleys—Old Mines—Cardiff—A Letter Finds a Friend Among Heaps of Gold—Cardiff Castle—Bute Docks—The Arcade—Names from All Europe—Grapes Under Glass—A Kind Family—Penarth and Hospitality—A Popular Man—The Esplanade—Queenly Cities Lulled to Sleep—Carriages Roll and Ships Rock — Guardian Spirits Are Anxious Where Men and Women Meet Destiny—Great Printing Press—A Busy City—Farewell.

## CHAPTER XXIII.

FROM WALES TO SCOTLAND, VIA ENGLAND . . . . . . . . 243

Traveling in London — Railways Flooded — Golden Apples—Leaving Wales—Old Castle Blood-cemented—"Can We Smoke?"—Writing on Wheels Rapidly Rolling—Towns, Castles, Farms, Rivers, Mountains—Birmingham—Leamington, Warwickshire—Going to Middlesborough—Hills and Dales—Purple Snow—Kind Cousins in an Iron City Visited by Ships—Parks, Etc.—Statues for Brains and Enterprising Wealth—Enroute to Edinburgh—Durham—The Cathedral—Powerful Newcastle—Twenty-five Thousand Men Making Great Guns, Ships, Chains, Engines and Cars—Jubilee Exhibition—A Big Gun—Thousands of Modest Girls Serving—Off for Edinburgh.

## CHAPTER XXIV.

EDINBURGH, SCOTLAND. . . . . . . . . . . . . . . . . . 255

Health — Fine Weather — Kindness — Places Passed Through—Things Noted—Edinburgh—A Queenly City—Gospel Hymns in the Street—Arthur's Seat—Castle Hill—Calton Hill—A Slough Turned Into a Flowery Vale Full of Locomotives and Business—The Old Cannon-crowned Castle—Sir Walter Scott's Fine Monument—The Mound—Granite City—Spires, Monuments, Etc.—Holyrood Palace—Bird's-eye View—Bagpipes and Artillery—Plaided and Plumed Soldiers, Etc.

## CHAPTER XXV.

EDINBURGH, SCOTLAND. . . . . . . . . . . . . . . . . . 263

Ancient Banners Waved Over the Birth of Kings and Queens—Her Beauty and Glory—A Grand Ride—Tall Buildings on Ledges—High Street—Knox's House—The Old Castle—Five Hundred Feet Above the Sea—Soldiers in Red Coats and in Kilts, With Swords, Skean Dhus and Sporrans—A Great City Dressed in Gray Stone—Grass Market—St. Margaret's Chapel—Mon's Meg—Stone Cannon-balls—Crown Jewels—Queen Mary's Bedroom—A Cannon Roars at One O'Clock, Touched by Fingers Four Hundred Miles Long—What is Man?—Calton Hill—Nelson's Monument—Twelve Columns—Scotland's "Pride and Shame"—A Temple Deserted its Portico.

## CHAPTER XXVI.

EDINBURGH AND DUNFERMLINE, SCOTLAND . . . . . . . . . 269

Edinburgh—Like Home—Sober People—Magnificent Squares—Oases in Chiseled Rock—Five Stories Cut in Granite—Giant Breaking from Glass Fetters—On the Way to Dunfermline—Steel Spanning Sea Waves—Through a Mountain by Inverkeithing—Scotland's Old Capital—Ruins—Electricity Flashes Greetings—Metalic Horses—Linen Factories—Wheels Thunder and Shuttles Flash—Thirteen Thousand Women—Kind Friends—Goods Pictured for Columbia—A Walk—Steel Columns Above Blue Hills—Andrew Carnegie—Princely Giver—Scotch Hospitality—Old Palace Ruins Interesting—Fine Old Church—Deceptive Pillars—Pictures in Glass—Tombs of Kings—Curfew Rings Here—The Looms Battle—Working in Factories—Parents of Friends—Hospitality Makes Angels.

## CHAPTER XXVII.

SCOTLAND: A WONDERFUL BRIDGE, ETC . . . . . . . . . . . 281

Sea-waves Crouch Before Rulers of Kingdoms and Commerce — From Edinburgh to Dunfermline — South Queen's Ferry — Port Edgar — North Queen's Ferry — Towers of Granite and Steel Planted in Water — A Highway for the Passage of Fiery Chariots, Balanced on Circular Towers Forty Stories High — Machine Shops Suspended in Air — Thirty-one Men Killed — Four Thousand Men Riveting Forty-two Thousand Tons of Steel — Halcyon Days — The Sun Kisses the Water by a Ruined Castle — Pleasant Drive — The Lovers' Walk — Quiet, Quaint, Old Crossford — Kind Hearts — Walking Toward the Lights of Dunfermline

## CHAPTER XXVIII.

SCOTLAND: STERLING AND GLASGOW . . . . . . . . . . . . 288

From Dunfermline to Sterling — Mountains Like Lions, Shining Like Velvet — Sterling — Going Up by Famous Objects to Rocks Marble-Decked and Castle-Crowned — Cannon Roar Between the Clouds and the Winding Forth — Bridge of Allan — Abbey Craig — A Plain Decked with Rocks, Rivers, Sheep, etc. — A Cemetery Clad in Marble, Granite, Glass and Roses — Old Churches — Relics of Kings, Queens and Knox — Scotland's Standards — Ben-Lomond — Water Looped in double S's in Meadows Five Hundred Feet Below — Soldiers — Highlanders — Singing Witch — Bannockburn — Curious Monument — On to Glasgow — Thirty-six Hundred Grouse — Winan's Deer Park — Six Hundred Thousand Busy People — A Chimney Breathes Four Hundred and Thirty-five Feet Above the Pavements — A Great Road Walled Eight Stories High — Great Buildings — Glasgow Names — St. Enoch's Roaring Station.

## CHAPTER XXIX.

SCOTLAND: GREENOCK AND PAISLEY. . . . . . . . . . . . . 296

Greenock — Ships and Sugar — The Clyde — A Morning Walk — Mountain Peaks — Fairy Lands — Looking Down on Greenock — Scene Unsurpassed — Ajax — The Largest Ship — The Lyle Road — Esplanade — Highland Mary's Grave — Watt's Scientific Library — Telegraphy in 1753 — The Ship Yards — Paisley — Shawls and Thread — School Children — Thannhill — Wilson — Kilbarchan — Moving Toward Dumfries.

## CHAPTER XXX.

SCOTLAND: DUMFRIES . . . . . . . . . . . . . . . 303

By Train From Glasgow to Dumfries—Things Seen—History—Location—Churches—Walk with Mr. Sharp—Famous Names—Robert Burns: His Dwelling, His Ale House, His Statue, His Church, His Arm Chair, His Mausoleum, His Poetry, His Admirers—Clydesdale Horses—Old Churches—Bridge Six Hundred Years old—Fine Railway Station—Viaduct Over Railways, etc.

## CHAPTER XXXI.

FROM SCOTLAND TO IRELAND . . . . . . . . . . . . . 310

Leaving Dumfries—Riding over Mountains Among Lakes and Meadows—Mountains Decked with Purple Heather, White Granite and Sheep—Old Stranraer—Home-like Hotel—Leaving Stranraer—Loch Ryan—Ships, Sea-birds and Green Hills—Locomotives Rush Down to the Ships—The Irish Sea "Like a Lake"—Ships Like Spirits on Eternity's Ocean—Mrs. Scott Siddons—At Larne, Ireland.

## CHAPTER XXXII.

IN IRELAND. . . . . . . . . . . . . . . . . . . . . 316

Interesting Country—Velvet Meadows—Clear Lakes—Picturesque Mountains—Leaving Larne—Enroute to Giant's Causeway—Port Rush—Dr. Adam Clarke's Monument—The Jaunting Car—The Electric Car—The Mowing Machine on a Cliff—Dunluce Castle—Strange Images and Shapes—Ocean Waves Moaning in Caves—Dined Near the Great Freak of Nature.

## CHAPTER XXXIII.

IRELAND: FROM GIANT'S CAUSEWAY TO DUBLIN. . . . . . . . . 322

Giant's Causeway—A Beautiful and Wonderful Freak of Nature—Forty Thousand Columns of Stone, Cut by Nature, on the Shore of the Sea—"Black North"—Wave-cut Rocks—In a Cave—Walking Over Pentagon and Hexagon Columns—The Wishing Chair—Finn McCue—Fingal's Cave—Famous Names—Going to Belfast—Fine City—Foggy Morning—Off for Dublin—Interesting Places Seen—The Round Towers—Arrive at Dublin.

CONTENTS. 13

## CHAPTER XXXIV.

DUBLIN: PLACES OF INTEREST AND BEAUTY . . . . . . . . . . 331

Ireland's Chief City—Position, Commerce, Etc.—Population—The Buildings—Sackville Street—Fine Monuments — Grand Edifices—Glasnevin Cemetery — Marble Crosses and Memorials in Colonnades— The Circular Vaults—O'Connell's Lofty, Round Monument—Phœnix Park—Carpet of Rainbows Spread by Artistic Gods—Wellington's Sublime Monument—The Corsican Corporal Heart-broken—Red Coats—Along the Quay—Beautiful Women—White Hair and Fresh, Pink Cheeks—Crowned With the Glow of an Indian Summer Sunset—Pies, Cakes, Creams, Coffees and Candies, on Sackville Street—Served by Ladies Incog.—Good Bye—" Good Bye."

## CHAPTER XXXV.

DUBLIN, AND VOYAGE TO LIVERPOOL . . . . . . . . . . . . 339

Dublin—Poetry and Romance—Stephen's Green—The Old Singer — Wealthy Families Remodel Great Churches—Driving Timid, Saucy and Wild Droves from Fields Into Ships—On a Blanket Among Trunks—Darkness Sits on the Sea— Rude, Furloughed Soldiers Sing and Dance—Rocked on the Sea Far from Green Hills—Holly-head — Great Railway Station at Midnight — Cars Full of Drowsy Passengers—Arrive at Liverpool—Finding My Friend's Hotel — Miles of Gloomy Buildings—Men Sleeping on Stone Beds—I Sleep on a Bench—The Busy Morning.

## CHAPTER XXXVI.

MEN AND THINGS BEYOND THE SEA . . . . . . . . . . . . 345

Fragments Collected — Coins of Two Nations — English People; Reading, Dressing, Eating, Drinking, Manners—Cool—No Flies—Pleasures and Palaces—Only One America — Her Starry Banners Wave Benedictions in Distant Lands — Great Britain's Headquarters — Kingdom's Admired—Acknowledging the Stars and Stripes—London's Crowds; Advertisers, Workers and the Poor-House — Wedded to a Great City — Thirty Thousand Houses a Year—Dream Life—A Fire in Wheatley's Fourteen-acre Store — Seven Hundred Drowned, but not Missed—Strange Sayings—Enterprising Barber—Prices of Various Things — Two Swift Monsters — England's Champion Horse—Died That Night—Dover's Fat Man.

## CHAPTER XXXVII.

NORTH BURTON AND SCARBOROUGH, ENGLAND . . . . . . . . . 356

Green Country Village and a Splendid Watering Place—Wyoming Compared with Other Valleys — A Sunset of Glory Seen Through "Gates Ajar"—The Author's Father at North Burton—Meets Junius Brutus Booth—Marries—Traveling by Rail in Yorkshire—At Hunmanby — North Burton — The Pudseys — Father's Chair — The Gypsy—Unique Old Church—Smuggling—Good Land—Scarborough the Splendid—In Steam-carriages on the Cliffs—Colored Sails Flap on the "Purple Deep"— Chiseled Beauty Between Hills by the Sea — Castle — Soldiers in Tents — Hotels—Ships — Fish and Fisherfolk — Elegant Buildings — Flowers and Lakes Under Iron Bridges—Men, Women, Children and Horses on the Sea Sands—The Aquarium—Poverty Mimics Pride—Going Home—A Delightful Evening.

## CHAPTER XXXVIII.

LEAMINGTON, WARWICK, STRATFORD, ETC. . . . . . . . . . . . 368

Grand Warwickshire—Leamington—Gardens—Drives—Medicinal Waters—Warwick Castle—An old Glory Surrounded by Beauties of Nature and Art—Peacocks and Cedars of Lebanon—The Dungeon, Dark and Dreadful—Stratford-Upon-Avon—Shakespeare's Birthplace—The Room Where the Great Poet was Born — No fire Allowed—Stealing a Place to Write a Name—Relic Hunters—Shakespeare's Curse—A Delightful Ride on the Avon—Coventry—Old Churches With Tall Spires—St. Mary's Hall—Lady Godiva Rides Naked Through the City—"Peeping Tom" is now Blind Tom—Leaving Fair Leamington.

## CHAPTER XXXIX.

FROM ENGLAND TO WYOMING VALLEY . . . . . . . . . . . 376

In England's Busy Sea-port—Going to the Ship—Miss Oliver—Thousands of People Sailing Out Into the Fog to Lands Beyond the Sea—Liverpool Fades Into Smoke and Fog—Sunset Smiles on the Sea—Moonlit Highway—Rockets Bursting Above the Waves—Weeping and Dancing—A Sunday Fair on a Great Ship—" Lovely Apples"

—Canes—Caps—Pipes—Bog Oak, etc.—Ireland Sinks Into the Sea—Sea Rough—The Snorer—The Winds Lift Up Dark Waves—Many Ill—Sea Grand—Alleghenies of Water — Chinaware Crashes and Lights go Out — Tossed in Bed — The Deck Like a Barn-roof — Not Afraid, but Satisfied—Comrades Recovering—Mr. G—— Ill.

## CHAPTER XL.

FROM ENGLAND TO WYOMING VALLEY—CONTINUED . . . . . . 386

Miss Oliver Wounded—Mr. G—— Preparing to be Buried in the Sea—Took Hot Rum and Quinine—"Get Out"—Miss Oliver Worse—The Surgeon Assists—Steamers Racing Through White-Crested Billows—Officers Kind—The Magical Sea—Ships Like Butterflies on Crystal Vases—Singers Cheer Miss Oliver in Darkness—Sandy Hook—Anchor Chains Rattle—A Great City's Crystal Gate—Ships, Forts, Hills, Mansions, Monuments, Churches, Bridges—On the Wings of the Morning—The Sea's Births Like a Resurrection—Letters from Distant Kingdoms—Custom House—Rough and Dusty—Officials Seem Unfeeling—Take Away My Watch—Tell who I am—Watch Returned—Miss Oliver's Brother—Shake Hands Amid Tears, Good-byes and Partings.

## CHAPTER XLI.

FROM ENGLAND TO WYOMING VALLEY—CONCLUDED . . . . . 398

In New York City—Five Hundred Thousand People in Cars on Stilts—Crossing North River—The Giants race Through Autumn-Crowned New Jersey—Bright Mountains and Flaming Furnaces in Pennsylvania—Oh, the Sunset!—Gazing with the full Moon, down upon Wyoming Valley—Meet Friends on Warm Hearthstones—The Wounded Girl tells her own Story; Crosses wide States While Suffering, and finds Lover and Brother—Gets Married—Better but not Well—My Trip and its History Terminates—A Panorama of Great Glory, full of music, love and undying Beauty—Kind Reader, Adieu.

# TESTIMONIALS.

*From Rev. L. L. Sprague, D. D., Principal Wyoming Seminary:—*
C. D. LINSKILL, ESQ.:
 *Dear Sir*—I have read your letters from Europe with much interest and should like to see them published. If you decide to do so, please send me a volume for library Wyoming Seminary.
 KINGSTON, Pa., Aug. 18th, 1888.     L. L. SPRAGUE.

*From Hon. L. D. Shoemaker:—*
 I have read some of your letters from Europe as they were published, and would be glad to have a copy of them all in book form.
 WILKES-BARRÉ, Aug. 27th, '88.    L. D. SHOEMAKER.

*From Hon. Chas. A. Miner:—*
C. D. LINSKILL, ESQ.:
 *Dear Sir*—I read your letters from Europe, as they appeared in the *Telephone*, with much interest. They renewed to me my own visit of several years ago as I read descriptions of the scenes I had passed through. I would be more than pleased to see them in book form.
 WILKES-BARRÉ, Sept. 3d, 1888.    CHAS. A. MINER.

*From Hon. H. B. Payne:—*
FRIEND LINSKILL:
 Acquainted as we have been since boyhood, I read with pleasure most of your letters from Europe appearing in the *Telephone*. Those letters together in a book would be almost yourself in book form. Hence I would be much pleased to have a copy.  *Yours truly,*
 WILKES-BARRÉ, Sept. 6th, 1888.     H. B. PAYNE.

*From Governor James A. Beaver:—*
C. D. LINSKILL, ESQ., Wilkes-Barré, Pa.:
 *My Dear Sir*—Your letter of the 11th instant has been received. I have read some of your letters, as published in the *Wilkes-Barré Telephone*, and found in them much that was new and interesting. Their publication would, I doubt not, secure a wider range of readers and an appreciative constituency.  *Very cordially yours,*
            JAMES A. BEAVER.
 EXECUTIVE CHAMBER, HARRISBURG, Sept. 20th, 1888.

## TESTIMONIALS.

*From Congressman Osborne:—*
MR. CHARLES D. LINSKILL:
   *My Dear Sir*—I read many of the letters written by you, while you were in Europe, with much satisfaction, and think you should publish them in book form. They would make an interesting volume and I would be glad to have it in my library. Very respectfully,
*Your obedient servant,*
   WASHINGTON, D. C., Sept. 8, 1888.     E. S. OSBORNE.

---

*From Calvin Parsons, Esq.:—*
   I have read, with the greatest pleasure, "L.'s" letters of his travels in Europe. I would be happy to receive a copy, in book form, for my library.     *My best regards,*
   PARSONS, Sept. 7th, 1888.     CALVIN PARSONS.
To Mr. Linskill.

---

*From A. T. McClintock, Esq.:—*
   If the letters referred to are published in book form I will be pleased to have a copy.     A. T. McCLINTOCK.
   Sept. 7th, 1888.

---

*From W. W. Loomis, Esq., Ex-Mayor, Wilkes-Barré:—*
MR. C. D. LINSKILL:
   *Dear Sir*—I have read your letters from beyond the sea with interest and pleasure, and if you publish them in book form, I believe hundreds of people will read it, and be entertained and profited thereby.
   WILKES-BARRÉ, Pa., Sept. 7, 1888.     W. W. LOOMIS.

---

*From Judge Stanley Woodward:—*
   I was very much interested in your letters from Europe, as published in the *Telephone*, and think them well worthy of preservation in a more permanent form.     STANLEY WOODWARD.
To Mr. Linskill.

---

*From Hon. Chas. D. Foster:—*
   I heartily concur in what has been said by those who have already written in this book. Have been much interested in the letters of my old school friend and neighbor, in the land of buckwheat, and shall only be too glad to purchase and read his travels in Europe, in book form.
   To Chas. Linskill, Esq.     CHAS. D. FOSTER.

---

*From Rev. R. W. VanSchoick, Presiding Elder Wyoming District:—*
   Mr. Linskill has made the public a great debtor by the publication of his letters from "Over the Sea"; and will immensely increase their obligations to him by putting his incomparable narrations in book form. Such a work will find a place in every library.
   KINGSTON, Pa., Sept. 11th, 1888.     R. W. VANSCHOICK.

*From Col. G. M. Reynolds :—*
    Mr. Linskill will confer a favor by including me among the subscribers to his forthcoming book.         G. M. REYNOLDS.

*From Geo. B. Kulp, Esq., Local Historian and Editor Legal Register :—*
    Your letters from beyond the seas were read by me with great pleasure and profit. I have several copies of travels in my library, but none of them are as entertaining as your letters.    *Yours, etc.,*
    WILKES-BARRÉ, Pa., Sept. 11, '88.         G. B. KULP.
*To C. D. Linskill, Esq.*

*From L. H. Taylor, M. D.:—*
MY DEAR MR. LINSKILL:
    I have read some of your foreign letters with interest, and will be glad to see them published in book form.
        *Sincerely yours,*         LEWIS H. TAYLOR.

*From Hon. Garrick M. Harding, ex-Judge Luzerne County :—*
MY DEAR CHARLES:
    Your European letters, originally published in the *Telephone*, are too interesting and instructive to run the risk of that oblivion which too often is the fate of a country newspaper. Resurrect them by all means and give them book form, so that our children and children's children may participate in the pleasure which their ancestors have enjoyed.
        *Very truly yours,*         GARRICK M. HARDING.
    WILKES-BARRÉ, Pa., Oct. 8th, '88.

*From William Puckey, Bookseller :—*
CHAS. D. LINSKILL, ESQ.:
    *Dear Sir*—I have read your letters from England, Ireland, Scotland, Wales and France with much pleasure and profit. I was never so much interested in letters of travels. Your letters are eloquent pen pictures of great and beautiful things, and are as attractive and reliable as the most carefully written history. I think your book will have a large sale. I shall at least take two copies.    *Truly yours,*
    WILKES-BARRÉ, Pa., Sept. 25th, 1888.         WM. PUCKEY.

*From Rev. A. Griffin, Pastor Central M. E. Church, Wilkes-Barré :—*
MY DEAR FRIEND CHARLES:
    It affords me very great pleasure, indeed, to add my unqualified endorsement to your project of yielding to the advice of your many friends and putting your European letters in more permanent form than a local newspaper can give them. The careful perusal of your familiar letters is next to a personal visit to the Old World. Publish them in book form by all means, and count me a subscriber to a copy of the first edition.         *Very truly yours,*
    Oct. 8, '88.         A. GRIFFIN.

## TESTIMONIALS. 19

*From A. H. Tuttle, D. D., Pastor First M. E. Church, Wilkes-Barré:*
CHAS. D. LINSKILL:
 *My Dear Sir*—Your letters came to us like a sweet breath from beyond the sea. They breathe the spirit of restfulness upon us in this busy, work-a-day life of ours. I am glad you are to put them in a convenient form for frequent use. They are as instructive as they are restful.   *Respectfully,*
 Oct. 8th, 1888.         A. H. TUTTLE.

---

*From Hon. J. Ridgway Wright:—*
CHAS. D. LINSKILL:
 *My Dear Sir*—I understand that you intend publishing your letters from abroad, that have appeared heretofore in the *Telephone*, in book form. That is good. I enjoy your style—your way of looking at things. I have enjoyed the letters and must have one of the volumes so published.  *Very truly yours,*    J. RIDGWAY WRIGHT.
 WILKES-BARRÉ, Pa., Nov. 5th, 1888.

---

*From Rev. F. B. Hodge, Pastor First Presbyterian Church, Wilkes-Barré, Pa:—*
 I will cheerfully become a subscriber for your letters from Europe when published in book form, as requested by your many friends.
              F. B. HODGE.

---

*From Hon. Chas. E. Rice, President Judge of Luzerne County:—*
MY DEAR MR. LINSKILL:
 I have read most of your letters from Europe, as they have appeared in the *Telephone*, and with the greatest pleasure. The simplicity of style and the closeness of observation manifested, give them a charm as well as a value, entitling them to preservation in book form.
     *I remain, yours truly,*
 WILKES-BARRÉ, Pa., Oct. 9th, 1888.    CHARLES E. RICE.

---

*From Mr. J. W. Hollenback:—*
MR. CHAS. D. LINSKILL:
 I have read some of your letters from Europe with much interest, and notice a style unique, and not usual to even our best writers. I will also be one of your first subscribers on the appearance of your travels in a book.        J. W. HOLLENBACK.
 WILKES-BARRÉ, Pa., Oct. 10th, 1888.

---

*From Major C. M. Conyngham, Wilkes-Barré, Pa.:—*
MR. LINSKILL:
 I enjoyed the reading of your letters from Europe very much indeed, and shall be glad to read them again in book form.
   *Yours truly,*     C. M. CONYNGHAM.
 WILKES-BARRÉ, Pa., Oct. 15, 1888.

*From F. V. Rockafellow, Banker:—*
FRIEND LINSKILL:
    I have read most of your foreign letters, and was greatly pleased with their style and language, and learned from them many useful facts. Your descriptions of great cities, and grand, old buildings, and of the sea, rivers, plains and mountains, were real, lifelike and satisfying. While your descriptive powers are remarkable, many of your sentences are as smoothly and eloquently worded as any thing I have seen in our language. I shall be pleased to see your letters in book form, and shall want one for my library. I am quite sure your book will have a large and extensive sale, for it possesses that which will interest and instruct English reading people everywhere, and for many years to come.
          *Yours truly,*           F. V. ROCKAFELLOW.
  WILKES-BARRÉ, Pa., Oct. 8, 1888.

*From Hon. D. L. Rhone, Orphans' Court Judge:—*
FRIEND LINSKILL:
    Your letters from Europe are worthy of being put in book form. There is so much in them of the aims, and cares, and works of the common people, not observed by other authors, and so much of general history related in a style so original and agreeable, as to give them an unusual interest.           *Yours, etc.,*
  WILKES-BARRÉ, Pa., Oct. 11th, 1888.     D. L. RHONE.

*From Ex-Judge John Handley:—*
    Publish your letters from Europe by all means. I have read them with great pleasure and much instruction.     JOHN HANDLEY.
  SCRANTON, Pa., Sept., 1888.

*From Col. J. D. Laciar, with Scranton Republican:—*
MR. CHAS. D. LINSKILL, Editor Wilkes-Barré *Telephone:*
    *Dear Sir*—I wish to express to you the gratification I experienced when the notice appeared that you contemplated the publication, in book form, of the series of admirable letters written by you while on your late European tour. I read many of the letters as they appeared from time to time in the columns of your paper, and regard them as highly instructive, especially as to their descriptive features of places of interest visited by you, and the evidences they bear of your close observations as a traveler. The letters are well worth preserving in permanent book form. May you have the great success you deserve.
          *Very sincerely,*
  SCRANTON, Pa., Oct. 20, 1888.     J. D. LACIAR.

*From Roger McGarry, Superintendent Wilkes-Barré Water Co.:—*
    I have read Mr. C. D. Linskill's letters with much pleasure and profit, and cheerfully subscribe my name among his many admirers.
  WILKES-BARRÉ, Pa., Sept. 11th, 1888.   ROGER McGARRY.

*From Mr. Charles T. Seymour, Importer of Havana Tobacco, 180 Front Street, New York:—*

MR. LINSKILL:

*My Dear Sir*—Incidentally, the other day, I took the *Telephone* from the postman's hands. * * I was soon enwrapped in your crisp, practical narrative of one day's sight-seeing in Paris. * * The scenes were vividly brought to my mind, and for truth and clearness I commend it beyond anything I have seen. * * In those articles I am sure, from the sample I have read, I shall be much edified, instructed, and a very pleasant trip recalled with a minuteness and grace that I, as an old reporter on the *New York Herald*, perhaps can appreciate as much as the majority. * * *Yours very truly,*
Jan. 17th, 1888. CHARLES T. SEYMOUR.

---

*From J. Arthur Bullard, M. D.:—*

MY DEAR MR. LINSKILL:

You ask me for an expression concerning your letters, and I reply without hesitancy that I have always found them interesting. You seem to have the gifts of observation and description, and your easy pen pictures of American as well as of English homely domestic life, its familiar scenes and incidents, strike the popular chord. * * * *

Having read the *Telephone* since its first number I was prepared somewhat for the letters of its wandering editor on the other side of the "big water," and therefore read them with comfort, interest and advantage. The man who can enter so naturally into the little things of life is certainly the one best calculated to hold a warm place in the hearts of the masses. I wish you all success with your book.

*Yours truly,*
J. ARTHUR BULLARD.
WILKES-BARRÉ, Pa., Oct. 11, '88.

---

*From F. C. Johnson, M. D., of the Wilkes-Barré Record:—*

MY DEAR MR. LINSKILL:

As I did not have an opportunity of reading all your letters, I will be glad to see them in book form. To me they were far more interesting than the pretentious foreign observations with which our literature is flooded. I like to look at Europe through your glasses, and you may put me down for a copy—not for review, but " C. O. D."

F. C. JOHNSON.

---

*From W. G. Weaver, M. D.:—*

MR. CHAS. D. LINSKILL:

*Dear Sir*—I read your European letters, under the title of "Here and There," with much pleasure, and I am glad to hear of your intention to put them into book form. They deserve to be widely circulated.

In these days, when literary piracy is so common, it is gratifying to meet with a really unique and original style, such as all your writings display. I wish you success in your publishing venture, and shall gladly subscribe for a copy of your book.

Sincerely yours,<br>W. G. WEAVER.

WILKES-BARRÉ, Pa., Dec. 11th, 1888.

*From Hon. E. C. Wadhams:—*

Having read with interest your letters published in the *Telephone*, think, if published in book form, would secure a large patronage.
To C. D. Linskill.

E. C. WADHAMS.

WILKES-BARRÉ, Pa., Oct. 8th, 1888.

*From Isaac P. Hand, Esq.:—*

MR. C. D. LINSKILL:

*Dear Sir*—I read most of your letters, written while you were in Europe and published in the Wilkes-Barré *Telephone*. I assure you it is with great satisfaction that I learn the same are to be issued in book form. Your descriptions of things seen and places visited are very instructive and interesting, and far from commonplace.

Yours truly,<br>ISAAC P. HAND.

WILKES-BARRÉ, Pa., Dec. 19, 1888.

*From Dilton Yarington, Esq., Carbondale, Pa.:—*

MR. C. D. LINSKILL:

*Dear Sir*—Now with regard to your book containing the interesting letters you wrote from Europe; consider me a subscriber. In my younger days I have read much of the history of Europe, but I must say that I never had a proper conception of English *home* matters and the English people at home until I read your interesting letters. My ancestors on my father's side were from England one hundred and sixty years ago; on my mother's side, from Ireland one hundred and eighty years ago. By all means make me a subscriber.

Respectfully yours,<br>DILTON YARINGTON.

*From Edw. Edwards, Paymaster Taff Vale Railway, Cardiff, Wales:—*

C. D. LINSKILL, ESQ.:

*My Dear Sir*—Myself and family are very pleased to learn that you were well. * * * It quite cheers us to find that you retain such a kindly recollection of your visit to Cardiff. It was so short that I feared you would scarcely be able to recall the circumstance, amidst the almost numberless incidents of your trip to the "Old Country." We feel

amply repaid for any trouble we may have taken to make your visit agreeable. * * * We, every member of the family, have been very much interested in your papers, and look forward to the future numbers with considerable pleasure. Should you again visit our country I trust you will find it convenient to give Cardiff a more lengthy visit.
*Faithfully yours,* EDWARD EDWARDS.

*From David Harris, Foreman on Forth Bridge, Scotland:—*
MR. LINSKILL:
I have received the papers you sent on to me, and I am glad to see the description that you have given of your travels in Scotland. You have not been idle the time you were here. You have given a splendid account of the bridge here. I am sure your readers will be very much taken up with your travels. *Yours truly,* DAVID HARRIS.
NORTH QUEEN'S FERRY, Scotland, March 25, 1888.

*From Alexander Farnham, Esq.:—*
FRIEND LINSKILL:
I have read your "Here and There" letters from Europe with great interest and profit. Your descriptive talents are peculiar and pleasing; simple, yet comprehensive; attractive, instructive and useful. I shall be glad to have a copy of your "Travels in Lands Beyond the Sea."
*Truly yours,* ALEXANDER FARNHAM.
WILKES-BARRÉ, Pa., Oct. 19, '88.

*From A. R. Brundage, Esq.:—*
MR. LINSKILL:
I read your letters of foreign travels with great interest. Having passed over very much the same ground myself, I can certify to the faithfulness with which you have described places and scenes of the Old World. *Very truly,* A. R. BRUNDAGE.

*From Col. C. Dorrance, President Wyoming National Bank:—*
C. DORRANCE LINSKILL, ESQ., Wilkes-Barré, Pa.:
*Dear Sir*—I have read your letters from England and France, as published in the *Telephone*, with much interest, and judge if you publish them in book form, as you propose, the work will have a wide and generous patronage. *Respectfully and truly yours,*
DORRANCETON, Pa., Nov. 8th, 1888. C. DORRANCE.

*From S. H. Lynch, Esq.:—*
CHAS. LINSKILL, ESQ.:
*Dear Sir*—In looking over the *Telephone* weekly, I have been particularly pleased with your very interesting letters on your voyage to Europe, with your rambles up and down the land of your forefathers

and elsewhere. Your descriptions of places and people met with by the way, with the incidents occurring daily, have made very attractive reading to me, and I have no doubt that the gathering together of your notes of travel will make an instructive and entertaining volume.

*Yours truly,*
WILKES-BARRÉ, Pa., Oct. 15th, 1888.   S. H. LYNCH.

---

*From C. P. Kidder, Esq. :—*
MR. CHAS. D. LINSKILL:

*Dear Sir*—I was greatly interested in your letters from Europe and derived much pleasure and profit in their perusal. Your descriptions of Old World cities and scenes are the next thing to being there in person, and your letters have renewed in me a desire to visit those countries—a desire I hope to gratify at some no distant period.   *Truly yours,*
WILKES-BARRÉ, Pa., Oct. 27, '88.   C. P. KIDDER.

---

*From E. H. Chase, Esq. :—*
FRIEND CHARLES:

I read a number of your letters from abroad, and was disappointed if, in opening the *Telephone*, I missed the interesting headlines, "Here and There." The letters were racy, and descriptions of the kind difficult to describe, but entertaining to read. I sincerely trust that if you do collect them in book form you will not overlook in its distribution,

*Yours very truly,*
WILKES-BARRÉ, Pa.   EDWARD H. CHASE.

---

*From F. J. Deemer, Asst. Supt. Susquehanna Coal Co.:—*
MR. CHAS. D. LINSKILL:

*My Dear Sir*—I have read your letters from Europe with considerable interest and profit. Your descriptions of the sea, of ships, of cities, famous buildings, and landscapes, are very pleasing and instructive. I am glad to learn that you are to enlarge and improve these letters, and publish them in book form. I shall be pleased to have a copy for my library.   F. J. DEEMER.
WILKES-BARRÉ, Pa., Nov. 6, 1888.

---

*From Robert Baur, Publisher, Wilkes-Barré, Pa.:*
FRIEND LINSKILL:

I have read all of your letters from the "Old World," and can heartily endorse what your many friends have said regarding them. I have been interested and pleased by your original style of expression, and your characteristic description of things, people, and places, "in lands beyond the sea." I am sure your book will find its way into many libraries, as it richly deserves to do.   *Truly yours,*
WILKES-BARRÉ, Pa., Nov. 8th, 1888.   ROBERT BAUR.

# CHAPTER I.

## INTRODUCTORY.

WHY AND HOW THIS VOLUME WAS PUBLISHED—THE AUTHOR'S FATHER—CAME FROM ENGLAND—SETTLED IN PENNSYLVANIA—ASKED HIS SON TO MAKE PILGRIMAGE—HIS SUDDEN DEATH—CORRESPONDENCE LASTING SIXTY YEARS—WHITE, ROARING BILLOWS CAN NOT DROWN LOVE LETTERS—BEREAVEMENT, SORROW, LABORS AND CARES CALL FOR REST AND CHANGE—A FRIEND INDEED—GETTING READY TO GO—PASSPORT, AND LETTERS FROM PROMINENT MEN—GOVERNOR BEAVER'S LETTER—CONGRESSMAN OSBORNE'S LETTER—OTHER LETTERS—TAKING LEAVE—AMERICA'S SHORES SINK IN SILVER—AT LIVERPOOL—THROUGH ENGLAND, IRELAND, SCOTLAND, WALES, FRANCE; PARIS AND LONDON—RELATIVES HELPFUL—WEATHER MOST AUSPICIOUS—THINGS PICTURED ON THE SPOT—GOOD WISHES—GRASP EACH READER BY THE HAND.

To tell the reader why and how this volume was written is a pleasing task.

In May, 1830, my father sailed from Hull, an old seaport town on the eastern coast of England, and in thirty days landed at New York. He settled in Lehman, Luzerne county, a few miles west of Wyoming valley, where, after residing for more than thirty-five years, he fell down and expired suddenly, on the morning of the 18th of August, 1865. He was by nature endowed with more than average physical, mental and moral powers. His memory was very tenacious and his judgment most excellent. Naturally, he often spoke to his children and friends of "Old England" and told us of the beauty, and glory, and romance, and history, and wealth of his native land. He once said to the writer, "I did intend to return to England, to again look upon dear friends and familiar scenes, but I am now too far advanced in years to go and will relinquish the thought; however, I wish you some day to go and see where I was born and attended school." These words were spoken with a sigh, while his tears were nearly ready to fall.

After his death I wrote to his brother, and ever since then, at unequal periods, I have corresponded with my uncle, or with cousins, in a land beyond the sea. I have often wondered that the mighty, rolling, white-capped billows of the Atlantic have not drowned in their awful and thundering depths, the feeble messages sent forth by loving hearts—hearts knit by the tender ties of consanguinity. But still, after nearly sixty years of family separation the waves of Old Ocean occasionally toss upon the white strands of America a letter for your humble servant.

For more than a score of years I had longed intensely for the time and means to visit my father's mother-land. At length, in the early summer of 1887, after a season of great bereavement and much care and labor, by the counsel and aid of a very dear friend, I began to prepare to sail for Europe. Of course, the project and its possibilities pleased me much. I told friends that I was going away and many subscribed for our paper. I also secured a passport and a number of letters from men high in social and political circles, believing that I would find them useful in various ways and places, as I certainly did find them to be. The letter sent to me by Governor James A. Beaver, of Pennsylvania, was certainly one of the best I received; in fact, it would not be easy for any person to receive from anyone a better or more neatly worded testimonial. I therefore will take the liberty to publish his letter here, which is as follows:

COMMONWEALTH OF PENNSYLVANIA, EXECUTIVE CHAMBER.
HARRISBURG, July 7th, 1887.

TO ALL WHOM IT MAY CONCERN:

Charles D. Linskill, Esq., of the City of Wilkes-Barré, in the Commonwealth of Pennsylvania, editor of the *Wilkes-Barré Telephone*, is about to travel beyond the seas. He is a reputable citizen of Pennsylvania, engaged in a most honorable calling, has respectable standing in his community, has served his country in a military capacity, and is in every way worthy the respect and confidence of all with whom he may come in contact. He expects to pursue some literary work incident to his profession during his absence, and is therefore cordially commended to all who can assist him in his laudable enterprise.

Very respectfully,
JAMES A. BEAVER,
Governor.

I also insert the pleasant letter sent me by Gen. E. S. Osborne, our Representative in the halls of the

National Congress at Washington.  The following is his letter:

House of Representatives, U. S.,<br>Washington, D. C., 29 June, 1887.

My dear Mr. Linskill:

I understand you are about to make a trip through Europe, intending to be absent until late in the fall. I sincerely hope you may have a pleasant journey and a safe return to your home and friends, and that your health may be benefitted and your fund of information enlarged thereby. I shall look for your letters in the *Telephone*, and shall enjoy their reading very much. If you come across Mr. Blaine be sure and make yourself known to him, and tell him you and I are old friends.

Sincerely hoping that a kind Providence may protect you from all harm, I am with esteem,

Your obedient servant,<br>E. S. Osborne, M. C.

To Charles D. Linskill, Esq., Editor *Telephone*, Wilkes-Barré, Pa.

Hon. L. D. Shoemaker, Hon. E. C. Wadhams, Richard Sharp, Esq., George A. Edwards, Esq., and Master Mechanic Charles Graham, Sr., and others gave me excellent letters, introducing me to people in public and private life.

On the 14th of July, 1887, I parted with friends at Kingston and was driven through the fresh, morning air across Wyoming valley, where golden grain and fragrant hay stood in shocks to be conveyed to the barns.

At Wilkes-Barré I said "good bye" to my kind and patient partner, Mr. Sanders, and to the compositors and other friends, and took the train for New York. On Saturday afternoon, July 16th, on board the magnificent steamer "Servia," we steamed out into the wide,

wide sea, and before sundown the shores of America seemed to melt to silver and disappear into Dream-land.

That afternoon as the shores of my dear, native land sank out of sight beyond gleaming waves of Old Ocean, the following short letter appeared in the *Telephone:*

### GONE.

Dear friends: By the time that most of you shall see these lines, I will be on board of a great steamship plowing the blue and trackless Atlantic, bound to walk and talk in England, Ireland, Scotland, Wales and France.

I expect to see many great, grand, old, beautiful and curious things which I hope to write of in a way that shall prove entertaining and useful.

Since I began to arrange for my transatlantic trip I have been befriended by many in various ways, and a number of eminent men have given me most excellent letters of introduction to persons beyond the sea.

I hope and expect to return, but, if He who holds the ocean in the hollow of His hand and binds its proud waves with tiny grains of sand, wills that I should meet you here no more I wish you to know, that I go from the shores of time with the fortitude and peaceful confidence of a humble Christian. Good bye. L.

In eight and a half days we cast anchor at Liverpool, England's mighty and far-famed seaport. I crossed and re-crossed England; visited famous and beautiful portions of Scotland; went into Ireland, "the gem of the ocean," and saw her most wonderful works of nature, and visited Dublin, her beauty, glory and pride; ran down through Wales and inspected Cardiff, her chief city. I crossed the English channel, where two seas meet and contend, and went down through the heart of "Sunny France" and walked along the banks of the Seine in her gay, grand, glittering capital, and gazed upon her mighty and beautiful buildings: places of worship, places of pleasure, places of glory and places of blood. Again, I walked the streets of vast, ancient, wealthy, powerful and ever-roaring London, and met hundreds of thousands of fellow-mortals wending their way through almost boundless forests of buildings—buildings gloomy and gay, massive and elegant.

While absent I managed to write letters for the *Wilkes-Barrè Telephone*. These letters, on my return, I found had been read by thousands of people with deep interest. Having cousins in London and other great cities in England, facilitated my seeing and learning useful and interesting facts. In the letters I have essayed to let the reader see what I saw and let him know the thoughts I experienced when standing in the presence of the objects described. I was also favored with the finest summer weather that western Europe had experienced in nineteen years, and rain and storms did not hinder my travels or prevent my sight-seeing. For me to speak of the character of these letters might seem as lacking in good taste, as it would be unnecessary, in view of the many remarkable and comprehensive testimonials which are published on other pages of this volume. These testimonials and hundreds of others, written and verbal, decided me to publish my letters in this volume. These letters have been carefully revised. A few typographical errors and unimportant matters have been expunged, while many things of considerable interest are added. I am confident that the new chapters on the "London Fog" and on "The Great Fire" of 1666 will prove very interesting and useful.

Dear readers, and fellow-travelers on the shores of Time, I close this prefatory chapter hoping that you may be interested and instructed in perusing the following chapters, and that I may some day grasp each one of you by the hand.

Very respectfully yours,<br>
CHARLES D. LINSKILL.

# CHAPTER II.

### FROM THE MOUNTAINS TO THE SEA.

SAYING "GOOD BYE" TO RELATIVES, PARTNER AND FRIENDS—LOOKING DOWN ON LUZERNE AND OTHER COUNTIES—IN NEW JERSEY—RUSHING THROUGH CITIES WHILE LONG, WHITE, GUARDIAN ARMS RISE AND FALL—IN NEW YORK—CENTRAL PARK—MONUMENTS AND MONSTERS FROM BEYOND THE SEA—CARRIAGES FOR PALE BABIES, AND PROUD MILLIONAIRES—TOOK BAGGAGE TO STEAMSHIP—AT CONEY ISLAND—ITS HOTELS—ITS FLOWERS—ITS SWIMMERS—ITS WINE, ITS WOMEN—ITS TOWER—ITS FRIENDS—A SEA SHELL CONTAINING SIXTY-FIVE MASTER MUSICIANS—THE GARDENS BLOSSOM WITH FIRE—A PLACE TO LEARN—A PLACE TO FALL—SHAM BATTLE—BAY FULL OF SHIPS AT NIGHT—THE HEAVENS FRESCOED WITH COLORED LIGHTS—STATUE OF LIBERTY—BROOKLYN BRIDGE, AN ARTIFICIAL MIDNIGHT RAINBOW—READY TO WAVE A FAREWELL TO MY NATIVE LAND.

On the morning of July 14th, 1887, I bid "good bye" to my sister, Mrs. Shaver, and her husband and two sons, and a number of neighbors at Kingston, Pa., and was conveyed with my baggage to the Lehigh Valley Railway Station in Wilkes-Barré. It took me about one hour to pass through Wilkes-

Barré, for there were my partner, John and Charlie at the office, bless them, if they do sometimes put in the wrong letter and leave out the right word, and a host of other acquaintances and friends to shake my hand and say "bon voyage." Well, at 8:40 the train started and I was on my way to Europe via England—one of the many dreams of my life. The morning was clear, warm and pleasant. The farmers were engaged here and there through the valley in harvesting grain and making hay and the valley generally, perhaps never looked more pleasant to me. Our train, with the energy of steam and steel, urged on by muscle and educated brains, climbed the mountain, and we could see not only Wyoming's fair vale, but we could see away beyond the Kingston mountain to North mountain, where Lake and Ross and Fairmount fields could be seen yellow with ripening grain. Yonder were the mountains around Shickshinny, and yonder were the high hills back of Centremoreland, and away there were the mountains west of Scranton. Now the train rolls through Solomon's Gap, and bidding farewell to Wyoming we look over Wright, Slocum, Dorrance, Dennison, Hollenback, Conyngham and Nescopeck to Salem and Berwick. We pass on by Glen Summit's spacious and pleasant hotel where a number of Wilkes-Barré people are seen with others sitting on the porches or moving about the grounds. We pass White Haven and on down the Lehigh valley, until at Slatington we begin to get away from the mountains and into a region of fine farms. On the train we met Sheriff H. W. Search and deputies W. A. Campbell, A. Barnes and Alderman Donohue. They were taking five prisoners to the Eastern Penitentiary. One was a Hungarian who had murdered a fellow-countryman of his. He was going to prison for seven years. They were fair-looking young men and we pitied them and detested vice the more.

Passing Allentown and Bethlehem we cross the Delaware at Easton just below where it receives the waters of the Lehigh. Through Phillipsburg and on through central New Jersey, and I was pleased with the country. Wheat and rye were about all harvested and oats were about ripe and some fields of corn were heading out. At Metuchen we run in on the Pennsylvania Railroad and now on through Elizabeth and Newark to Jersey City, all the way much like a city. How we did dash and roar right through these cities whose streets were barricaded with long arms that rose and fell as we rushed by.

At Jersey City we leave the train and going upon a great ferry-boat are soon in the mighty and bustling city of New York. I put up at Smith & McNell's popular hotel and eating-house, opposite Washington market. After dinner I went up to great Central Park, wishing to see the famous place, in her cool, summer dress of green, spangled with flowers, as each time when I was there before she had on her too cool robes of white snow. I there met thousands of people rambling among rocks and trees, on green fields, beside lakes or in shady bowers. What a host of children in baby carriages and in arms, or walking; many of them looked as if they indeed needed fresh air. Again I gazed a long time on the odd and very ancient obelisk from distant Egypt. It stands on an eminence of three layers of great stones about 17 feet square at the base. The obelisk, or needle, as it is sometimes called, stands on a great stone which was brought with it, measuring nine feet square by seven feet in thickness. The top of the obelisk is, say, sixty-five feet from the ground. The turnouts or carriages of all kinds, shapes and colors which you see here by the thousand are an interesting feature of the place. The coachmen are dressed in livery. However, many of the vehicles are driven by the owner himself as he goes out with his family, or with some friend, or alone. Here I saw the lightest and most graceful and easy carriages that I have yet seen. I went down by the menagerie and saw a large herd of elephants feeding in a field. The wonderful variety of birds, some to swim, some to wade, and some to sing and others better adapted to aerial flight, all make an interesting show. I bid good evening to the park and go down on the "Elevated," which means, of course, the elevated railroad.

On the morning of the 15th I took my trunk up to Pier 40 and gave it in care of the great Cunard Steamship Company. I went aboard the "Servia," a magnificent ship, and looked about awhile, but I will know her better before I try to tell you of her.

In the afternoon I paid fifty cents for an excursion ticket to Coney Island, and stepped aboard of a great iron boat with hundreds of others and steamed down New York Bay. Yonder is Brooklyn, the great bridge, Long Island, Governor's Island; yonder Jersey City, New Jersey, Bedloe's Island, bearing above the waves the mighty Statue of Liberty Enlightening the World; Staten Island, Forts Hamilton and old Lafayette, light houses, Sandy Hook, etc. Oh, what a breeze! it is almost cold! and so hot in New York! See that straight line in the water which tells where the brown waters of New York Bay meet the clear blue waters of Old Ocean. The air seems to smell slightly of salt. Oh, how delightful it must be to sail salt seas! Now we turn a point and land at a great iron pier which runs more than a thousand feet into the sea.

We are now at Coney Island on the eastern coast of Long Island. I wish I had time to describe the place. It is perhaps the most wicked place in America, though very handsome. Fun and pleasure, and money-making here hold High Carnival all summer. Like a holiday every day and on Sundays like two holidays. I stood on the white sand and saw men, women and children bathing. Some contending with waves far out, others holding on to ropes, while others stood or lay in the sand with sea waves dashing over them. You must know that the sea is always in motion, its waves always either sigh or roar, coming up and going back. It is alive and doing business where it has done business for thousands and may be millions of years. Here are great hotels covering acres. West Brighton, Brighton and Manhattan Beach, and miles away across the waves may be seen the gigantic hotel at Rockaway Beach. To the east is the great, blue, everlasting sea. Paying five cents I rode on the Marine Railway which runs over a corner of sea water for nearly a half a mile to Manhattan. What a beautiful place!

I paid ten cents and went in to hear Gilmore's great band of sixty-five musicians play. The bright-colored cloth canopy tinged all below charmingly. Oh, what enrapturing music for an hour or two! "Unequalled." Yes, P. S. Gilmore, that is the word. They blend thunder and clang and ring and cling and roar and whistle and sighs and sobs and shouts and bird songs, twang of catgut and ring of anvil and exultations of all kinds into music so rare that when you do not laugh or cry you either write poetry or plan for greater and better things. They played in a place that made me think of a great sea shell set up at the edge of the sea with open part turned inland. At another place I heard the 7th Regiment band of nearly fifty pieces play. They do grandly also.

Toward evening I was taken, for ten cents, to the top of the great steel tower, three hundred feet up. There you have a strange and awful feeling as you gaze out over sea and land for fifty miles. Men and women below look like children. Say ten miles away stands the dark Statue of Liberty. Away on the sea the white sails glisten and wave. Music rises from below and you see the merry-go-rounds in the form of all kinds of animals, birds and fishes; and there are a cluster of balloons flying around and around. Now the lamps are lighted and the beach is all ablaze with colored lights, clustered and single, and one almost thinks the flower-beds have begun to send out lights as well as fragrance. Now we descend and as we are just "too late" for the boat we must wait an hour.

Life is something intense here at night. Oh, I wish each one of my readers could be for an half hour at the top of that lofty steel tower. They would see and learn so much of the sea, of geography and of this mysterious thing called human nature or life. On the ground amid things, glorious and otherwise; amid painted things animate and inanimate, you are asked to come and sit, free of charge, to see and hear shows of acting, dancing, singing, sleight of hand and the drolleries of clowns, but while you listen they hope you will order something to eat or drink, which we about always do, for you know, if we Americans are not "dry" we can always eat, if it is only ice cream, in July. It is dark, or rather it is dark somewhere else. Coney Island does not believe in physical darkness.

We go to the 8:40 p. m. boat and sit on the top deck. The whole beach for miles blazes with gas and electricity like a hundred political torch-light parades. Yes, "the lights along the shore" are burning. Where a great sea strikes a great land there the fire flies, so to speak. Now our monster boat glides up the bay. See yonder the fire-works at Manhattan! A sham battle with cannon and mortar is going on! The whole canopy of darkness blossoms with gay colored fires that scatter their brilliant leaves slowly down toward the earth. Oh, enchanting spot! let men, women and children beware, for we cannot live forever on ice cream, and fire-works, and music, and beer, and hope, and envy, and ambition, etc. The bay is full of ships small and large. Now we see the great Statue lit up. The light should be ten or twenty times as great. Yonder is the Brooklyn bridge spanning the east river; see the lamps! How like a great row of lights in the heavens.

We got off the boat at Pier 1 and took the elevated railroad to Smith & McNell's, where I rested well last night, and now I must stop writing and go and trade off a few "green-backs" for "British gold;" to use in Liverpool, Whitby, London, etc., for in about two hours that English Captain of the "Servia" will say "all aboard" and we will wave a farewell to America's shore and at three o'clock I will wave my—white, yes, white handkerchief, to all my friends and readers and to those dear little, tender, wondering, hopeful hearts in Lehman. But, what is the matter? I seem to need spectacles! Farewell.

# CHAPTER III.

### "BEHOLD ALSO THE SHIPS."

TWENTY-THREE HUNDRED MILES OF BILLOWS—PASSENGERS VARIOUSLY ENGAGED—LOOK THROUGH THE GREAT SHIP—WHERE BUILT—HER SIZE—ONE-TENTH OF A MILE LONG—HER WEIGHT—HER MINES OF COAL—PASSENGERS—CREW—TWO STORIES UNDER WATER—THE STEERAGE—THE GILDED SALOON—TEN THOUSAND HORSES OF STEEL TO CONQUER THE SEA—THE RAGING FURNACES AND SWEATING FIREMEN ON THE FLOOR OF THE SHIP—"YOU ARE CHALKED"—THE VAST, VIRTUOUS OCEAN—NOON IN THE DEEP—TIME ANNIHILATED—THE IRON TUNNEL—THIRTY-FIVE BOAT LOADS OF FUEL—MAN MOVES ALL THE OCEANS—QUEENSTOWN—LETTERS—ON TO LIVERPOOL.

Twenty-three hundred miles of Atlantic billows rise and fall between our good ship "Servia" and New York, in the "Land of the Free." I sit by a brass-bound porthole, which is closely locked each night with its round door of heavy, clear glass. The ship rolls gently from side to side. Men are talking, children are prattling and playing. Ladies are sitting in easy chairs reading, novels in nearly all cases. Many of the young men are resting or sleeping in their berths. It is three o'clock in the afternoon of Friday July 22d. The water roaring, and white with foam, rushes in waves from the black, steel sides of our great ship as if angry at being thus disturbed, while the deep blue waves roll away to the north many hundreds of miles farther than we can see. The whole sky is covered with clouds of light lead color and has been so shrouded for days and nights. They say we are about six hundred miles from Queenstown, Ireland, where we will land before sailing to Liverpool.

The Royal Mail Ship, "Servia," is a large and magnificent steamship worthy of a few words of description. She was built in 1882 at Glasgow, on the Clyde, Scotland, and cost about two hundred and fifty thousand pounds, or over twelve hundred thousand dollars. She is 530 feet in length and about 54 feet wide. Think of it, she would reach from the middle of Franklin street to River street, Wilkes-Barré. She sinks into the water when loaded about 26 feet, leaving about the same number of feet of her hull above water, while her upper decks are nearly or quite sixty feet from her lowest timbers or the steel frame-work of her keel. Three great iron masts rise above the deck more than a hundred feet. Her weight without cargo is about eight thousand tons and with her present burden weighs about thirteen thousand tons. Her tonnage is set down at seven thousand two hundred tons, i. e., the number of tons she can carry. We have on board nearly seven hundred passengers and the ship's crew, numbering about two hundred and fifty, making a total of nine hundred and fifty persons. She is constructed of steel and iron: I mean the hull and frame work. One coating of steel outside and a lining of iron within. She is one of the very largest ships in the world. The saloon and first-class cabins are finished and furnished magnificently. The captain gave me permission to go, and attendants to show me, through the ship. I went down under the forecastle deck and saw where the steerage passengers have to eat and sleep. The darkness and closeness and seasickness of many and not over-clean people make it a dismal and unpleasant place. Away down near the bottom of the ship where the waters are always dashing on the outside of the steel-plating I saw the common sailors' bunks, and on the other side the firemen or coal heavers have their quarters, while just above a great store of provisions are kept, meat, vegetables, &c. The fresh meats and fish are kept cool and sweet in a chemical refrigerator run by a steam engine, which is going nearly all the time. In some rooms of the steerage part of the ship, I counted bunks or sleeping places for twenty persons.

The intermediate department is capable of accommodating but a hundred or two of passengers, but the berths are clean and comfortable, being supplied with spring beds, blankets and all necessary articles.

The first-class cabins are very elegant. I was shown the room of the Earl of Aberdeen and lady who are on board, and also where the Queen of the Sandwich Islands had her home when she came over to New York the early part of July. I visited the barber shop, the grand saloon, the music gallery, the pantry, the dish room and the cooking department, the fruit room, the library, the bath rooms, the ladies' boudoir, the smoking room, the wheelhouse, the captain's room, the mates' room, the drug store, &c. The saloon, as I above stated, is fine. It is lighted by many electric chandeliers, and will seat in cushioned chairs at dinner 309 people The beautiful hard wood with its inlaid pictures representing art, science and commerce, and the beaten brass, and crimson curtains about the portholes, and the large hanging nickel-plated goblet racks over the tables, all have a pleasing effect.

Mr. Julian De Ovies, a young and polite Spaniard, who is proud of his old Castilian blood, Fruit Steward, showed me around. At the printing office he gave me menus and concert programmes, charts, &c. Probably the part of the ship that impressed me most was the engine and fire rooms where the power is generated and exerted to force this monster of the deep, in one week, against and through three thousand miles of winds and waves on the stormy Atlantic.

Near the middle and at the bottom of the ship the mighty engines are located. Open work of steel like ladders form the decks or scaffolds above this portion of the ship so that the hot air may ascend and cool air find its way down. When I went down where these steel giants were every second lifting three monster piston-rods seventy-eight inches upward and heard the labored breathing and felt the powerful pulsations I said, "a great institution to conquer a great ocean!" The engines are 10,000 horse-power. The employees were courteous and pointed out the various parts of interest. This vast riveted chest of steel is the condenser where the steam is pressed back to water to use again. You see much smoke float away from an ocean steamer but little or no steam. We walked along the great twenty-inch shaft that revolves the screw that propels the ship. The sides and top of this long tunnel through which runs the shaft, is of heavy boiler iron with water-tight doors here and there, which in case of accident are closed, and though one portion of the vessel were filled with water, other parts might be all right and keep all afloat. The water-tight doors are closed at noon each day to be sure that all is in working order.

I went into the fire-rooms, where few passengers are admitted. Here were thirty-nine roaring furnaces, where twenty-one sweating men were heaving the coal and keeping up the fires. I also went into the coal bunkers or bins where 2,100 tons of coal are stored for each trip. It looked like a Wyoming valley coal mine near a number of raging furnaces. It was, between the fires, the most oven-like place I had ever seen. I then contrasted the difference between the position of these firemen and the gentlemen and dudes in the luxurious ice cream and wine palaces overhead. Indeed, I fancied I found as good and trustworthy men down there on the floor of the deep as could be found above, though some of them did draw a shovel on the smooth iron floor in front of me, thus saying, "you are chalked," in other words, "a fee is expected."

I acknowledge, the trip cost me a number of English shillings, but it was a "big show" for me, and I was quite satisfied. The men stay down here four hours at a time and then go up to rest for eight hours. When not really in front of the roaring furnaces they stand under ventilators, whose funnel-shaped mouths are turned to the windward, on deck, fifty feet above. By the way, perhaps there are a hundred ventilators in various parts of the ship to suck up and carry down fresh air to the lower portions of the ship, for at night, and especially in very stormy weather the portholes, (windows) and doors and hatchways are all closed nearly or quite water-tight, as the ship plunges under and through the awful waves of the sea.

Great is man, but greater is the Maker of the sea! Man may use Old Ocean, if he walk uprightly, for legitimate purposes, but she is too vast and virtuous to be poluted by the pigmy, man. Now I hear a clanging and a ringing, and the engineer says it is twelve o'clock and he turns the good clock ahead nearly half an hour, for as we run toward the sun we gain time; as it were, we help the sun to do his work. He writes on a bulletin that we have made 366 miles since yesterday at twelve. The smooth, oily floor of the engine room is hard to walk upon when the ship rolls and they give me a handful of clean waste to help me grasp the smooth, greasy iron stair-rail as I go up to the free, open deck in time for dinner.

The engineer said, "we work up to nearly ten thousand horse-power," and the captain said "we burn from two hundred to two hundred and five tons of coal per day."

When a boy I wondered at the greatness of a canal boat that could float away with sixty tons of coal, but this leviathan of the deep required thirty-five boat loads of coal to enable her to say "good afternoon" to America and "good morning" to queenly old Europe.

These powerful engines displace or dash out of the way about four hundred million tons of water in going from New York to Liverpool and doubtless agitate trillions of tons more.

This is certainly long enough for one letter and in my next I will mention our voyage, our fellow travelers and the "great deep" and some of its wonders.

We are now in sight of Queenstown, Old Ireland, where they take our letters to mail them for America. Some of our company disembark here, but most of them cross the Irish sea, nearly three hundred miles farther to the world-famous shipping port of Liverpool, England. Adieu, across three thousand miles of deep, blue water.

# CHAPTER IV.

### ON THE GREAT DEEP.

ON BOARD THE SHIP—HOT DAY—AN ACRE OF WAVING HANDKERCHIEFS, DAMP WITH TEARS AND PERSPIRATION—BAND PLAYS "AULD LANG SYNE"—MOVING OFF THROUGH A LABYRINTH OF GREAT THINGS—OTHER EUROPE-BOUND STEAMERS—OFFICERS VIGILANT—HILLS SINK WITH THE SUN AT THE WEST END OF A BROAD, SILVER AVENUE—HOT BELOW DECK—MY BEDROOM—MY COMRADES—THE SPOUTING WHALE—SHIP FARE—SUNDAY ON THE SEA—RELIGIOUS SERVICES—FOG—BIRDS—PORPOISES—BIG FISH—COLORED FISH—THE SEA TRIES TO MIMIC THE HEAVENS—A WORLD OF WATER FIVE MILES DEEP—ITS GLEAMING ARMS ENCIRCLE THE ICY NORTH AND THE SPICY GROVES OF "FAR CATHAY"—FRIENDS ON DECK—WHAT SEA WATER IS LIKE—PEOPLE FROM ALL OVER THE UNITED STATES AND CANADA—A GALLANT EARL AND HIS FAIR COUNTESS; GENTLE FOLKS; THEY AMUSE AND TREAT POOR CHILDREN—NAMES OF SOME FELLOW PASSENGERS—OCEAN ROUGH—MANY ILL—THE WRITER KEEPS WELL AND SWAYS IN A HAMMOCK WORTH FIFTEEN HUNDRED THOUSAND DOLLARS—COOL ON THE SEA IN JULY—IRELAND SEEN THROUGH FOG—PLEASANT SIGHT—THE OLD "STOW-A-WAY" RECEVES A SOVEREIGN—OFF QUEENSTOWN—SAILING UNDER BIRDS ON THE IRISH SEA.

About 1 o'clock on Saturday, July 16th, I found myself, by street car and on foot, wending my way to

Dock No. 40, on the North River, to go aboard the Royal Mail Steamship "Servia." The weather was very hot. Why men and horses did not drop down more frequently than they did is a wonder to me. Hundreds of people were hurrying down to the great covered pier, many to sail on the "Servia," and others to see us off. Trunks, baggage and merchandise, and provisions for the trip, were being hoisted on board by great hoisting machines, and people were passing up the gang-planks or bridges. There were people of nearly all ages, sexes, and conditions in life.

Many visitors came on board to take leave of their friends. Soon the word came for us to let go and put off. Then hand-shaking and embraces and tears, and finally the last bags of mail came on board, and visitors walked down the planks and a few later ones hurried up, and, while a band was playing on the pier, the connecting links between us and the shore were drawn up, while our great ship with her deck crowded with people, moved slowly out into the river.

As we headed toward Old Ocean I heard the familiar notes of "Auld Lang Syne," and looking I saw the whole outer end of the pier was crowded with people, many being ladies, waving handkerchiefs, and, of course, our decks were all a-flutter with handherchiefs, mine with the others, for, though no one there on shore knew me, I could wave adieu to my country and her people.

The day was clear, and the ride down New York Bay, near so many interesting objects, was very enjoyable, notwithstanding the heat. It was remarkable how plainly we could see the really great and lofty buildings in New York. It is a fact, that large and great things are seen best from a considerable distance.

By the way, I was told that the music given us at leaving was due to the fact that we had on board with us some great person or persons, as it is not common for steamships to be thus serenaded by a fine band at departing, and I afterward learned that we had as fellow-voyagers the Earl of Aberdeen and his Countess.

As our great ship, (530 feet long) with nearly one thousand people on board, plowed the waters of the bay, we counted four other large steamers also leaving, bound for England, France and Germany. Our good Capt. Horatio McKay stands on the bridge, his vigilant eye sweeping the wide stretch of water as we begin to leave Sandy Hook on the west and Coney Island and Rockaway Beach on the northeast; and the old pilot stands near him, while the first mate, Robert S. Simpson paces to and fro at the bow, on the forecastle. As I did not then know his office or business, I walked near him and found him to be civil and not unwilling to give information, but when I noticed a rope was stretched between us and others, I saw it was proper for me to retire, as I afterwards learned that until a ship is fully out to sea there is always more or less danger from sand-bars, rocks or collisions.

Now the hills on the New Jersey coast begin to look silvery and sink down with the sun, and as the sea is covered with a strange, beautiful light to the west, twilight sets in and we lose sight of America. As the ship plows along, the white, foaming waters roll away from her prow and sides and many of us gaze on the pleasing sight for hours, for though the breeze that fans our cheeks is cool, the ship, all below deck, is still very warm.

At about 10 o'clock I retire to my state-room, and find that I have a neat little bed, upon a wire spring mattress, about two and a half feet wide by six feet long, and Assistant Steward W. W. Kennedy has put me in with three young men, each having a bed in our state-room, which is, say 6x8 feet, where we can look through a round port-hole upon the sea. Two beds on one side and two on the other side, one above another. The names of my fellow-travelers are Joseph Groves, of Pittsburgh, Pa., P. W. Rafter, of Richmond, Va., and B. McDonald, of New York City.

Sunday morning I arose at half-past four; so hot and close in state-room I could hardly rest or sleep, but cool and refreshing on deck. As I walked the deck an elderly lady and young man were pointing and looking off northward, and there I too saw the white water-spout of a whale thrown up in the form of a great ox-bow, and probably a portion of his black back, but he did not gratify our curiosity by coming nearer. About seven o'clock the bell rang for breakfast and nearly every one found himself possessed of an appetite. The passengers in the steerage, or most uncomfortable portion of the ship, would be served with coffee, bread and meat, and sometimes oatmeal and soup. The intermediate passengers, having it clean and comfortable, were provided with coffee, tea, butter, milk, fresh bread, mutton, beef, potatoes, bacon, oatmeal, puddings, etc., in liberal quantities. The saloon or first cabin passengers were provided with all the luxuries as well as the substantials, soups, fish, fowls, meats, vegetables, bread, pastry, fruits, nuts, wines, etc.

Yes, for say ten, twelve or fifteen dollars a day one can fare sumptuously even on the "great deep," as our lordly ship pushes on at the rate of four hundred miles a day. You will see that there is great difference in the treatment and board furnished, but you must remember that one pays $20.00, another $35.00, others from $60.00 to $120.00, or even more if they ask many extras. Being an ordinary man, as you know, I chose the medium position and was thus permitted to reach out my right hand toward gentility, wealth and culture, and my left hand to the worker, the poor, the humble and the sailor.

Our first Sunday was a lovely day; the sea was "smooth as a lake," and at 10:30 a. m. the bell rang and we, that is, many of us, gathered into the saloon and our captain read a very suitable service from the prayer book of the Church of England, and we sang two or three hymns. While engaged in worship a fog sprang up and the fog-horn, or gong, was blown every minute or two until the fog lifted, or until we ran through it. You probably know that we could see but a few rods into this sea-fog and the whistle was sounded to prevent our colliding with another vessel; as much as to say, "look out there! I am coming!" The afternoon was fine, and after dinner all seemed to enjoy themselves as they sat or lay upon deck, or occupied easy rocking-chairs and read, or gazed out upon the waters, while others promenaded the deck for exercise; generally men with men and ladies with ladies, as we had not yet become acquainted with each other; but later in the voyage the young men and women, and old ones, could be seen walking briskly up and down, talking and looking out to sea, and watching the sea-birds as they flew through the air a short distance above the water or rested themselves upon the swelling waves. The stormy petrel, or Mother Carey's Chickens, were seen all the way across the ocean at intervals.

Quite often we would come into a school of porpoises; perhaps hundreds of them. Sometimes a dozen or more at different places would shoot up and out of the water with their swinelike-looking heads, reminding one of hogs springing over a low wall. They appeared to follow the ship a short distance, and you could see them gliding along some feet under water. They seemed five or six feet long, a foot or more in diameter, and with brown backs, and sides of gray or whitish color. I saw one large fish, say eight feet long, which I think was a shark, and as the ship rushed by, he curved his body and darted away like a pike. I saw green, red, yellow and white fish of smaller size, and one bright, purple mass, like a peacock's tail, which was probably a jelly-fish. Readers and children, imagine yourselves on a world of water—water all around meeting the sky; the sun coming up out of the sea and going down into the sea; and this water looks as blue, far out at sea, as indigo, especially when the sun shines from a clear sky. You see, the heavens are older, and greater, and higher, and what can the sea,—the unstable sea do but to mimic the heavens? When the heavens frown with dark clouds, then the sea frowns dark, and great waves roll and toss like clouds on its surface, and the white foam of the billows' crest and the sparkling phosphorus may be compared with heaven's lightning, while her almost constant roar may be called the imitation of thunder.

Consider, also, that this world of water is from two to seven miles deep, and that it touches all the rest of the water in the world, for all the rivers and lakes of Earth (above or below the surface) stretch down their gleaming arms to the sea. The dew, and the shower, and the water-spout are all fed from the sea. The calm, beautiful sea that we gazed upon that Sunday, stretches away to the frozen north and the icy Antarctic of the south, many thousands of miles away. It encircles islands and continents from California's Golden Gate to the pearly and spicy isles of " far Cathay."

I must hasten, for I have notes already which would demand a score or two of letters. I retired that evening at 8.30, and as the ship had cooled off in the ocean breezes, I slept well until 4.30 next morning and arose about 5 o'clock, feeling well. Going upon deck, I walk to and fro with friends, for I have found some friends already, or. sit in my own hired chair, for sailor Sullivan found a chair which he let me have for the trip for " four shillings," so near to a dollar that I gave him a dollar. Was the chair worth a dollar?

Probably not, but its use was worth a dollar to rest in and save one's clothing clean and uncontaminated by the floor of the decks, for how can one rest in poor or soiled garments?

Let me tell the young and those unacquainted with the sea, that sea-water is perfectly clear and white, and as salty as very strong brine, and while a small quantity might be wholesome and settle the stomach, a larger quantity would surely make one ill, however, it might be an illness that would later bring a better feeling and health. I found that many of our comrades had crossed the sea before, some of them a number of times.

Have you understood that our great ship took out four hundred and fifty saloon, or first-class cabin, passengers, one hundred and seventy-five steerage passengers, and say seventy-five intermediate passengers, besides the officers and crew of two hundred and fifty? Mr. Hendrickson, of Brooklyn, N. Y., was in charge of a European excursion numbering about two hundred persons, composed chiefly of lady teachers of Brooklyn and New York.

I met people from nearly every part of the United States and Canada. I met Mrs. Davies and her son and daughter, from Nebraska City, Neb., who were neighbors there of Mr. and Mrs. W. L. Wilson, formerly of Plymouth, Pa. Of course, I made a number of acquaintances among the officers and crew, and passengers, and took the liberty to ask them to write their names in my memorandum book. The best known and most distinguished passengers we had were the Earl of Aberdeen and his wife, the Countess of Aberdeen. They had been traveling quite extensively in America. They are indeed gentle people, and much beloved on land and sea. The reader will remember that the Earl was formerly Lord Lieutenant of Ireland. The Earl is a young looking man, say five feet nine inches tall, slender, fair complexion, dark hair, and a slight tinge of Scotch in his appearance and accent. The Countess is about as tall as her lord, complexion fair, hair a beautiful reddish brown. She is young, and has children, at least one. When I saw her I was ever reminded of a fine, tall, healthy girl of education, taste, and gentle refinement, such as we occasionally meet in the country in America, in favored localities and well-to-do families.

The Countess came out occasionally and made the little children of the steerage and intermediate departments presents of confectionery, little books and toys; however, a few other ladies of the first cabin did the same, on at least two occasions. One evening much pleasure was afforded many of the passengers, when the Countess came to the fore of the ship and got the humble children to run races on the deck, and the winners were rewarded with some little prize of a toy or book. Finally, when she began to undo a rope to get up a tug-of-war among the little ones, the Earl came out and assisted her, and much mirth and good feeling was promoted by the harmless tugging at each end of the rope by the little ones, gazed at on each side by a wall of spectators.

I will give a few of the names I have in my book written by themselves, viz: Earl of Aberdeen, Countess of Aberdeen, (the Earl wrote merely "Aberdeen" with date and address, and the Countess wrote "Ishbel Aberdeen," date and address); Horatio McKay, Captain; Robert B. Simpson, Chief Officer; Edward T. Richardson, Second Officer; Thomas Fleming, Purser; Andrew Finnie, Chief Engineer; Edward M. Finucane, Surgeon; John B. Lyle, Chief Steward; William W. Kennedy, an assistant steward; Julian de Ovies, steward in charge of the fruits and nuts; Mr. Hoy, Chief Cook; Charles Bycroft and William, assistant stewards in intermediate department. Among the passengers I mention a few : Thos. Edwards, Louis F. Landers, Daniel Hockaday, P. Pearson, Wm. Cowley, P. Crowley, Miss Nellie Craig, Miss G. A. Normanton, Frank Sloan, Harry Footner, Thos. Goffe, Benj. Richards, Thos. Burke, Edward Stone, Fred. Leslie Chapman, of Amherst College, Mass. Thomas Davies, George Dibben, Fred. G. Davies, Miss Annie Jones, Miss Eleanor Birket, James Coventry, Boatswain on "Servia," Miss E. A. Dibben, Mrs. Booth, Mrs. G. Dufton, John Murphy and William Courtney, of "Servia;" and W. G. Graham.

The third day the ocean was quite rough, and our ship rolled and pitched, and the billows were wreathed with white foam, and as it came toward evening the clouds were dark and threatening, and the sailors climbed aloft and furled the sails and set the ship in order, and as the waves dashed upon the deck occasionally it looked as if we were to have a wild night.

The rain fell fast and nearly all the passengers went below, and we could hear the boatswain giving orders with his shrill little whistle. Many were sea-sick, and that evening, and for a day or two following, they were a sad looking lot for they were obliged to "pay tribute to Old Ocean," in other words, "feed the fish." If the children do not know what these words mean I will tell them when I return.

I did not get sick. I liked the motion of the ship. It was like a swing, a cradle, a see-saw, a rocking-chair, and merry-go-round, but most of all it reminded me how, when a boy, I climbed a very tall and slender hickory tree in a high wind, and as I rocked to and fro my mother on the ground begged me to come down. Poor mother! I wish I had caused her less anxiety. But, really, many sailors and others wondered that I was not sea-sick. I thought if the Cunard people could afford me a hammock on the billows, worth fifteen hundred thousand dollars, I might try to keep well and cheerful. I think if one stands on deck and watches the billows rise and fall and breathes the fresh air, he will see what rocks him, and expect it, and resolve to let accounts with Old Ocean rest as they are and keep well.

For four or five days we scarcely saw the sun, but we did not have much rain. I feared rainy weather in England, but for ten days now, the weather has been fine, and English people tell me they have not had so fine a summer since 1868. I am cool all the time and wear my winter clothes, barring the overcoat, but I wore one on the sea.

To bring this letter to a close—on Sunday morning, the eighth day, we faintly discerned the cliffs of Old Ireland through the fog, while sea-weeds floated on the waves and white gulls sailed through the air. After a while the fog lifted and we saw the green fields, and hills, and woodlands of Ireland more plainly, and they were a pleasing sight. To see land after many days is like "good news from a far country," or like "the shadow of a great rock in a weary land," or like the rainbow after the tempest.

Between ten and eleven o'clock a. m. we arrived off the beautiful harbor of Queenstown, Ireland, and lay there until the "tender," a small steamship, came and took off the passengers who wished to land, along with their baggage, and the mails for Ireland, and the letters we wished sent back to America. We shook hands with our new-made friends, and amid cheers and jollity, and some repartee, we waved them adieu.

I might tell you that our old "Stow-a-way" left us here. A man had hid himself in the ship at New York and came out of his hiding-place when he got hungry. A cheap passage, you see! they made him work his way, but the sea was so kind to us that they were kind to him, and I was reliably informed that the Earl of Aberdeen gave the old "Stow-a-way" a sovereign, about five dollars. I am quite sure that the Earl is very lenient and kind to Ireland and the Irish people.

Here, in the Irish sea, gazing on the distant and inland mountains of Ireland, and faintly discerning bays and towns along her coast, while beautiful sea-birds circle above us, I will close for the present, as it is mail time.

# CHAPTER V.

## THE IRISH SEA, AND LIVERPOOL.

SUNDAY AFTERNOON OF BEAUTY AND PEACE—HEAVEN WEDS EARTH—MOUNTAIN PEAKS IN WALES—NOBILITY, PEASANTRY, BEAUTY, AND GENIUS SING ON DECK—TWILIGHT ENCHANTING—LADIES SCREAM AND FAINT—REVOLVING LIGHTS TWINKLE ON ENGLAND'S SHORES—LIVERPOOL—OUR SHIP LINKED TO 18,000 POUNDS OF STEEL ON THE FLOOR OF THE SEA—MR. PUCKEY FINDS ME—LIVERPOOL DOCKS—COST HUNDREDS OF MILLIONS OF DOLLARS—A VAST SHIP-SAFE—THE WORLD'S MERCHANDISE PILED ON CHISELED ROCKS—ACRES OF AMERICAN PORK AND LARD—HANDSOME LADIES—HORSES A "TON WEIGHT"—A HORSE UNDER SEVEN TONS OF PLATE GLASS—GREAT BUILDINGS—FORLORN CREATURES—RAILWAY TRAINS ROARING UNDER HUNDREDS OF SHIPS—A WILKES-BARRÉ GIRL MET—MIGHTY SHIPS CUSHIONED IN GRANITE VASES—THE ANGEL OF LIGHT PLACES HER JEWELED FOOT ON THE FLOWING MANE OF THE SEA.

When I laid aside my pen the other day, we were sitting on the deck of a great ship while it was rapidly plowing the bright green waters of the Irish sea. The sea along the coast of Ireland looks very green. It is Sunday afternoon, and for hours we sail in sight of the quiet green hills of Ireland, while the serrated and pyramidical mountains away inland look blue and most beautiful. We pass bays, and harbors, and lighthouses, and ships, large and small, while many seabirds wing the air above and about us.

The afternoon draws toward evening and after supper the decks are all filled with passengers, sitting, walking or talking, and gazing toward the northwest where the sun is going down between two mountains in Ireland and lighting up the sky and the sea in most beautiful colors. The following words I take from my note-book just as they were written that evening:

The Earl of Aberdeen and Lady having invited the people to assemble on deck and enjoy a praise service of song from the Sankey and Moody gospel hymns, Mrs. C. Laty, a sweet singer from St. Louis, led the singing, while nearly all joined the chorus. We sang "Homeward Bound," "Out On The Ocean Sailing," "Sweet Bye And Bye," and other appropriate hymns. The Earl and Lady and a minister standing, holding books and assisting to please and edify the large company of singers and spectators.

At the same time we could see just above the waves on the east, three or four dark peaks of mountains in Wales, and at the west a most gorgeous sunset was seen over Ireland, and the bay of Dublin and the Irish sea were painted crimson, while a line of dark green was seen near the shore, and the deep blue mountain chain stretched between the blazing ocean waves and the brilliant, flaming clouds. It was difficult to tell where ocean and the heavens met. People stood in wonder and delight, saying beautiful! indescribable! while the horizon glowed half way around the world. This was 8:30, and at 9:10 I could still see to sing, or try to sing, from my little pocket edition of gospel hymns.

It had been gloomy for a number of days, and now to add to the beauty of the scene the new moon hung its crescent in the western heavens. It was not really dark at 10 o'clock, at about which time a fog sprang up, and like an arrow a smaller steamer flashed by on our port side within a few feet, and many declared within a few inches. The officers shouted, ladies screamed, and a few fainted, and the steam fog-horn sounded its warning at brief intervals. Many realized that we had narrowly escaped a sad ending to a lovely and pleasant day, and expressed their gratitude that the sea was not claiming us or those of the smaller ship as screaming victims, for we were many miles from land, though at sundown we saw the tops of hills on either hand.

An old gentleman from Omaha, Nebraska, named Joseph Hensman, on his way to native England after an absence of many years, asked the name of the lady that led the singing, and when I told him he said he knew her, as she was formerly a neighbor of his.

A few evenings before this a concert had been given in the saloon for the benefit of a Sailors' Home in Liverpool. The programme was interesting and the Earl of Aberdeen was called to preside, and truth impels me to say that the richest part of the whole affair, notwithstanding two addresses by American reverend gentlemen, was the closing address by the

Earl. His manner is peculiar and pleasing and his words were not only very humorous and laughable, but politic and wise in reference to uniting commerce, nations and castes. Whatever his lordship is on land he is certainly a gentleman on sea. I do not say this because he subscribed and paid for the *Telephone* and also wrote out the directions for me to find the finest scenery in the highlands of Scotland.

This is what he wrote: "The Highland railway, from Perth, passes through beautiful scenery. The pass of 'Killiecrankie,' is between Pitlochry and Blair-Athloe—about six miles between."

At 11 o'clock there is still a bright streak along the northwestern horizon, where the sun went down, for you see, these northern regions have such long winter nights that they do not like to give up the sun, so they have a long, grand twilight. Now we see the revolving lights winking and blazing at Hollyhead and all along the English coast, and at 11:30 I retire to my berth, as they say we will reach Liverpool about 2 o'clock in the morning. Falling asleep, I awoke two or three hours later, and looking out of the porthole I saw a long line of bright lamps, on a level along the water, and I knew we had reached the great and famous port of Liverpool. I lay down and soon after an awful rumble, and rattle, and roar gave me to know that our true and tried ship was casting anchor in the Mersey river, as the tide was not high enough to float her into the dock.

Yes, those great, heavy chains, that ran through the nostrils of our sea-monster, connected us with the anchors weighing 18,000 lbs. that lay in the sand on the river's floor. After resting awhile we arose and the stewards with cheerfulness and cordiality prepared us our last breakfast of the voyage. Then the sailors opened up the large hatchways or doors in the deck and hoisted out tons of trunks and baggage by steam machinery, and it was let down upon a tender, a steamboat on purpose to unload ships so they need not wait until high tide to land. The tender made two trips.

My feelings when we packed up to leave the ship and her crew, and new-made friends, were similar to those of an old-time last day of school. I knew we should never in this world or any other world all meet in the same way, and though I saw no tears fall, yet my handkerchief arrested and absorbed a good many. Yes, there is my trunk, or rather Percy's trunk, bright as ever; thirty-four hundred miles from Huntsville, Pa. Now, I have mentioned my son! How can I go on? An "only son!" "Greater love hath no man." Stubborn hearts surrender.

Oh, here is Mr. Thomas Puckey, who has brothers in Wilkes-Barré; he is an emigration agent and has heard of my coming. Our tender, or boat, moves away from the ship and after a run of a mile we are landed at a great building on the stone dock, where we wait until our baggage is conveyed into the examining room of the Custom House. What noise and commotion, ringing of bells, roaring of wheels and waves, and rumble of iron-bound trunks and boxes on stone floors, rolling trucks, talking and laughing of men, and the petulant scream of the almost omnipresent child. Soon doors are opened and we go up an incline into a large room where the letters of the alphabet in large size are seen on the wall. Opposite " L," I find my trunk, and being in a hurry, as Mr. Puckey is waiting outside, I tugged it over to a low platform near the door, and unlock it in the presence of an officer, and take out some things, and open collar boxes, etc., for him to see. He asked, if I had any tobacco or cigars. I said, " No, sir." I was very willing he should see all, but he said, " What is this in your pocket?" "Got any cigars?" "No, I don't smoke." " Oh, note-book and papers." " That will do." The trunk was handed to a porter, and a boy carrying my satchel and parcel went before me to 18 Dutton street, where Mr. Puckey lives and also keeps a boarding-house.

The school-boy knows that Liverpool is one of the greatest seaports in the world. I might write columns about Liverpool, but I must compress it to a few lines, for I have already seen several great cities in England, and to-morrow I expect to start for London.

The docks of Liverpool might be termed a great marine depot or station, where many hundreds of ships from the four quarters of the earth come to load and unload great cargoes of human beings and all kinds of merchandise; timber, corn, cotton, pork, lard, molasses and oil from America, tea from China, coffee from Java and Brazil, leather from Peru, flax from Russia, silks from Italy, wine from Spain, furs from the North, fruits from the West Indies, and spices from the East Indies; all these in quantities sufficient to stock thousands of great wholesale stores.

To describe these docks, I might ask the reader to imagine a canal eight miles long; think of it! a canal a thousand feet wide running from Wilkes-Barré to Pittston, or from Wilkes-Barré to Nanticoke, all locked in by great walls of heavy cut stone and divided into many compartments of various sizes and forms, holding thirty feet of water; and some of these compartments are dry-docks where vessels being floated in at high tide are left on blocks, dry, to be repaired, painted, etc. These docks cost hundreds of millions of dollars, and here and there on their broad walls are solid stone towers, some built for light-houses and some for clock-towers, and probably some erected for appearance only. I was permitted to ascend a light-house to the lamp and reflector and look through the keeper's telescope.

Many vessels, large and small, were coming and going, and I saw three large ocean steamers start for America. There come two steamers crowded with excursionists from the Isle of Man, and soon a boat crowded with visitors is seen rushing out to sea, bound for the Isle of Man. The keeper said, the "Prince Albert" and the "Victoria," two new Isle of Man boats, are the fastest boats in the world, one going 25 miles and the other 27 miles an hour. I asked if I could see the "Great Eastern," and he said "She went up to New Castle a week last Sunday, to the Exhibition there."

Across the Mersey river we see New Brighton, Lisceard, Birkenhead and Waterloo. I walked along the great stone highway that separates the ships from the restless tide and saw acres of American lard, pork, cotton and timber. How strange, to see great logs of trees here carted about, swung under carts with immense, broad wheels, say twelve or fifteen feet in diameter! See the immense logs of mahogany, roughly squared! I presume I saw timber and lumber enough to set up twenty wholesale lumber yards. Yes, and there is a saw-mill! Is it possible? in the city of Liverpool, where you will not find one wooden house!

I rode along these docks six miles for two pence (four cents) on the top of a tram car. Street cars here are called tram cars and they carry about as many people on the top as inside. Ladies, well, they dressed well and were handsome and modest, also ride on the top of these conveyances. You, or we rather, go up by winding steps from the rear platform. Some of these cars or 'busses have no flanges to their wheels and they can run anywhere on the smooth stone pavement, and thus avoid delays.

Nearly all along these docks runs a wall of brick or stone, say fifteen feet high, which separates the business of the docks from the regular city streets, with broad gates here and there. It is within this wall that the tram cars and 'busses and great freight wagons and carts chiefly run. For long distances tall, gloomy buildings of brick and stone stand holding many thousand tons of the world's merchandise.

One of the sights that claimed my attention almost by the hour, were the magnificent draught horses moving along with tons of goods on great broad wagons that reminded me of flat freight cars. These horses, were bay, gray, roan, iron-gray, and jet black, perfectly matched. I said to a policeman, (oh, how attentive, how ready to answer, how handsomely uniformed! There are nearly fourteen hundred of them in this city,) "I do not often see such horses, do you know what they weigh?" He said, "Come along," and crossing the street he said to a wagoner, "John, can you give the gentleman some information about horses?" I ask, "Do they weigh sixteen, seventeen or eighteen hundred pounds?" He replied, "A ton weight; Mapes, the sugar merchant, has one that weighs one and twenty-hundred." I thanked him and stood by a lamp-post to note it down, while the commerce of millions roared around us. I do not say rush, for they do not rush here as in New York. The reasons are, the gangways of trade are kept more free from people and pleasure, and the docks are so broad and long, and the river front is nearly level and all paved with hard rock which is kept clean and smooth. Here come two of those grand iron-gray horses with eight immense hogsheads of oil, and here another pair, with nine great casks of tobacco, each cask weighing, say fifteen hundred pounds, and here two more with about fifty solid bales of raw cotton. These wagons weighed about three tons each. The policeman, "No. 647," George Quilliam, said, "One horse yesterday took seven tons of plate-glass on a two-wheeled cart, three miles and a half—a bonny horse,"

As I said before, the streets are paved quite evenly with hard rock all along these great docks and out and up through the city. A man said, "the granite comes mostly from Scotland and Ireland, and the paving stones from Wales." After I have seen thousands of acres of stone pavements and millions of cords of granite walls, I am more thankful for mountains of rock.

I visited the post-office. The building is very large and massive, of dark gray stone, and with its pillars in front reminds me of Girard college. I walked up to St. George's magnificent town-hall and saw the great equestrian bronze statues of Prince Albert and Queen Victoria. The expression of the prince is really most kind, intelligent and benevolent, and has in it a strong tinge of pity. If this is a correct likeness, then I say the prince was a good man. See the monster lions of granite guarding the gateway! There is the tall and handsome column uplifting the gigantic statue of the Duke of Wellington! Here is an excellent statue of Disraeli, late Earl of Beaconsfield. The building is very grand within, but I did not enter it. As I stood on the asphalt pavement near St. George's fine hall, where immense granite lions and lofty columns glorify England and uphold marble and bronze portraits of her great ones, I saw three people who looked like well-to-do people from a country district of Pennsylvania. I asked a question of them and said I was a stranger. They replied, "So are we."

I said, "I am from America." They said, "So are we from America." The Adelphia Hotel, a fine building, stands opposite.

As I stand taking notes, I notice scores of healthy, good-looking girls and women passing to and fro. I think I must acknowledge that in complexion, at least, they surpass Americans—for bloom and freshness. They are dressed about the same as ladies in America, many of them in good, rich black.

One thing surprised me—to see so many, or even a few, wearing fur capes. True, the weather was not very warm, yet the idea of furs the last of July. I will say I have not felt a hot day here and I have not seen a fan used since leaving New York.

I would have had a wonderful idea of Liverpool women for dress, modesty and beauty, if I had not happened to be the next evening in a certain portion of the city where the cotton factories closed for the day. In that quarter I saw miserable creatures indeed. Poor, folorn creatures; they looked as if they were either drunkards or had lived with drunkards for years. See the specimens of female humanity, carrying bottles and pails to or from liquor saloons! Yes, if you wish to see poverty, you must walk near the base of magnificence and luxury, or stand by a fountain that foams and spurts strong drink; for gold is harder than human hearts, and strong drink corrodes the stomach, and wreaths the head in a worse fog than a London fog.

Here is truly a modern Goliath, in bright uniform with bright metals, and gay plumes, and belt, and sword! "Oh, that is Lewis' man, nearly seven feet tall! He is door man and directs people to any part of the extensive store." An advertisement, you see! If I had time I would tell how I went under the river Mersey, an arm of the sea, while the world's shipping floated above us.

We enter a great stone building, buy a ticket, walk down a few steps, get upon a "lift," i. e., an elevator, large enough to hold a hundred or more people. We go down say fifty feet into the rocky foundations of the earth, and leaving the lift, walk down a flight of steps, and there, away under ground, we find a depot i. e., station, and an engine, and a train of cars. I enter a compartment of a car; there is room for ten persons in a compartment, in the third class; a first-class compartment has room for six, with fine cushioned and armed seats. The doors close, and we start through the tunnel under the harbor of Liverpool and run rapidly through the darkness, and flash by a train going in the opposite direction. In a few minutes we are in Birkenhead and ready to be elevated into daylight. As I have a return ticket for three pence (six cents) I will go back the same way.

I wend my way to 18 Dutton street, where I am pleasantly cared for by Mr. and Mrs. Puckey. Mr. Puckey said, "That man who ate supper with you, has been in Wilkes-Barré." "Indeed!" "Yes, that is Dr. Romain, the 'King of Dentists.'" Later in the evening, as I sat writing, an English "lass" walked in with her bundles and sat down on a bench, and as she looked to be a traveler I helped her to an easy chair;

she was not unwilling to talk and I found she was from the United States—had been over in Dorsetshire, visiting her sister and was now on her way back across the ocean. She seemed to prefer America to England. When I found she was from Pennsylvania I took an interest and asked her what part, and she said, "Wilkes-Barré, in Wyoming valley." "Indeed! I have been there." She was Miss Daniels and had lived at C. E. Ayars' for years, in the same part of the city where we lived, I mean Percy and his mother and myself. Thus we see the world is so small that people cannot really get far away from each other.

Now, I think of Joseph Groves, of Pittsburgh, who was one of my room-mates on board of the "Servia." He had lived with the Chambers family, near Pittsburgh, for years. He left us at Queenstown, to visit his native land, and had authority to buy a few good horses to take back with him.

In writing of the Liverpool docks, I wish the young and inexperienced to know, that these immense stone docks have great water-tight gates that are swung open at hightide, which is every twelve hours, for ships to go in and out, and when the sea or tide begins to fall, go back, the gates are closed, and thus the largest ships float all the time in thirty feet of water, which they could not do if it were not for these locked docks. People away from the sea should remember, that noon or night, summer or winter, storm or calm, the waves of the sea are always rippling or dashing on the sands or rocks—always coming up or going back; making difference between high and low tide of from twelve to forty feet in various parts of the world. Here at Whitby, where I write this, the difference is about fifteen feet.

Yesterday the wind blew hard from the north, across the German ocean, and as I stood on the "West Cliff," Whitby, I watched the high, angry waves roll in and break on the shore and lash the rocks and great piers. The white, foaming, hurrying waves made me think of regiments of mad war-horses with white manes, charging upon the land. Look! it is near evening and a slight shower has helped to form the beautiful rainbow, which, like an angel, sets one jeweled foot right where the great waves moan and die on the white sand, while the other foot rests in a green field by the old Abbey. Glorious scene! I think of the one who shall shout, " Time was, time is, but time shall be no more." This angel seemed merely to say, "Here shall thy proud waves be stayed."

## CHAPTER VI.

### LIVERPOOL, MANCHESTER AND LEEDS.

LIVERPOOL BUILDINGS GLOOMY — SEEMED TO SHOW MOURNING — DEATH ON SHIPBOARD — PET NAMES — TRAVELING UNDER-GROUND — ENGLISH CARS, LOCOMOTIVES, AND STATIONS — THIRTY-SIX MILES IN FORTY-FIVE MINUTES — OAKS KILLED BY SMOKE — ENGLISH LANDSCAPES — GREAT, BUSY MANCHESTER — SHIP CANAL — MAGNIFICENT HALL — FORTY ACRES OF MASTERPIECES IN ART, MACHINERY, ARCHITECTURE, AND FLORA — CROWDS OF HANDSOME, WELL-DRESSED WOMEN — GARDENS BLOOMING WITH COLORED LIGHTS — FOUNTAINS OF GILDED WATER — A SWEET VOICE — RIDING THROUGH LONG, DARK HIGHWAYS IN GRANITE — HEDGES, STONE WALLS — UNDER THREE MILES OF ROCK — ACRES OF SMOKING CHIMNEYS — THE GUEST OF KIND PEOPLE — PLEASANT WALK — EXTENSIVE BUILDINGS — GREAT CO-OPERATIVE CONCERN — STREET CARS — DUMMIES — ROAD ENGINES.

I am now at cousin Henry's in London. I have seen many great, ancient and remarkable things in England. Yesterday I visited Hyde Park and Kensington with cousin John and his wife, where are clustered many beautiful and interesting sights, within great buildings. However, it will hardly appear fair to write of London before mentioning how I came here.

At Liverpool one of the first things which attracted my notice was the black appearance of the buildings, brick and stone, which looked as if they might be a thousand years old. The damp atmosphere with the steam and smoke have done it. The stores, dwellings, and great stone halls were the same, and caused me to imagine that they mourned for departed ones who had fallen on distant battle-fields, in foreign lands, and for those who had gone down in lonely seas in the north and south, and for others who had been burned or crushed in dark mines.

Perhaps I should also have mentioned that an elderly invalid lady died on our ship a few days after we sailed from New York. Her name was Mrs. Trude, of Chicago. I presume she was the grandmother of "Percy" Trude, a bright boy I met on the ship. Her remains were carefully placed in a life-boat, swung far above the deck, and conveyed to England, on our good ship. After all, it is not singular that passengers being carefully carried over dashing, roaring Old Ocean, should speak of the ship as "good," "grand," "noble," etc., and that sailors should speak of the ship as "she," and give her pet names.

Now I enter a railway station and purchase a ticket for Manchester, and entering a compartment of a car, we soon roll out of a great station and run under-ground a long way before coming to sunshine. I presume we ran right under broad streets and great buildings to be out of the way, for railways here must go under or over traveled streets. The cars are not so long as those in America and are divided into compartments by partitions which run right across the car and are say 6x8 feet square and have two seats running across and facing each other, so that half of the passengers ride backward, there being room for from six to ten persons in each compartment, according to the class. Some are fitted up very finely with cushioned seats, curtains, mirrors, water, and so forth, and are labeled "First" or "Second" on the doors, while those marked "Third" have plain, carpet-like cushions and backs, and often only the bare boards. Perhaps five out of six who travel go "Third-class." Fare third-class is about two cents a mile, second-class is about two and three-fourth cents a mile, and first-class about three and a fourth cents a mile. The compartments have glass doors and windows on both sides, and passengers, of course, enter on the side, so there may be five passengers stepping into a car at the same instant. The doors on one side are locked so people cannot step out on the wrong side. The station-master and guard turn the handles of the doors that are not well closed, and at the sound of a shrill whistle the engineer hears and sees, that all is right, and away we go.

The depots are called stations here, and in large cities are very extensive, say ten or twelve times as large as the Lehigh Valley station at Wilkes-Barré. I saw far larger and more expensive stations, but none more beautiful and convenient than the one at Wilkes-Barré, Pa.

The platforms at the stations here are paved with

large flagstones and are all on a level with the side doors of the cars. The locomotives are good-sized, and in the hilly regions of the north they are very heavy, and dark green paint seems a favorite color for them. Formerly the locomotive had no cab to shield engineer and fireman, except a steel plate in front with a pane of glass in each side. This would keep off the wind but not the rain and snow. Now the shield or front piece turns back over the engineer from twelve to thirty inches on different engines.

In large cities the tickets (you cannot enter the car without a ticket) are generally punched when you go upon the platform to enter the train, and are taken from you when you are leaving the station at the end of your journey. Sometimes you go up from twenty to sixty steps to enter a car, and sometimes down the same distance. At a station you cannot cross the rails, but must go up and over a bridge, or under a "subway." Enough, I may mention railroads hereafter. We ran from Liverpool to Manchester, 36 miles, in 45 minutes.

We ran through Warrington, a large manufacturing place that made the whole city and farm country around smoky. One old gentleman said: "The smoke is killing the hardy oak and other trees." On this trip I enjoyed my first views of English landscapes. It was a pleasing scene; the country generally level, was diversed with trees, spires, gardens, fields, hedges, grain fields, turnip fields, pasture fields full of sheep, cattle and horses, farm-houses and villas surrounded by trees, shrubs and flowers. I may say that traveling in England is like moving through great parks, gardens and tombless cemeteries.

At Manchester I found a great city, or centre, of nearly a million inhabitants, and a great exhibition was in progress. The Manchester people are enterprising and ambitious, and are now about ready to commence the making of a ship canal from here to Liverpool, which will make Manchester a great inland port and add immensely to her business and wealth. Liverpoolians are opposed to this mighty undertaking.

I went to the post-office, and buying some stamps and "post-cards," sent off some mail. Then I went to see the magnificent town-hall, which cost twelve hundred thousand dollars. It is of gray stone and is four hundred paces in circumference. It was twelve years building, has "three hundred" rooms, and is six stories high. Buying a ticket for sixpence, I entered the building and was shown around by a handsome, well-dressed man; by the way, some of the most pleasant and affable men I ever met are acting as guides and vergers in some of the old castles and cathedrals here. I am now thinking of the very kind and intelligent man who showed us through the quaint old Shakespeare house at Stratford-on-Avon. The chimes, and the fine, polished granite and marble columns, and the fine historic paintings costing ten thousand dollars each, at this great town-hall, I shall not soon forget.

Seeing 'busses and tram or street cars passing almost every minute, labeled, "To the Exhibition," I climbed to the top of one and sat there with a dozen or more of my well-dressed and orderly English cousins of both sexes, and enjoyed a pleasant ride of two or three miles along pleasant streets,—well paved —all English towns or cities are very well paved with rock, wood, asphalt, brick, pitch, and gravel or something—streets, alleys, lanes, squares, markets, etc. Here, where stand long rows of conveyances, large and small, public and private, is the great Exhibition building, including the old Botanic gardens, all covering thirty-six and a half acres. I put down a shilling (24 cents) and pushed through the revolving gate which gave a click, showing it to be a recording or counting gate.

They said, twenty thousand a day would attend. Entering, I found myself surrounded by plants, flowers, statuary, paintings, all kinds of bazaars, and there a great building devoted to machinery, which was a grand and extensive display. Almost a second Corliss engine gave the power to run the machinery. Here are a number of large and beautiful locomotives, fifty feet long, and some with seven-foot driving wheels. Here is a very handsome teak passenger car fitted up first-class, with all the conveniences of a modern parlor and sitting-room.

The art gallery, occupying many large rooms, was crowded with many fine paintings from all over England, and embraced things of such rare beauty as to keep one looking, and loving, and wondering for days. The old Manchester streets, which were shown, guarded and occupied by people in quaint and ancient dress, were an interesting feature.

At night, the Botanic gardens, which are a part of the grounds, were lit up by thousands of colored lights, in form of stars, crowns, roses, initial letters, etc., and the edge of the serpentine lake and all the walks and thicket edges blazed with beautiful mellow light, which made the place one of enchantment. About 9.30 o'clock, the great central fountain was unsealed, and for a half hour it threw lofty columns of water glittering with many and changing colors beautifully blending—a scene of beauty never to be forgotten. While I stood viewing the scene a pleasant-voiced lady looked at me, and said, "Are you enjoying yourself?" I answered, "Yes, very much." I presumed she was some one who thought she knew me. The voice was so kind and cheery, like old times in Wyoming valley, that I thought it was a voice I had heard there. Do such voices fall on our ears and hearts sometimes from Spirit-land to soften, and remind, and guard us? I afterward remembered that I had met her and her mother during the afternoon, and enjoyed a pleasant chat with them, while resting near the great throng. I must leave old Manchester for the present, but I shall not forget her great Exhibition, nor fine town-hall, and her thousands of beautiful, modest girls and women.

I left Manchester for Leeds about 4 p. m. Ran through a fine, hilly country full of farm-houses and hedges, the fields reaching up and over the hills. Now we run among the hills; all the houses are stone or brick; now we dash into a tunnel and run rapidly for some minutes through the darkness under a mountain for say four miles—the longest tunnel I have seen. Think of the money and labor required before a train can dash through the solid foundations of a mountain! When we emerged we were still in a vale between hills, the hedges have given way to stone walls, and the hill-tops are more dark, rugged and barren, and I begin to think of Yorkshire heather and the "dry, dark wolds" of which the poet wrote.

Now we roll through quaint, old towns of gray stone buildings—no paint. Here is Huddersfield, a considerable town, noted for making woolen goods. Now we dash into another tunnel, and rush and roar for three miles. At last the smoky chimneys of old Leeds are seen. As we roll in on a "high level" the thousands of red chimney pots on the houses and the very tall brick chimneys of the factories remind me of large fallows just burned over, as I have seen them in America.

Leaving the train at Leeds, I find my way to Mr. F. I. Wing's. He is father of Mr. H. K. Wing, of Plymouth, Pennsylvania. Mr. and Mrs. Wing (Mr. Wing has been at Plymouth) treated me very kindly and hospitably, and after tea Mr. W. and I took a very pleasant walk through the chief streets, Bridget, and Bow, of old Leeds. He has lived here many years and has seen great changes. He is a cloth merchant and is quite well-to-do. We saw the fine town-hall in which many men and boys were reading and studying, also some fine stores, markets, churches, hotels and residences.

Mr. Wing said, the place was once famous for making woolen goods and cloths, but is now noted more for making up cloth into garments. Leeds has about 350,000 population, say ten Wilkes-Barrés. There is a great co-operative society here in which 25,000 men are interested. Mr. Wing says it works well. Here I first noticed the low, American street car, and the "dummy" engine, like a little house, drawing cars through the streets, and here, also, I noticed great road engines, or locomotives, hauling heavy cars or wagons through the streets; up and down, without a track.

I left Leeds about nine a. m. for the ancient city of York, being much pleased with the kind, neighborly treatment paid me by Mr. and Mrs. Wing.

# CHAPTER VII.

## YORK AND WHITBY.

THROUGH FARMS—AUGUST FIRST, WHEAT NOT RIPE—CITY OF YORK—ITS BEAUTY—ITS ANTIQUITY—PROMENADE ON ITS OLD AND BEAUTIFUL WALL—ROMAN STONE COFFINS—OLD PLACES—OLD CHURCH HIDDEN IN A CITY—MAGNIFICENT OLD YORK MINSTER; A WINDOW FOUR HUNDRED YEARS OLD MAKES THE SUN PAINT RARE PICTURES, "WORTH A KINGDOM;" COVERS TWO THOUSAND FOUR HUNDRED AND FIFTY-SIX SQUARE FEET—A TALL STONE LADDER—ANGEL TONES—CHOIR UNIFORMED—HISTORY OF THE CATHEDRAL—ON THROUGH YORKSHIRE HIGHLANDS—GROUSE ON PURPLE HEATHER—RIVER ESK—COUSIN JOHN WEARS LIVERY—WHITBY—COUSIN EDWARD—ONE LINSKILL—HIGH CLIFF—WHITE WAVES DIE AT THE FEET OF BEAUTY AND INNOCENCE—THE PANORAMIC SEA—GRANDPARENTS' GRAVES NEAR GREAT COLUMNS AND ARCHES IN RUINS.

After leaving Leeds, the railroad runs through a beautiful agricultural country till we arrive at York, and many fields of wheat, oats, barley, peas and turnips are seen. Although it is August first, and after a dry, hot summer, the wheat is not yet ripe. I noticed a field of oats here and there which was ripe and, at least, partially in shock.

The city of York, which has about 70,000 inhabitants, is one of the most ancient cities in England. Perhaps the most modern thing in York is the very large and handsome railroad station with its iron columns, and arches, and glass roof, covering perhaps three acres of ground. Near this fine station may be seen the old wall of ancient York, with its battlements, running along on the eminence of a green, well-kept mound. The wall is from ten to fifteen feet high and is of light, gray stone. It is about two feet thick at the top, and inside there is another wall or walk of from four to six feet wide, which is now used as a promenade, and one may look through the battlements or open places on the wall, where in days long past the soldiers stood and cast their arrows, lances and stones at besieging armies. The wall is kept in good order by the city. The wall encloses but a small portion of the present city, and the old gates or bars, as they are called, are quite imposing stone towers, arching the streets at three or four different places.

York Minster, one of the oldest and grandest cathedrals in England, is here, and is visited by thousands of people from all over the world. I went through the building from the crypt to the top of the great tower. I heard the chimes, and the very sweet singing and chanting by the choristers at time of service, and saw the magnificent colored glass windows. I also went into ancient towers and churches and saw many old relics of times long past, such as the ruins of St. Mary's Abbey, the old Roman Tower and the great number of Roman sarcophagi, or stone coffins, weighing perhaps two or three tons each. While visiting the Museum of Antiquities, Roman relics, and so forth, my attention was called to liberal folds of dark, flowing hair, which had ornamented the head of a young lady about 1600 years ago.

As Edward and I strolled through a quaint old street in York, we came where an old house was built, from the second story, out over the sidewalk. While we looked at it a young lady (Miss Outhwaite, yes, I remember, it was in Goodramgate street,) came out to hang up a show-case of plain needle-work and I asked her if she could tell how old the building was. She replied, "Probably two or three hundred years; one family has owned it one hundred and fifty years." "Indeed! Thank you." She continued, "There is an old church in the rear of these houses; it is very old and interesting; they have services in it but three times a year; if you would like to see it you may pass through our house, as our's is the only one on the street with a back door leading to it." "Thank you!" Edward and I passed through the humble store, through sitting-room, through kitchen, and came to the open, or rather the enclosed square, and tombstones confronted us at once. Cousin Edward, in telling his wife of our little adventure, said, "The tombstones were so near the back door, that the people dried their dish-cloths on them." I had not noticed this, all of which proves that I am not observing, as I have so frequently remarked.

The church was walled in by houses on all sides, and I was told there were but two or three doors leading to it. It was very old, say six hundred years, very unique, and interesting, with stained glass windows, altars, high pulpit, and galleries, and high box-pews.

The guide-book says of this edifice: "Holy Trinity, Goodramgate, appears to be of very great antiquity; principally decorated, but with a perpendicular tower. The chantry on the south side is decorated. In the large east window is some excellent glass, date about 1450—80, representing various saints and evangelists, the Holy Family, the Virgin and Child, St. Ursula and her Companions." Not far away, in the city, we found people who had not heard of it, nor seen it. This is the only church I have seen literally hidden in the heart of a city.

This city is one of such great beauty and antiquity and so full of rare relics that I will devote a little space in trying to describe it. The guide-book says, "It was a flourishing place about two thousand years ago." Here soldiers, politicians, priests, poets, artists, architects and farmers contended for love, for money and for supremacy, a thousand years before Columbus was born. The Cathedral, or "Minster," as it is called, is one of the oldest, grandest and largest places of worship in England. I saw its most magnificent east window of rare old stained glass, put in four hundred years ago, over seventy-seven feet high and thirty-two broad, worth a kingdom, and could not now be duplicated. I walked up more than two hundred feet through narrow, dark stairways cut in rock, and stood on the lead roof and gazed down on the rare and beautiful old city framed in green, level farms, while the gleaming Ouse wended its way to the sea. Oh, see the beautiful light-colored wall as it winds up and down to surround the older portion of the city! What a place for lovers to promenade! Oh, hear the chime of the rich-toned old bells! Can angel tones be more charming? Father, I do not wonder that you often spoke of York and its "fine old cathedral!"

I shall try to describe the other cathedrals and palaces I see in my own language, but for lack of time to do this one justice, let me take the following pages from a guide-book:

### SHORT HISTORY OF THE CATHEDRAL.

The first building for the purpose of Christian worship on this ground was of wood, erected by Edwin, King of Northumbria, in 627, who, on Easter Monday, was publicly baptized by Paulinus, a Roman missionary, afterwards first Archbishop of York. Edwin commenced a church of stone, which was destroyed soon after its completion by Penda the Pagan, and again thoroughly restored by Oswald. About this time the revenues of the church were considerably increased by a munificent donation of territory made by Ulphus, Prince of Deira, now the East Riding. His horn, given at the same time as a pledge, may still be seen in one of the vestries. In 660, the Minster, having again become very dilapidated, was repaired by Archbishop Wilfrid, and the windows glazed.

Some years later, being nearly burnt to the ground, it was re-built in the finest style of Saxon architecture by Archbishop Albert. Guthrum, a Danish monarch, who reigned seventy years in York, embraced Christianity upon his defeat by the Saxons, and was baptized in the Cathedral, Alfred the Great standing as sponsor, and giving him the name of Athelstane. From this chieftain, Goodramgate, the site of his palace, takes its name. At the time of the Conquest the Cathedral was again destroyed by fire, and re-built in the Norman style on a larger scale by Archbishop Thomas, in 1080. After another conflagration in Stephen's reign, Archbishop Roger re-built the choir in the same style to correspond with the rest of the building. The present erection dates from 1215, when the south transept was begun and finished by Archbishop Walter de Grey. The north transept was the work of John le Romayne, treasurer to the Cathedral; his son, Archbishop le Romayne, laid the foundation stone of the nave, which, with the magnificent west front, was completed by Archbishop Melton. Then followed the building of the choir by Archbishop Thoresby, succeeded by the the erection of the western towers, and completion of the entire edifice as it now stands in 1472, having occupied about 244 years from first to last. At the Reformation, forty chantries were suppressed. During the Commonwealth a large quantity of the ancient stained glass was demolished. The pavement in the nave was laid down so recently as 1736, by the Earl of Burlington. On the 2d February, 1829, a fanatical cobbler, and brother of Martin, the painter, made his attempt to fire the Minster, and succeeded in completely gutting the choir, which was restored at a cost of £65,000. Another fire occurred on the 14th May, 1840, through the carelessness of a workman, in which the southwest tower and roof of the nave were entirely destroyed. Three years afterwards, upon its restoration, a new peal of bells was hung in this tower; and in 1845, the monster bell, "Big Peter," was placed in its fellow on the northwest. Since 1860, through the liberality of the late Dean Duncombe, and by means of public subscriptions, the following improvements have been effected:—The organ on the screen remodeled, the chapter-house restored externally, the nave furnished with a new organ and seats, both choir and nave lighted with gas from the clerestory, and the interior of the south transept completely restored.

DESCRIPTION.—*Exterior.*—The Cathedral is of magnesian limestone; cruciform, and of many styles of architecture, from early Saxon to the late Perpendicular. Approaching it by way of Duncombe street we have a magnificent view of this stupendous pile, the western front and towers enriched with great profuseness of ornament, in the foreground. Round the deeply recessed doorway the story of our first parents in Eden is elaborately sculptured. Of the three statues, that in the centre niche, is Archbishop Melton, in whose time the front was completed; the other two represent a Percy on the north and a Vavasour on the south, each holding pieces of stone in their hands, as a memorial of having contributed that material from their quarries for the erection of the building.  Passing round to the north side, which we find very plain and devoid of ornament, we arrive at the north transept with its light and chastely shaped window known as the "Five Sisters." Next comes the octagonal chapter-house, and then the choir, remarkable for its two small transepts (north and south) which are pierced by windows on three sides in each case; the clerestory lights are guarded by a stone screen of a light and elegant character.  This feature of transepts in the choir is not found in any other cathedral.  The great east window is glazed outside with thick semi-opaque glass in order to protect the rich colored work within.  Beneath is a row of heads, the Saviour in the centre, with six apostles on each side; at the apex of the window is the figure of Archbishop Thoresby holding a model of the Minster—this eastern portion of which he built.  The south side is similar to the north, but disfigured in the 14th century by the erection of some low buildings, now used as vestries.  The south transept is the oldest part of the Minster, and in the gable is the magnificent rose window, above which on the summit, is a crocketed pinnacle.  The dimensions are as follows:—

|  | ft. | in. |  | ft. | in. |
|---|---|---|---|---|---|
| Extreme l'gth, E. to W. | 519 | 0 | Nave . . . . . height | 99 | 6 |
| Transepts, extreme l'gth, |  |  | Width . . . . . . . | 139 | 6 |
| north to south . . | 249 | 0 | Choir . . . . height | 98 | 6 |
| Width, with aisles . . | 117 | 0 | Width . . . . . . . | 129 | 0 |
| East End . . . . width | 129 | 0 | Great Tower . . height | 213 | 0 |
| West End . . . . width | 140 | 0 | Width . . . . . . . | 65 | 0 |
| Chapter-house. . height | 67 | 10 | West Towers . . height | 201 | 0 |
| Width . . . . . . . | 99 | 0 | Width . . . . . . . | 32 | 0 |

*Interior.*—Entering the building by the south doorway (underneath the rose window), it consists of four principal divisions, viz.: Nave and choir forming the length of the cross, and the two transepts the arms. Each of these divisions again has a large central part or nave, and two side aisles. In the south transept is the beautiful monumental tomb of Archbishop Walter de Grey, said to be the finest specimen of canopied work in existence. The rose window, and the four stained windows below it, should also be noticed. With the exception of Ely and St. Paul's, the nave of York is the largest in the kingdom; the capitals of the columns in this part are particularly rich in ornament, and the west window, considered the finest known example of the decorated style, is filled with figures of archbishops, saints and representations of the resurrection of our Lord, and the coronation of the Virgin, the date of the workmanship being 1330-1350. The "Five Sisters" window, looking like a piece of fine lace work, so intricate is the design, and unequalled for its noble proportions and quiet simplicity, is the special feature in the north transept. In the corner to the right is the entrance to the chapter-house, containing beautifully stained glass windows, and numerous specimens of grotesque carving. In the choir, all the beautiful effects obtained by grandeur of conception, united to minuteness of detail, appear concentrated, the wondrous east window forming a fitting climax to the whole. In the aisles north and south of the choir, and in the Lady chapel, are a great number of monuments, principally of military men and ecclesiastics. The remains of the earliest foundations, Saxon and Norman, are still easily discernable in the crypt under the choir. In the Zouch chapel and vestries a collection of curiosities of great historical value is preserved, the most remarkable being the horn of Ulphus, virtually the title deed by which the dean and chapter hold several of their estates. The organ screen, crowned by one of the largest and most complete instruments in Europe, is a wondrous work in sculptured stone, containing statues of fifteen kings of England, commencing with the conqueror, and several smaller musical figures, termed the "celestial choir." The peal of bells consists of twelve, of dimensions varying from two and one-half to five and one-half feet in height, and weighing from seven to fifty-four hundred weight. "Big Peter" is seven feet two inches high, eight feet four inches in diameter, weighs ten tons fifteen hundred weight, and is, with two exceptions, the largest bell in England. Dimensions externally—

|  | ft. | in. |  | ft. | in. |
|---|---|---|---|---|---|
| Extreme length | 483 | 0 | Chapter-house .. diam. | 63 | 0 |
| Nave ..... length | 264 | 0 | Height | 67 | 0 |
| Width | 103 | 0 | Great Tower .. diam. | 44 | 9 |
| Height | 96 | 0 | Height | 180 | 0 |
| Choir ..... length | 156 | 6 | Organ Screen .. length | 50 | 0 |
| Width | 52 | 0 | Height | 24 | 0 |
| Height | 101 | 0 | East Window .. height | 76 | 9 |
| Lady Chapel | 66 | 6 | Width | 32 | 0 |
| Height | 101 | 0 | West window .. height | 54 | 6 |
| Width | 52 | 9 | Width | 25 | 6 |
| North Transept . length | 96 | 6 | "Five Sisters" . height | 53 | 6 |
| Width | 94 | 6 | Each width | 5 | 0 |
| South Transept . length | 104 | 6 | East End .... width | 99 | 6 |
| Width | 93 | 0 | West End ... width | 109 | 0 |
|  |  |  | Rose Window .. diam. | 30 | 0 |

## YORK AND WHITBY. 93.

Visitors are conducted through the building by the vergers during stated hours, at a charge of sixpence each person. The ascent to the top of the central tower, 212 feet high, is sixpence extra.

Leaving York, I ride fifty-six miles to Whitby, which lies on the North sea, on the northeastern coast of England. The railroad runs through a beautiful green and level country for about half the distance, when it begins to wind between high hills or moors. The dark green heather is beginning to blossom out into its delicate purple or pinkish dress. For many miles we run through the Yorkshire highlands, following streams of water up and then following others down. Here and there is a quiet little nook or pass in the hills, and there you will see a lonely-looking little stone house with a small barn and a few trees and shrubbery near. Away off, on the tops of these dark hills or knolls, the hunter loves to shoot the moor-grouse.

Now we come to the head of the river Esk, which runs into Whitby harbor. At Grosmont we go down a heavy grade, soon we come to Sleight's station, a cool, pleasant village between the well-tilled and lofty hills. Here I met cousin John, as station-master. I had time to shake his hand for the first time and say a few words, and off we went, through Ruswarp, and now we enter the covered station at Whitby. Engineers and railroad men had said, "Yes, we know Edward Linskill, he has been an engineer on this road for many years;" and, when we stepped on the platform, an employee said, "There is your cousin, looking for you," and soon we cousins, who had never met, were embracing each other in my father's native town.

Cousin Edward carried one of my bags, and a porter looked after my trunk, and so we wended our way through the narrow, winding, and clean, busy streets of dear old Whitby, until we arrived on West Cliff, the most pleasant and modern portion of the place. Now, I have the pleasure of taking cousin's wife and daughter by the hand, and they give me a hearty welcome. Cousin's wife is a plump little Englishwoman, with red cheeks, with dark hair, and bright eyes; her hands and feet are busy, and so is her tongue, at times. Their daughter, May, is a pleasant-looking and intelligent young lady, having some culture in music, painting, short-hand writing, and housekeeping. I could not help thinking it strange that there is but one male Linskill to be found in this old town where the Linskills have lived for hundreds of years. The name appears in the earliest official records of the place.

Whitby is an old seaport town, at the mouth of the river Esk, and contains 14,000 inhabitants. The cliffs along the sea are over two hundred feet high, and where the Esk comes down and breaks through into the sea, the valley is very narrow, and so the town has been terraced up the cliffs until the west side of the town extends over upon the level or high tableland.

I wish all our readers could stand for awhile on West Cliff and see the white waves die out on the sands near the feet of a thousand or two of children and women and men gaily dressed. These are chiefly visitors who have come from London and elsewhere to breathe this fresh, cool sea air for a few days or weeks. Now, look off on the sea and see scores of sailing ships and fishing-boats, and perhaps five or ten steamers, some of them large, going north or south.

What a panorama is the sea! always changing, like a kaleidoscope. Now, look and see the white stone piers that run out into the sea for more than a thousand feet at each side of the harbor. These piers nearly always are gay with promenaders. See the fish boats come in with their cargoes that have cost a hard night's work. Across there, half a mile away, on the East Cliff, you see the ruins of St. Hilda's Abbey, one of the grandest and oldest ruins in England. See the lofty arches, and columns, and walls, and great masses of masonry that have fallen generations ago.

Near the Abbey ruin stands a quaint old stone church surrounded by an acre or two of old, dark-gray tombstones. This church is very ancient and of unique structure inside, and contains the ashes of some notable persons of this region. Near one of its doors lie the bones of my grandfather and mother. This cliff, to the church, is reached by climbing one hundred and ninety-nine stone steps, but as it is mail time, and Cook's guide and four-in-hand are about ready to drive me and my friends around great, grand, beautiful and wonderful Paris, I will close and write more of Whitby, Birmingham and London another time. Written at Paris, August 29, 1887.

# CHAPTER VIII.

### WHITBY, JET, WHALING, SHIPS, ETC.

A CLEFT CLIFF—HOUSES HANGING ON ROCKS ABOVE SHIPS—RED TILES—NARROW STREETS—THE MARKETPLACE—STRAWBERRIES IN AUGUST—FISHWOMEN—TONS OF FISH GASPING ON GRANITE PAVEMENTS, AND BURIED IN SALT AND ICE—ELEGANT WEST CLIFF—LONDON VISITORS—COLD—MANY SHIPS—A WALK WITH EDWARD — SHIP-BUILDING — WINDMILL — BY THE SEA—UNCLE JAMES—A RAILWAY ON TALL, IRON STILTS ABOVE A GRANITE HAMLET, AND HAY-MAKERS BY THE CHAPEL—A WALK WITH FRIEND WADDINGTON—HIS VARIED AND AGREEABLE ATTAINMENTS—A WALKING AND FREE LIBRARY—CAPTAIN COOK—HILDA'S FINE RUINS—ANCIENT CHURCH—HUMBLE ELLIOT WRESTED A TITLE FROM FATE AND ROYALTY—A FEAST AT A SALOON IN A CLIFF—MEN GONE DOWN TO THE SEA TO TAKE WHALES, FISH, GOLD, AND KINGDOMS—JAW-BONES OF WHALES SET UP FOR GARDEN AND FARM GATES—ALUM—JET-WORKS AND JET-WORKERS—WHEN THE LORDLY DIE, JET-DEALERS THRIVE.

Whitby, as I have already mentioned, is in a very narrow valley, where the Esk, a small river, cuts through a high cliff, on its way to the sea. The harbor is not large, but it is protected by a pier on the west and one on the east. The valley along the river and piers, between the high cliffs, is literally crowded with houses, as are also the sides of the cliffs. The houses, many of them, have an ancient look and are roofed with red corrugated tiles. The sides of the cliff are irregularly terraced, and the houses rise one above the other to the top of the cliffs, and many narrow and winding walks go up between and around the houses, especially on the west side.

The streets along the river are very narrow and full of curves and angles, but are kept clean, and crowds of orderly, well-dressed people, especially on market days, are met, and they walk in the middle of the streets as well as on the pavements, which are in many places but two or three feet wide. The scenes in the market are interesting to a stranger. Here, in August, I saw the strawberries and vegetables that we would see in Wilkes-Barré in June.

Along the pier, a morning after the fish boats come in, an interesting and busy scene is presented, for here cart loads of herring, cod, ling, etc., are hoisted out of the boats, and while fish-women bear off a portion of them in baskets, on their heads, crying— "Fi-sh, fi-sh, nice fresh fi-sh, any herring? any f-i-s-h," others are laid out in rows on the stones or packed in barrels and boxes, in ice or salt, to be sent away to London and other cities. I am informed that as many as thirty thousand tons of herrings have been caught here in one season.

(7)

I have found, thanks to cousin Edward's wife, that herring right out of the clean sea, most skillfully cooked, are very palatable. In the steep, narrow streets you will frequently see donkeys laden with two large milk cans, one on each side, and often led by some young boy who is proud of the chance to show his governing powers.

A stranger is much surprised to see the fine plate-glass fronts, and the finely filled shop and store windows in streets so narrow. I think that I have mentioned that on West Cliff the town is quite new and modern, and numbers of quite fine, large houses stand here along streets reasonably broad. In this quarter the visitors from London and inland cities chiefly locate for some weeks of summer, say August and September.

I may here mention that hundreds of visitors come here each summer to enjoy the almost unequaled scenery and sea air on these cliffs, and also take enchanting drives or walks up the Esk valley and other pleasant little vales just back from the sounding sea. I could wear an overcoat nearly any August day on the high, breezy cliff overlooking the sea, and below on the sands were hundreds of people sitting, lying or walking, while others were bathing, and all the time sail-ships and steamers were passing north and south. These visitors or sojourners, as a rule, hire a house, or portion of a house, already furnished, and either run it themselves or engage with the house-owner or housekeeper to do the cooking and serving generally.

Whitby, at the last census, showed a population of 14,000. Walking, with cousin Edward, through the streets and out on the west pier, which runs nearly a fourth of a mile into the sea, many pleasing features are noticed. We meet many old men among the eighties, and some of them remember my father, and say, "Aye, I knew 'im; 'e was a tailor." Here is the public house, named "Nelson's Flag," near the pier, where my father lived, when a lad, with his parents. Here is the little terrace, where father was born. Here is the turn-bridge, where the old draw-bridge of my father's time used to be, and where crowds used to collect while ships passed.

We passed by the ship-yard, where men were engaged in building a steel ship of three hundred feet in length. A number of retired sailors were met here, and affable, intelligent men they are. We passed along the top of the cliff, near the old windmill, on our way to Sandsend, nearly three miles north of Whitby, where I found my uncle, James Linskill, a man eighty years of age. He was very ill, and said I had only come just in time. (He died two weeks after I left England, to return home.) He looked much as my father did, and his mind seemed as clear and active as ever. He had been, they say, a very steady, industrious, and economical man, and filled, for nearly forty years, a responsible position as station-master for a railway company, and, when he left the office, his son took the place. He distinctly remembered the day, in the summer of 1815, when Whitby rejoiced over the downfall of Napoleon at Waterloo.

Sandsend is a very quaint and pleasant little hamlet, in a small ravine, or gap, in the tall cliff; on one side the sea breaks, white and musically, on the sand, while, a few rods up the vale, over which a great railway leaps on tall, iron pillars, some men are building a hay-stack, and a neat little church gives sanctuary to the few worshipers that the sweet-toned bell called together. We return to Whitby by the railway, which runs along on top of cliffs, and occasionally passes over a deep ravine, on lofty iron columns.

At Whitby I met George W. Waddington, a man of varied attainments, a good and edifying companion, one who has seen much of life in England, South America, and California nearly forty years ago. His reminiscences of California, while they possess the attraction of intense fiction, have the advantage of being literally true and historical. Here he is known as an antiquarian, or, rather, a genealogist, for he is well versed in the origin and history of very many people and family names in the great county of Yorkshire and other portions of England. He is a general favorite and a regular walking and almost absolutely free library. I know of no other man so conversant with thousands of names. I went to the East Cliff with him one afternoon, and on the way he pointed out where Captain Cook, the circumnavigator, had lodged, and where my uncle Thomas had built houses and lived for years. When we came to the old church on the hill, which is still used, and which dates back hundreds of years, and which has a good chime of bells, his words among its ancient columns and monuments were full of instruction. We also wandered about the extensive ruins of St. Hilda's Abbey.

I went with cousin Edward to the Saloon, at West Cliff, where Sir George Elliott has terraced and beautified the cliff, and erected a spacious and comfortable building for the purposes of refreshments, music, dining, dancing, fairs, festivals, etc. We were there on the occasion of a fair and dinner in the interest of the Brunswick Wesleyan Chapel, and I will say that no dinner at Paris pleased me more.

Sir George Elliott is an enterprising and popular man of much wealth, who has, by great energy, risen from a lowly origin. He owns considerable property, in good buildings, on stately West Cliff, where many visitors love to reside, promenade, and rejoice, and recuperate for a while. The saloon grounds, above mentioned, are at the top and on the face of the cliff, and are enclosed, and can only be entered by the payment of a small fee. Of course, I have been in a hundred much finer places free of charge. These grounds embrace but a small portion of the cliff view.

This old town was famous in past years as a shipbuilding town, where hundreds of men went down to the sea in ships to do business on great and distant waters. From this old place many ships went into the northern ocean to capture great whales, and force them to surrender up tons of whalebone and thousands of barrels of fine and superfine oils, to light the miner and the mariner, the cottager and the palace-dweller. Here, also, sailed out many quaint and curious crafts into the waters of the North sea, and after a dark night of work on the waves, they came back laden with bright, fresh herring, cod, haddock, soles, eels, ling, etc.

Here, many good, stout, wooden ships were built, which went out to various parts of the world, for merchandise and pleasure. There are still standing in Yorkshire the jaw-bones of whales, which were set up many years ago for gate posts and archways; some of their jaw-bones were so immense as to stride wagons loaded with hay. I did not see this, but was told it by the most worthy people; but I saw those at dooryard gates. Formerly alum was made here, and in the vicinity, in large quantity.

Here, also, the manufacture of jet jewelry and ornaments was carried to great perfection, and many women and men were engaged in the business; some as miners and laborers, others as designers, choppers out, grinders, polishers, carvers, engravers and salesmen. The jet found here is the hardest and best in the world; in fact, it is so superior to the jet found in Spain and France, that the latter can hardly be called jet. Jet, as its name signifies, is a black, coal-like substance which admits of fine carving and a brilliant polish. Whitby jet ornaments are famous the world over. Years ago there were many factories running here, but now there are comparatively few engaged in the business.

I visited the factories of Charles and Thomas Bryan, and saw the work going on in all its stages. They were courteous, and permitted the workmen to make mementos for me. The operations are interesting in all the stages, from the rough material to the polished necklace. The trade, owing to foreign jet of an inferior quality being used, is not flourishing at present. Some years ago, when the Duke of Wellington died, and later, when the Prince Consort died, the business had great booms, and some dealers who were favorably circumstanced date the permanent establishment of their business from those periods of general mourning.

## CHAPTER IX.

### LONDON: GREAT AND BEAUTIFUL THINGS.

HEART OF ENGLAND—LEAMINGTON—WARWICKSHIRE—OXFORD—WISDOM CROWNS WASTING STONE—ON TO LONDON—SIXTY-THREE MILES IN SEVENTY-FIVE MINUTES—SUBURBS OF THE GREAT CITY—PADDINGTON'S GREAT STATION—HOUSE OF PARLIAMENT—CHAMBER OF COMMONS—MUSIC WEDDED TO TIME—SIR JOHN PURLESTON—HOUSE OF LORDS—WESTMINSTER ABBEY—COUSINS FOUND—TRAFALGAR SQUARE—NATIONAL ART GALLERY—THE "WILD WEST"—BLANKETED INDIANS UNDER STARS AND STRIPES IN THE WORLD'S LARGEST CITY—AWFUL LIGHTNING AND THUNDER—BUFFALO BILL, WHILE GALLOPING, SHATTERS GLITTERING BALLS AMID LIGHTNING AND FALLING RAIN—"BROTHER JONATHAN" AND "JOHNNY BULL" CONTENDING AMID CLASHING ELEMENTS, ETC.

It would take too many columns now to tell how I traveled down through the green, shady heart of old England, to the world's metropolis, but I will try to do so later. At bright, beautiful Leamington I found a cousin, and we visited wonderful Warwick, and quaint, old Coventry, and dear, cool, green, "Stratford-on-Avon." Pleasant days were those!

Enroute for London, I stopped at old Oxford, the city of ancient colleges, where Wisdom lifts up her voice from the top of many a gray stone column, spire and dome; where the tooth of Time has eaten deep furrows in hard stone,—stone and granite created by the "ancient of days," which skillful, pains-taking and honest men chiseled and laid up hundreds of years ago. I asked a man near the station, "What do you do here?" and he answered, "We make Parsons." After I had walked around and through a score of great, gray, old colleges, with their chimes, clocks, columns, arcades, porticos, courts, libraries, and halls of art, learning, antiquities, and halls for dining, I saw plainly the character of the city, and concluded there was but one Oxford on earth. They pointed out a place in the street where men had been burned, ages ago, for their religious faith.

Sometime I must try to tell you how I went from Oxford to London that pleasant afternoon. How we galloped, how we rushed, how we whizzed the sixty-three miles in seventy-five minutes. How we leaped green-banked canals and willowed rivers, and darted through broad meadows, where fat cattle and sheep lay content; through fine fields of wheat, barley, oats, peas and beans; by great towns and smoky cities, so rapidly that we could not read the boldly painted name of the station; on by the hedges, which look like smooth ribbons of satin; on through regions of brick kilns.

At length we come where beautiful mansions stand on shady hills, and in sunny vales, and now long rows of neat, new tenements, stand like an army speaking for peace and prosperity. A few miles farther, and our noble engine draws us into the great railway station at Paddington, not many miles from the heart of great London.

The station is a great building of stone, with iron and glass roof, with room for many trains to come and go at once. Just read the signs: "In," "Out," "Booking Office," "Cloak Room," "Left Luggage," "Refreshments," "This Way Out," "Gentlemen," "General Waiting Room," "First Class Ticket Office," "Second Class Ticket Office," "Ladies' First Class Waiting Room," "Station Master's Office," "Cross the Lines by the Subway," etc. Similar rooms and offices are on each side, and the great stone platforms are about level with the car doors, which are all along the side of the train, and fifty people may at once step into the fifty open doors. The doors are marked in plain letters, "First," "Second," "Third," denoting the class, and you enter the class for which you have a ticket. It is near 5 o'clock, and I have a ticket to the Speaker's gallery in the House of Parliament. So I leave my largest bag at the cloak-room, take a receipt on paper, pay two-pence, (four cents.) Looking around, I find I am a good way from the House of Parliament, and am told to take the under-ground line to Westminster Bridge.

I wend my way down under-ground, pay two or three pence, and away we go into the dark caverns under the busy and crowded streets of the old city. Trains flash by, and we stop now and then at a station; a shrill whistle, in the mouth of the master, sounds, and away we go. Now, on the lamp-globes in the station, I read, "Westminster Bridge." I go out and pass upward through a gate-way, and give up my ticket, and come out upon the pavements crowded with people going to and fro, while the streets are full of cabs, carriages, omnibuses, etc. Handsomely uniformed policemen stand at the corners to keep order and help pedestrians to cross the streets. Right in front, across the street, stands a gray stone building of vast extent and graceful proportions. In the massive and lofty tower is the largest clock-face I ever saw, thirty feet across it, and, as it is six o'clock, I hear sweet music fall out of the sky, and the bells chime, one, two, three, four; one, two, three, four; four times over, and then we hear six loud, soft tolls of the bell. This most magnificent building is the House of Parliament, where England's law-makers, born and elected, assemble to transact business of state. It stands on the banks of the famous Thames (temz), where historical things have had birth for two thousand years. And here is Westminster Bridge, across the Thames, a grand and substantial structure. There are many bridges over the Thames, and strong stone and iron ones they are, too. They are free, and broad, and would, probably, bear up a million tons. This fine building is hundreds of feet long, and would require about a half mile walk to go around it. The towers are lofty and very elaborate. Having a pass, which cousin Edward and Mr. Nicholson secured for me, through their member for Whitby, I enter the House of Commons. I enter a great doorway, and go through a hall, and up a flight of broad steps, into another great, lofty hall, where the light falls like lovely angels through colored glass. Almost every step is guarded by doorkeepers and guards, who ask your business. In this large hall stand marble likenesses of England's great men on massive pedestals. Going up more steps, I enter a great circular hall, with lofty and finely ornamented ceiling, and the columns surrounding it have niches, one above the other, in which stand, say, sixty statues of famous people of the past. Here stand many doorkeepers in fine uniforms, some of them busy examining cards and letters. A crowd are waiting to go into the Chamber of Commons, which is in session. We, or some of us, pass the guards and go along another hall, where, in large panels, are painted some of the important events of English history. Then up a stairway, and we sit down on a well-cushioned seat in the Speaker's Gallery, and gaze down on a finely furnished room of say 60x90 feet. The chief points I remember are the handsome and elaborate carvings in dark, old oak, and the fine, soft light coming down through glass in the ceiling from gas jets. The speaker and his associates wore long, white wigs. I was impressed with the slow, studied, business-like words and delivery of the speakers,—not much in the manner, but much in the words. I could not hear all that was said, yet I was glad to hear they were discussing safety-lamps, and were interested in the subject of preserving the life of the poor laboring man.

After an hour or two I went out, and as I was entering a clean, light restaurant-room, a pleasant-looking woman, dressed neatly in black, asked me to take her in to supper, but she was dressed too well, I thought, to be really in need of a supper, and I said, "No!" She followed me in, and I said "No" two or three times before she departed. My first night in London! Yes, "Alone in London." A policeman pointed out a public house, in King's street, where I staid all night, and the people were as kind and neighborly as Wilkes-Barré people could be.

Every fifteen minutes, when awake, I heard the music of the bells in the tower of the House of Parliament, tolling the time. It seemed more like rejoicing at the birth of new time, than tolling the death of past or dead time. At a later day I handed Sir John Puleston, member of the House of Commons, a letter from Hon. L. D. Shoemaker, whom he remembered along with other Wyoming valley people, and he was apparently pleased that he was remembered west of the Atlantic, and he said, "I am as much American as any of you." He also said, "I am sorry you did not give this to me sooner, then I could have given you a seat to hear Mr. Gladstone to-morrow, but now every seat is engaged. He also said, "I would have given more than one five dollar bill to have had you admitted." I thanked him, saying, "It's all right, it was my oversight." He took me into the House of Lords, and pointed out the Prime Minister, and the Lord Chancellor sitting on the woolsack with white wig, etc., looking ancient and dignified. He also took me to other parts of the building, which is about as beautiful as marble, and gold, and glass, and oak, and silk, and leather, can make it.

Near this grand building stands the very ancient, beautiful, and historical "Westminster Abbey," the burial place of English kings and queens, and some great men. A guide took us all through this ancient cathedral and tomb, which is so crowded with lofty columns, and arches, and statues, and monuments of strange and beautiful forms; but I must leave a more detailed account to another time.

I traveled many miles through the crowded streets before I came to cousin John Linskill's, at Brixton. He is a dealer in jet jewelry. Then I went to the Ely place, near the Holborn Viaduct, where I found cousin Henry and his wife. Henry is an expert carver and finisher in jet ornaments. In the afternoon Henry said, "Let us go." We went out to grand, busy Holborn street, and ran up to the top of a "'bus," and thus we went to "Trafalgar Square." A granite paved square, almost surrounded by granite palaces, where Nelson's lofty column stands, and many famous men stand in marble, on solid pedestals, and where granite lions, and sea monsters, throw rivers of sparkling waters into the air.

We went into the national art gallery here, and saw hundreds of fine paintings immortalizing famous scenes of love, of friendship, of genius, of natural scenery, of mythology, and of blood-red war on plains, on mountains, in cities, and on the billowy sea. There was a wealth of them. Henry said, "Would you like to see 'The Wild West,' Buffalo Bill's 'America Exhibition?'" "Yes." We took a train, and a few miles' ride brought us to the grounds, where, for a shilling, (24 cents) each, we entered the extensive buildings and grounds. All free except the refreshments and the reserved seats. We walked under the glorious "Stars and Stripes," and England's royal banners, and met English men, and women, and Americans, side by side, with the wild, red men of North America, who stalked about in gay blankets as if they were "to the manor born."

Here are booths, stands, arcades, castles, bazaars, saloons, studios, and factories, where mechanics, artists, and handsome lady clerks preside. The art gallery is a very worthy display of American genius, life and scenery. We are under broad roofs of glass, and slate, and metal, upheld by wide arches of steel, and the rain descends in torrents, (the first England has had in weeks!) Now the lightning flashes in and contends with the electric lights—man-made lightning—and heavy peals of thunder crash in, and drown partially the hum of human voices, and the roar and clash of machinery, and the multifarious sounds of business life.

About 7 o'clock p. m., we went up into the great circular stand, which partially surrounds the field where the "Wild West" performances take place An hour in advance of the time, there are hundreds, if not thousands, assembled waiting for the performances to begin. While we sit and look upon the open circle, which is swimming with water, and the great rain drops still fall, while most vivid flashes of lightning appeared to rend the black sky, followed by peals of thunder that seemed to jar all of great London.

For an hour this awful display of heaven's pyrotechnics and artillery continued, and to add to the terror of the scene, the chief part of the lightning started earthward from the black heavens directly in front of us. The lightning was so bright that when the continuous streak flashed out, a long line of bright, red dots took its place. Many seemed frightened and left the place. At 8:10, when we thought the exercise could not go on, the electric light, from great reflectors, flashed into and across the watery ring, and a man came out through the water and rain and announced, in a loud voice, the programme of the evening. And very soon, through gaps in the painted mountains, companies of horsemen, Indians and Cowboys rode in, and soon the riding, racing, shooting, yelling, etc., commenced, and for an hour and a half, the wildest and most bloody scenes of the very wild American West, went on in the heart of the world's greatest city, while the terrible thunder shower slowly abated. Amid a continuous rattle of rifle firing and yelling, of almost entirely nude savages, the frontiersman's house, and the old mail coach, were set on fire, and the former burned to the ground. Buffalo Bill rode rapidly around the ring, shooting into fragments the glass balls thrown up by a rider.

Taken all in all, so wild and grand a show I never witnessed before, and why the show went on, under such circumstances, was a wonder to me and my cousin. I hardly knew whether it most meant "Yankee" courage and enterprise, or "Johnny Bull" determination and stubbornness. I tell you, we two hundred millions of English people are not to be despised! I told my cousin, that this awful American thunder shower in steady, cool Old England of the north, surprised me more than anything I had yet seen here. He said we might wait years for such thunder again. The rain and the shower is over, and cousin and I find a train which takes us nearly home. The queen and her family visited the "Wild West" show, and "Buffalo Bill" was also complimented by other people of high degree.

## CHAPTER X.

LONDON: THE FOG, THAMES, AND PARKS.

SMOKE FROM A MILLION CHIMNEYS—ONE HUNDRED AND FIFTY SQUARE MILES OF BUILDINGS—A MODERN JONAH—PLAIDED WITH RAILWAYS—SEVEN THOUSAND MILES OF STREETS—LONDON FOG—DINNER BY LAMP-LIGHT—LOST IN THE STREET—WALKED INTO THE DOCK—BEEF CATTLE CHOKE—TRAVEL BLOCKADED—MAILS LATE—CRUSHED BY WHEELS UNSEEN—WHAT MAKES THE FOG—PARTICLES OF SOOT ENCASED IN OIL AND CLOGGED IN MIST—FOGGY DAYS ELSEWHERE—MORAL—THE THAMES; A RIVER, SEA, SEWER, HIGHWAY AND HARBOR — EMBANKMENT — OBELISK— MOSES, NAPOLEON AND OTHERS—ROYAL DWELLINGS — PARKS—PALACES—BLACK THORNS AND BRIGHT BAYONETS.

I made some mention in last week's letter of London, but it would take many columns to describe the great city. There is, perhaps, never a day clear enough from smoke and haze to permit one to see even half of London at once.

Imagine a city with nearly a million buildings, covering one hundred and fifty square miles; nearly six Huntington townships, or seven Jackson townships; with seven thousand miles of streets, and containing nearly as many people as the great State of

Pennsylvania. No wonder that fog and smoke hang over it nearly constantly. I would not greatly marvel if a modern Jonah should tramp down the Strand, or along the Thames Embankment crying, "Yet forty hours and London shall be overthrown!" or an angelic messenger declare it another Babel, and confound the tongues again, and thus disperse the vast multitudes to greener, fresher, and more salubrious habitations and pursuits.

However, I do not consider London the most wicked city; I think many far worse; yet, it does not seem wise to rear human beings in such a dust, and rush, and roar, and smoke. Imagine, or as the English girl says, " fancy," the tens of thousands of cabs, 'buses, and street cars, carts, and wagons, that rattle and rumble over these thousands of miles of granite-bound streets, and the thousands of steam cars that run like a net-work over and under ground. London is completely checkered and plaided with railways, both over and under the streets. If you wish to go anywhere, all you have to do is to go up or down into a station, or get upon a 'bus or tram-car, pay a very few pennies, generally two, and you are there. Still, after riding for miles, London yet roars around you.

Through London streets beggars, princes, kings, queens, lords, ladies, artists, mechanics, laborers, and the rich and poor pass, some reclining on cushions of velvet and morocco, and others are led by a child or dog. These streets, which thunder with business, sometimes throb and rejoice with music, and waving banners, and nodding plumes. The smoke, ascending from hundreds of thousands of chimneys and engines, form a cloud which nature can seldom lift or waft away, and sometimes, when the fog comes up from the Thames and the sea, and mixes with this smoke, you have "a sight to see," in other words, you can hardly see anything, and street lamps, though burning, are seen but a yard or two.

The time for the London fogs is in the winter. They begin in November and occur until the following March. The day I left London I could see but a few rods in the streets. Sometimes these fogs last two or three days, and partially suspend travel and business, as the 'bus-drivers and cabmen cannot see to drive about the streets. My cousin said, he knew a fog to continue for nearly three weeks, and it was a curious sight to see boys with torches running just ahead of the cab horses to show the way. Sometimes you could not see a lamp across a small room. This must be much like the Egyptian darkness, for it can be felt by those with weak lungs and throat.

Cousin Eleanor said, "One Sunday I had to get dinner by lamp-light." Another one said, "On one occasion, in a protracted fog, many beef cattle died." This subject is so curious and wonderful, that I will here clip, from an English paper, the best explanation I ever read of a London fog:

"At most of the junctions of important streets in the metropolis, great confusion, danger, and delay were caused yesterday, from morning till night, in conducting the vehicular traffic; and in the midst of vehicles of almost every class, pedestrians found that to cross the street was a very hazardous operation. Lads and men earned many a copper by conducting people from one side of the street to the other during the day; and in the dismal obscurity of last night, link boys, with torches, and others, with bull's-eye lamps, were found at the corners of important suburban thoroughfares, ready to assist pedestrians across the roads. The day traffic of the city was carried on under circumstances more favorable than in other parts of the metropolis, because the public lamps were lighted. But, notwithstanding this, there were some awkward blocks during the day at Ludgate circus, upon which four busy thoroughfares converge; and for some minutes omnibuses, railway vans, carts, and cabs, were, at times, pressed together promiscuously in almost inextricable confusion. At Holborn circus, at King William's statue, west of Gracechurch street, and at the top of Cheapside, close to the general post-office, similar blocks occurred, the inconveniences and dangers of which the city police did much to alleviate. In the same way, the metropolitan police did excellent service on the great lines of traffic, such as the Strand, Oxford street, and Regent street, in extricating jammed vehicles from their perilous position, in stopping traffic where its further progress would add to existing confusion, in getting out of the way cabs, carriages, and carts, that were blocking up the roadway, and in clearing a free and safe passage for persons crossing the streets. Along the suburban lines of railway, passengers by the trains could see large fires blazing in open iron cages close to every signal post, the fire answering the double purpose of warming the fog-signalman, who could not leave his post, and of conveying, by its strong light, a good idea of the locality of the signal-post to the engine-drivers. On long stretches of line the numerous fires had a singular appearance. The attendance of children at Board and other schools was very small yesterday. Last night the fog cleared away somewhat on the Surrey side by half-past eight; and was not so thick in the city as it had been during the day. Over the northern area of the metropolis it was very dense; and that was also the case in Norwood, Forest Hill, New Cross, Hatcham and Lewisham. The atmosphere was raw and cold. The wind was exceedingly light, from the west-northwest.

"Late on Tuesday night a porter, in the employ of the North London Railway Company, found the body of a respectably dressed man lying on the rails in the Dalston Junction Station. The poor fellow was terribly mutilated, and most probably had been run over by more than one train. Dr. Callaway, of Dalston lane, was called, but life was extinct. The deceased was identified by some papers in his pocket as Mr. Nathaniel Andgrase, aged 55 years, a meat salesman, residing at 25 Oxford road, Finsbury Park. It is supposed that he fell or walked off the station platform in the dense fog. About the same time Arthur Charles Faulkner, of 131 Bouverie road, Stoke Newington, was found lying on the Great Eastern Railway, at the London-fields station, with both of his legs terribly crushed by a passing train. He was conveyed to the German Hospital, where he remains in a precarious condition. He, too, had walked off the platform in the fog just as the train was approaching. A young woman named Arnold slipped off the platform at Dalston Junction, and was struck on the side by a train. A bystander, at great risk to himself, jumped down and pulled her from the front of the engine. She was taken to the German Hospital, and after a time was able to proceed home. People were lighted across the roads in the outskirts of London, with lanterns and torches, and locomotion was exceedingly difficult. The railway services were carried on with extreme care.

"Billingsgate Fish Market only received five hundred packages of fish on Tuesday, and there was none to hand yesterday morning, and when the cargoes arrive they will be greatly depreciated in value through the delay. There are many colliers lying below Gravesend waiting to proceed up the river. The wharves and warehouses on the Thames are virtually at a standstill, waiting for the goods that are afloat, but unable to reach their destination. The railway ferryboat, between Tilbury and Gravesend, was unable to run after mid-day yesterday, and the daily passengers by the London and Tilbury Railway Company were subjected to the greatest inconvenience. At 9 p. m. an impenetrable fog hung over the river from Gravesend to London bridge.

"Two men, named respectively Govatt and Forster, who were employed in the London docks, were making their way, on Tuesday, along one of the quays, when, owing to the thickness of the fog, they missed their way, and stepping over the edge of the quay, were both drowned. Their bodies were afterwards recovered near Millwall.

"The fog enveloping the estuary of the Thames and Medway was the densest known for years. All water traffic was at a standstill, and the mail service from Queenborough to the Continent was suspended. Sheerness Harbor was enveloped in the thickest fog known for many years. The mail cart, which brings the London and provincial mails from Chatham, was four hours late, the driver having great difficulty in finding his way along the roads which connect the Isle of Sheppy with the mainland. On the water it was impossible to discern objects only a few feet ahead. The mail packets for Flushing, with the Dutch and German mails, were unable to leave Queenborough Pier, and no boats arrived from the Continent yesterday. The troop-ship Wye, Staff Commander Alfred Thomas, is still lying in the harbor unable to take her departure for Gibraltar, whither she is bound with cadets for the Channel Squadron. Communication with the ships of war in Sheerness Harbor yesterday had to be kept up solely by fog signals.

"The fog continued yesterday in the Channel, and along the coast. It was denser than on Tuesday, objects being obscured at a distance of a ship's length. The navigation of the Channel was so difficult that yesterday the Bologne steamer did not leave Folkestone, and the passengers went on to Dover, where the mail steamers ran regularly, although considerably delayed.

"The fog at Sittingborne yesterday was worse than on Tuesday. Several barges, ready freighted, are detained at some of the wharves along the creek, waiting to be despatched. The owners, however, decline to let them depart while the fog lasts. The driver of the mail cart from Sheerness to Sittingborne met with an accident on Tuesday night in consequence of the fog. He ran into a fence at the side of the road, and was thrown out dangerously near to a dyke full of water. Fortunately, he escaped with a severe shaking, and resuming his journey, arrived at Sittingborne two hours late. Such a dense and long-continued fog has not been known in this district for many years.

"A plate-layer named Hammond, while engaged last evening laying fog signals on the main London and North-Western line at Vauxhall, Birmingham, was knocked down by a goods train and killed. In the thick fog which prevailed he did not observe the train. His body lay on the metals for over an hour and a half before it was discovered. At Bilston a woman walked into the canal and was drowned. At Willenhall a carrier was driving to Walsall, when his horse got off the main road and fell into an open work. The cart was smashed to pieces and the horse was killed, but the man escaped, receiving only a few bruises."

An editorial in the same paper, among other things, says: "There are fogs in Liverpool and Manchester, in Dublin and in Amsterdam, which, in unmitigated murkiness, fall little short of those 'London particulars' for which Mr. Guppy apologized to the wards in 'Jarndyce.' Only, as there are more people in London to write and read and talk about them, so we are apt to hear more of the metropolitan darkness than of that which is every winter seen elsewhere—just as the 'miseries of the Channel passage' have a wider literary notoriety than the greater inconveniences of much more important voyages. All true fogs, from London to Behring Straits, from Greenland to Peru, are primarily due to mist, and their greater or less depth of hue is owing to the greater or less quantity of foreign matter with which the mist is associated. We have them in winter simply because in winter there is more moisture in the air than at any other time of the year, and less warmth to dissipate it than during the summer.

"On the continent there are usually fewer fogs during winter, mainly because at that season there is generally less rain, and, therefore, less moisture to be evaporated in the shape of mist. Over the greater part of Europe and America the sky from December to April is often as clear as at any other period of the year. For the upper reaches of the air, instead of holding in suspension a thick layer of vapor, discharge it in the form of snow, and then what little evaporation goes on from the snow is speedily precipitated in the same form as before. Hence the comparative immunity of the continental cities, and, it may be added, of those of America, from the pest which afflicts our milder and moister latitudes.

"This immunity does not, however, apply when the ground is saturated with water after a thaw, such as happens to be the case at present in many parts of Europe. Then, unless the wind is in such a direction that the ascending vapor extracted from the soil by the warm air is driven to a distance, it accumulates in the atmosphere, and becomes more or less impregnated by the smoke and other impurities which get entangled in its meshes. Nor do the most favored of cities escape if the sea fog is driven far inland. It is a sea fog which is at present enveloping us. Sometimes, on a clear day, it may be seen rolling in from the German ocean, and advancing up the river, and the streets running parallel with it, in a distinctly visible cloud. Then in a few minutes all is in darkness. The smoke of a million chimneys does not ascend or get blown away, but hangs within a few feet of the earth, and blackens the veil which has come between the sun and planet, dependent on his rays for heat and light. The sea fogs are generally wetter than those which owe their origin to evaporation from the land, for the palpable reason that in them the terrestrial impurities—the soot, the chemical fumes, and the other nastinesses which blacken our faces and our linen, choke our lungs, and, as the Registrar General's returns show, shorten our lives—are less abundant than the watery elements. Over the sea the air is usually supersaturated with evaporated moisture, and in some parts of the world, the Newfoundland Banks for example, this fog hangs almost continually, though it is not so black and so foul as in cities, because in the ocean there are no 'products of combustion' to befoul it. Fogs on land are more common in valleys through which large rivers flow, since, a cool body coming in contact with one that is warmer, the humidity is apt to be precipitated in the form of fog. The fleecy cloud which the painter loves is a near relation of the dirty London pall. The Scotch mist is another stage in its intensity as regards precipitation, while if the precipitation is still more copious, rain is the result, or if the strata of air through which the moisture falls is sufficiently chilly, it reaches earth in the form of snow.

"Fog in London is, therefore, in no way different from fog elsewhere, except, possibly, that it is a trifle dirtier, and, therefore, a great deal thicker. Dr. Frankland will, no doubt, have us to believe that the dewy particles of fog are each covered with a wonderfully thin envelope of petroleum, formed by the imperfect combustion of the London smoke, which keeps the watery vapor from being dissipated. But, whether this hypothesis is well founded or not,—and it has the unquestionable merit of not being easily disproved—it does not alter the broad principles with which we have to deal.

"These are, indeed, confirmed by the fact that, long before London was as large and as smoky as it is at present, the citizens complained bitterly of what Crashaw calls the 'profane fogs' that 'sit and scoule upon night's heavy brow.' Even in John Evelyn's time, he records that one week the fog was so thick that 'people lost their waye in the streetes.' A little earlier in our history we seriously thought of checking the consumption of coal by the universal panacea of hanging the offenders. We may come to that again.

"Meantime, though London fogs enjoy an unenviable notoriety, our 'brumous isle' is in no respect more foggy than some countries to which no such celebrity attaches. In London the foggy days are, on an average, thirty-eight, which is the same as in Stuttgart. In Munich they are forty-seven; in Hamburg, fifty-two; in Tegernsee, in the Bavarian Alps, one hundred and thirty-four, while so few are the clear days on the St. Gothard that this lofty pass may be said to be enveloped in mist during the greater part of the year. Its foggy days are two hundred and seventy-seven and a half out of the three hundred and sixty-five, an average which compares well with that unhappy town on the west coast of Scotland, where, according to the legend, it is always raining, 'except when it snows.'

"The moral of all this is simply that we must bear with what nature has given us. We cannot prevent the London fogs. But by consuming our own smoke, using gas fires, or in some other way ceasing to defile the air, we may render them no worse than the honest watery mists with which Northern folks are so familiar."

The Thames, a tidal river, say eight hundred feet wide, or like the Susquehanna at Wilkes-Barré, winds through the city and affords, with its docks, room for thousands of ships, and much local travel and traffic are done on its waters by long, narrow, uncovered or low-decked steamers, which glide rapidly up and down under many grand and substantial bridges. The river here looks to be filthy and much like a sewer, for, though Old Ocean sends her waters up and down the Thames like a throbbing vein, yet the mud and filth is rolled back by the tide before it reaches the open sea. However, the water looks more like mud than sewerage matter, and I noticed no disagreeable smell when I was along or upon its waters. The sewerage to a large extent is carried far down the river and more or less filtered for purposes of farm and garden fertilizing. London is nearly sixty miles from the open sea.

I walked along the Thames Embankment for a mile or two and was pleased with the wealth and solidity manifested. Here was a great wall made of immense blocks of granite, from the street level to the bottom of the water, say thirty feet, with a heavy parapet or guard wall—all so heavy that it seemed done for the sake of giving employment to workers and to evince wealth and substance.

Here stands on the solid embankment a beautiful obelisk, a "Cleopatra's Needle," from the ancient and classical Nile, where Abraham, Moses, Joseph, Alexander, Christ, Cæsar, Anthony, Napoleon and Nelson thought and did great things, in the sight of the almost everlasting pyramids. Our obelisk in Central Park is taller and finer, yet ours standing on a hill is enhanced thereby in appearance. Opposite this embankment, across the streets, stand tall and elegant buildings of gray and light colored stone, columned, turretted, domed, arched, spired; castles, temples, banks, cathedrals, hotels and palaces. Here a great, gray stone hotel is being erected. See the mast timbers and scaffolding around it like dead forest trees before a ledge of gray granite. Here stands the Somerset House, a government building for internal revenue business, etc. It is apparently six hundred feet long, and with its great and lofty columns, looks indeed substantial. Indeed, there are buildings here which would almost bankrupt even a city of some pretensions to erect.

Yonder stands the House of Parliament with its great clock, "Big Ben," and it chimes and tolls four o'clock. You would not soon tire of hearing these chiming bells. I went on into St. James' Park, Regent Park, and Hyde Park, and was much surprised and pleased to see such fine and extensive parks near the heart of so great, and busy, and struggling, and suffering a city—pleased that they, with their trees, flower gardens, seats, ponds, fountains, swans, ducks, walks, green lawns, lamps, drives, policemen and all, were free, and many poor people were resting and walking about therein. I saw the residence of the Prince of Wales, near St. James' Park, but it had high walls and trees, and shrubbery, on nearly every side. It is a plain, old structure, but I dare say it is very neat and comfortable within. Yes, it is most likely to be well furnished with beautiful things—things dear-bought and far-fetched. Opposite the prince's house is St. James' palace, a large, low, old building, well guarded by soldiers. It contains government property, and affords a residence for officers, and probably some relatives of the reigning family. As I wandered through these great parks I could imagine I was in the country, but when I came to the other side I again heard the roar of wheels and the clatter of hoofs like the roar of many waters. Yes, the pent-up waves of vast London roll on beyond the great parks, and stately hotels, stores and residences rear high their haughty heads.

I passed Buckingham Palace, a residence of the queen. It is very large, and with its fine grounds, covers much territory. It is not tall, nor stately, nor elegant looking on the outside, but you may depend there is a fine suite of household utensils and ornaments within, and comfort and happiness for human beings, provided they have health of mind, body and conscience; however, I do not imagine that royalty is very happy in Europe, nor anywhere else:—I mean royalty without wings. All these public buildings and places are guarded by blue-coats and black thorns; and red-coats and bayonets, carbines and swords, on foot and on horseback. It is dark; after calling on Minister Phelps, I start for home, I mean my London home.

# CHAPTER XI.

LONDON'S VASTNESS, ST. PAUL'S CATHEDRAL, ETC.

FIFTEEN MILES THROUGH MIGHTY BUILDINGS—ASKING FOR BREAD ON STONE BEDS—ST. PAUL'S MARVELOUS CATHEDRAL; IT WHISPERS—MARBLE HORSES KNEEL DOWN WITH SHERIFFS WHILE SAUL OF TARSUS ASKS A QUESTION—ANGELS, WOMEN AND WARRIORS, IN POLISHED MARBLE AND BRONZE, GLORIFYING DEAD HEROES — TRAVELING WITHOUT LOSS — A PURSE THRUST INTO A STRANGER'S BOSOM—A DIGRESSION — FRAGMENTS — ANOTHER DIGRESSION — HOSPITAL FLOATING THROUGH SALT BILLOWS—THE CRUEL GOD OF THE SEA—THREE GRAND SIGHTS—THE LAND OF INDIAN SUMMER—GLORY UNDREAMED OF.

I have already written two letters from London, but I have scarcely made a beginning on the great city, or "big village," as many call it. So, notwithstanding I have visited the large cities of England, France, Scotland, Ireland and Wales, I cannot refrain from writing again under this head. It is difficult to get the reader to form his ideas large enough when thinking of this vast city. Let us begin in the green fields, just out of the city, and walk through the great town. Here are fields of wheat with shocks of eight or ten sheaves, standing very thick ; there are meadows full of fat cattle and sheep. I think if David, the mighty warrior and immortal poet, had been an Englishman he would have written, "The cattle upon a thousand plains and the sheep on a myriad hills are His." Handsome mansions stand on beautiful eminences, surrounded by fine trees and brilliant and fragrant flowers; gardens arranged in symbols and letters that speak the praises of the King celestial and the queen terrestrial. Now, we come to long rows of neat, new tenement houses, for London builds thirty thousand houses a year. Now, we go on and come to substantial business blocks and the streets begin to teem with tram-cars, 'busses, cabs, drays and people. We pass on by stately mansions, palaces and extensive parks; on by temples, towers, cathedral domes, castles, monuments, fountains and great buildings of state, and arrive at the Thames Embankment. Now the heavens are smoky and the sun looks a dull red, for we are many miles from the green, fresh country. Here is the river Thames crowded with steamboats and business. Let us cross Waterloo bridge, a bridge apparently as solid as old Earth herself. We pass on for miles through streets so crowded that you wait at corners for a chance to cross. All kinds of business is going on in the streets and in great granite markets, and some beggars ask for money and others try to claim your attention with a box of matches, and bootblacks say: "Shine your boots, sir; only a penny?" We pass Ludgate circus, Holborn viaduct, the post-office, Smithfield meat and fish markets, St. Paul's vast dome, go on by Bunhill fields, where Bunyan, Wesley, Clarke and others are buried, and so on into localities which for hundreds of years have been the abode of poverty, misery, crime and unrest. The pavements, doorsteps, and worn, dusty hallways seem to reek with tears and blood violently shed, and the cracks, creases and wrinkles on pavestones, bricks and doorways seem to speak weird, ruffian and piteous languages. Going on, we pass great railway stations with columns, gates, clock-towers and broad arched roofs of glass on ribs of iron; on by stores and mansions, and having made a trip of say fifteen miles, we again came into the God-made country among groves of trees, gardens of flowers and vegetables, and fields of grass, grain, sheep, cattle and brick kilns.

I thought it was somewhat strange that on the steps of the monuments reared to commemorate the great deeds of great men, for instance, in Trafalgar Square, London, and in Dublin's wide street, Sackville, I saw so many idle men. I thought that a poor way to gain a monument. My cousin in Trafalgar said: "These men are out of work and they sleep here all night." Oh, yes; I see. They ask for bread and receive a stone. We cannot say that many men are built for monuments. Monuments are built for men who at their birth receive a genius, a spirit of unquenchable, undying determination to do or to be something. They say, "Let this blood drip out, let these bones crack, let this body decay, but let this idea, this brave, eternal genius, live and shine." So they smile at labor and pain and face death in mines and markets, studies, studios and garrets, and sail through great billows, and wave bright swords over bloody and screaming battle-fields, where angels and demons invisible look on with tears and amazement as mortal spirits burst away from mangled bodies. The monuments to soldiers are tall and beautiful, but the monuments to philanthropists, patriots, artists, martyrs and saviors are lovely and ennobling.

I said to my cousin, "If England ever becomes bankrupt, she may sell her works of art, her palaces, and her relics, and her things of great beauty, value, and antiquity, and pay off her debts." The task of telling about all these grand and beautiful things is so great that I am slow to begin it. I stopped at the Central post-office and I found it to be comprised in two great granite buildings, one each side of the street; one 375 feet long and two stories high, the other 300 feet long and five stories high. A man said, "They have recently added a story to that building which made room for over five hundred more clerks." They are preparing to build a larger and grander building. A report states that in one year there were 238,000,000 letters delivered from the post-office to the people of London.

Now I am at St. Paul's Cathedral, perhaps the most impressive edifice I have yet seen. I walk into the beautiful church-yard grounds and look at ancient tombs and see the fine display of shrubbery and flowers. I paced around the building and counted five hundred and thirty-three paces; more than a fourth of a mile! The flowers, all colors, sweet vegetable angels, grow in crosses to honor the place, while their patriotic hearts spell out the words: "V. R. 1837, God save our Queen, 1887." In the gable over the the great portico is a representation of "Saul's Conversion." It is a grand sight to see men, and horses, and soldiers, in hard marble, fall prostrate in the presence of the supernatural light and voice. This massive church, one of the largest in the world, is crowned by one of the largest and most wonderful domes on earth, and is surrounded by a great, gilded cross. The structure is said to be three hundred and sixty-five feet high, and its great dome is seen towering aloft for miles around when the atmosphere is favorable. Entering the church the spectator is almost awed by the magnitude and grandeur of the place. A forest of columns and arches uphold the lofty roof and dome, and as you walk the marble floor, light falls through many windows of stained glass like angels on errands of peace. Oh, what a labyrinth of rich and rare monuments stand around in marble and bronze to the honor of great soldiers, statesmen, divines, philanthropists, and artists. Those to Wellington, Nelson and General Gordon appear the grandest. England is remarkable for honoring her great soldiers. "Great murderers!" one man said. Here angels, and men, and children, and gods, and goddesses, and nymphs cluster in marble at the feet of the great ones to do them honor, while lovely women in pure white marble, draped in thin lace, stand about these departed heroes as if fain to warm them into life once more. Coming to a most kind and handsome face, cut in marble, I paused to see whom it represented, and read the name of "Howard." Coming to the centre you look up to the Whispering Gallery—a great height—and above it to the great pictured dome, and away to the top of the dome, where a small hole in the floor, or rather roof of the dome, permits the spectator to look down three hundred and twenty-five feet upon the people below, who "look like flies."

Walking around and around, up well-worn stone steps, we came at length to the "Whispering Gallery," of which I had heard so much. The attendant, Mr. William Parker, said, "Go around yonder, please," and he motioned me around to a place on a narrow gallery opposite to him, and there I heard a whisper apparently near my ear saying, "The architect of this building was Sir Christopher Wren. It was commenced in 1675, nine years after the great fire, and was thirty-five years in building, and cost fifteen hundred thousand pounds. The building is three hundred and sixty-five feet high. This dome is one hundred and twelve feet in diameter, and my voice travels around about one hundred and seventy feet to where you are. Sir Christopher lived to see it finished, and died at the age of ninety-one years, and was buried in the crypt of the church." I whispered, "Is it possible you are saying these things?" The whisper came back, "Yes." I said, "Wonderful!" and he whispered back, "Yes, it is wonderful." I went on up to the Stone Gallery, and there I found William Rumford, as guide. He said, "Since the dynamite outrage we do not permit people to go up to the ball." We walked around the dome and looked off on the city. He said, "Yonder is the river Thames, Blackfriar's bridge, House of Parliament, Victoria tower, St. Bride's steeple, Bow church spire, Bank of England, Mint, Guild hall, London bridge, St. Mark's hospital, tower of the great fire, Shoreditch church, St. Luke's church, post-office, etc." "Oh, that is the great bell of St. Paul's. It weighs seventeen tons, and is tolled for five minutes every day at one o'clock."

The watchman on top gave me a piece of the stone from the top of the dome, cut out in making repairs. I, of course, gave him a piece of silver for the favor. By the way, let me here say that, after traveling many years and thousands of miles in various countries, I have not lost nor been robbed of a single dollar. One gentleman this morning told me how he lost sixty dollars in London by the "confidence game." He actually put his pocket-book into a stranger's pocket, and, of course, never saw it afterward. The stranger had dazzled my fellow-voyager by shaking five hundred pounds in Bank of England notes before his eyes. Yes, a man is unwise when he wishes and expects something for nothing. The worlds of which we have knowledge are not built and run that way. Is this a digression, or is it slang; or, is it both? If it is, make the most of it, for "you pay your money and take your choice." I do believe there are men who would be willing to be accounted fools, if thereby they could save some—I mean save some fragments. Fragments? Yes, fragments of humanity. Now, for another digression. I am sitting near the port-hole of a great steamship in the middle of the Atlantic, and the great, blue waves roar hoarsely as they rush up nearly to the window where I am now writing. I am on my way back to see Percy and May, and sisters and—and you. We have had a storm (equinoctial) for two days, and the ship has become a great hospital, floating through salt waters and fresh breezes where health is supposed to gather her stores of bloom and cheerfulness. Oh, Neptune! you cruel god of the sea! How deathly you cause some of my dear fellow-travelers to look! But doubtless a rose will yet glow warm, bright and fragrant where a snow-bank now lies. Yes, weeping may endure for a night, but joy, joy cometh in the morning, "in the morning," "surely cometh."

Beautiful! Yes, the sea and truth are beautiful. I have not been ill an hour since I left "America, darlint, the land of the free;" yes, more—the land of the brave and beautiful, the land of the wild and wide, the high and low, the great and the grand. If I ever have seen three grand things, they are, a great thunder storm, Niagara, and the sea in a storm. The chief steward said I ought to have been a sailor. Well, I used to think my two crowns meant something; but I fear the barber can not trace two now, for, "you see," my hair begins to part in the middle—i. e., you will see, when I get back where the sun sets over the Plymouth mountain, in beautiful Indian summer, painting more glories in and along the Susquehanna than most people ever dream of.

# CHAPTER XII.

BILLINGSGATE, TOWER OF LONDON, FIRE, GREENWICH.

FISH, CARLOADS AND SHIPLOADS—WHERE SLANG WAS BORN—MONUMENT OF LONDON—A THOUSAND ACRES OF BUILDINGS BOW INTO ASHES—WILD FIRE DARTS ITS RED TONGUE AT THE KING AND AT THE HEAVENS—THE TOWER OF LONDON—DUNGEONS DARK FOR A THOUSAND YEARS—OLD WEAPONS OF WAR BLOSSOM IN BOUQUETS AND DECORATE THE CEILING—LADY JANE GREY—TRAITOR'S GATE—FIFTEEN MILLION DOLLARS WORTH OF JEWELRY—GARMENTS WORN BY LOVERS AND WARRIORS—CANNON FROM THE FLOOR OF THE BONE-PAVED SEA—RIDING ON THE THAMES—GREENWICH—NAVAL SCHOOL—FOREST OF FINE COLUMNS—PAINTED HALL—SHIP MODELS—NELSON PAINTED A GOD—TRUE TO THE VISION.

From London bridge we walked through Billingsgate fish market, where we find many men and women, in buildings, large and small, and in courts and streets handling and selling fish. Some were packing, others unpacking, counting, assorting, etc. There were fish of nearly all sizes, shapes and colors, red, white, yellow, blue, black, brown, bright and dull; with scales, claws, shells and pincers; dried, smoked, skewered and corded; in boxes, bales, tubs, kegs, barrels, baskets, carts, barrows, wagons, etc. Oh, what a Babel! The narrow streets are crowded with vehicles, horses and people. Hundreds of cartloads of fish are handled here each day.

Near this quarter stands the tall monument erected to commemorate the great fire of 1666, which breaking out near this spot, burned down many thousands of buildings. The column is two hundred and two feet tall, and is crowned by a great urn that represents a flaming fire and glitters in the sun. For threepence one can go up inside to a gallery near the top, where a good view can be had, on a clear morning. Some years ago people fell into the habit of jumping from this tower, which caused the gallery to be covered with an iron screen. So we see that human beings have to be saved from themselves as well as from their "friends."

The greatest fire ever known on earth deserves more than a passing notice, and I will here make room for a few lines on the subject clipped from my own work, and from one, Pepys, who witnessed this awful exhibition of wild-fire.

In London, in September, 1666, a little fire sprang up, and roared, and spread, and darted its red tongue into the black heavens as it dissolved long streets full of houses. Armies of firemen could not tear down the houses fast enough to starve it out, and it slumbered not until 13,200 houses and 89 churches lay in ashes. It cared not for the king, nor lords, ladies, soldiers, beggars, nor firemen.

The story, as Pepys gives it, may be regarded as

one of the first and best bits of realistic description in English literature, pre-Raphaelite in its accuracy. From the first moment, when the maids who have sat up to finish some preparations for a "feast" the next day, call their master at three in the morning to tell of a great fire in the city, to the end, when he wanders among the ruins trying to recall landmarks, one sees every inch of the fiery progress. Pepys goes to sleep again after a short look and rises late, setting at once to work with his usual love of order in arranging the closet, disturbed by the women's cleaning the previous day, and undoubtedly swearing under his breath at their theories regarding the relative value and place of papers. But when at last he is told that the fire has reached London bridge he hastens down, noting by the way how the poor pigeons, "loath to leave their houses, hovered about the windows and balconies till they burned their wings and fell down."

The people seemed equally distraught, staying in their houses till the fire touched them and then running into boats or clambering from one pair of stairs by the water side to another.

Back to the king's closet in Whitehall, and "I did tell the king and duke of York what I saw, and that unless his majesty did command houses to be pulled down nothing could stop the fire. They seemed much troubled and commanded me to go to my lord mayor from him and command him to spare no houses, but to pull down before the fire every way." A hand in an affair of this magnitude was altogether to the mind of the busy little man, who hastened by coach, seeing "extraordinary good goods carried in carts and on backs."

The Lord Mayor is met at last, "like a man spent with a handkercher about his neck," who, when he heard the king's message, "cried like a fainting woman, 'Lord! what can I do? I am spent. People will not obey me. I have been pulling down houses, but the fire overtakes us faster than we can do it.' So he left me, and I him" Pepys goes on, and walked home, gazing at the distracted people, not forgetting his passion for fine clothes even here, but noting, "I saw Mr. Isaac Houblon, the handsome man, prettily dressed and dirty at his door, at Dowgate, receiving some of his brother's things." Later on, as the day wanes, "we had an extraordinary good dinner, and as merry as at this time we could be."

"Here all merriment ended. Even the light-hearted king felt anxiety enough to go and come restlessly in his barge, watching the fire from one point and another. The wind has risen. Flakes of fire were carried and dropped in a horrible shower, and as it grew darker, and they could endure no more on water, they retreated to a little ale house. We saw the fire grow and appear more and more, and in corners, and upon steeples, and between churches and houses, as far as we could see up the hill of the city, in a most horrid, malicious, bloody flame, not like the fine flame of an ordinary fire. We staid till, it being darkish, we saw the fire as only one entire arch of fire from this to the other side of the bridge, and in a bow up the hill for an arch of above a mile long; it made me weep to see it."

So for days, the story goes on, till nearly a week has passed. The fire reaches the foot of the lane the day after Pepys and Sir William Penn have dug a hole in the garden and buried their wine in it, not forgetting a Parmesan cheese and some papers, and he and the pretty, silly wife, with some friends, carry the gold to a boat and escape to Woolwich, Pepys leaving the treasure there with a charge that it must be watched night and day, and hastening back to watch once more the march of fire and flame.

At last it ends, when all have lost reckoning even of the days of the week, and Pepys, with a long drawn breath of relief, celebrates the release from anxiety by hurrying to a friend's lodging, "where," he writes characteristically, "I borrowed a shirt and washed." A week later the wine and "Parmesan cheese," are once more in the proper place, furniture is set up again, and Pepys goes to church and a thanksgiving service that the fire is over, objecting strongly to the cheap wit of the preacher, who tells them the "city is reduced from a large folio to a decimo tertio," and gives them altogether "a bad, poor sermon."

The Tower of London: This famous old castle, for it is more like a castle than a tower, stands on the north bank of the Thames and dates back to the days of William the Conqueror, more than eight hundred years ago. It has been used as a fortress, a castle, a palace, a state prison, a place of execution, the residence of royalty, an armory, a record office, a menagerie, a museum of warlike antiquities, captured arms, cannon and banners, and a safe for crown jewels. Of course, as the Tower, with its walls and many buildings, covers more than twelve acres of ground, it could answer a number of these uses at the same time. When we came to its massive walls and gates we found them well guarded by soldiers.

We get tickets at the office and pass in over the old moat, which is now used as a vegetable and flower garden and a place for drilling and exercising the soldiers. As we arrive near the White Tower we hear music from an excellent drum corps and a band of Highland bagpipers, and soldiers are drilling on the stone-paved court. Here are a great number of cannon, mostly ancient and of unique pattern, long, slender, graceful, and others short, clumsy and of large calibre, for throwing shells, etc. These bear foreign inscriptions, showing that they have been captured from France, Spain, Russia, Africa and India, but I saw none from America, while many of them were from France. Nearly every city and castle in England is ornamented with Russian cannon. Yes, there are thousands of tons of almost useless cannon in England, giving a warlike aspect to castles and parks, to say nothing of the thousands of very efficient guns which darken the port-holes of forts and thunder from the decks of great war ships.

I wish my readers could see a few of Armstrong's one hundred and ten ton guns—mighty engines of modern warfare, which flash lightning and hurl nearly a ton of hard, cold metal like a black thunderbolt through space, splintering massive ribs of oak, grinding walls of brick and granite to dust, and making great rents in manifold plates of fine-grained iron and steel, honestly riveted. Italy and China are paying England for making them many great guns, and when the world has a full supply of these artificial thunder storms with which men hurl lightning from ships to cities and from kingdoms to empires, war will be a thing of the past.

Yes, gold and silver are monarchs now, only slightly limited; but friendship, justice and love will ere long wave their fair, bright banners over the mountains of land and the mountains of water. Then, when the sun rises, a halo of glory will surround his bright face, spelling out the word "Millennium," and billows Atlantic will crouch at his feet, while tempests rest and steel-harnessed steam does the work on broad, blue seas.

To return to the Tower of London, the guide points out the spot where Lady Jane Grey's beautiful head fell into the cruel and bloody basket. I gathered up a few brown leaves, and pebbles from the place. There is where prisoners of state looked through iron bars, or carved pictures on the cold, gray stones within, until cruel, envious, bloody and fickle politics opened the door to lead them to death or to glory. There is where princes were smothered, and there is where princes were born and tutored, and there is where queens dressed, and bowed, and smiled, and sighed, and wept. There is the "Bloody Tower," the "Lion Tower," and yonder the "Traitor's gate," which opens into the river Thames. If a prisoner passed in under this great spiked gateway, he might never hope to see the outside world again.

We entered a stronghold through doorways, hallways, and stairways of granite, well guarded by doorkeepers, and come to where the crown and crown jewels are kept. They are placed in plain sight in a large, upright show-case, and well protected by glass and an outer frame-work of iron. There is the crown and scepter, and maces, and badges, and sashes, glittering with precious stones, said to be worth $15,000,000.

Now, we pass on to old verdigris-eaten armor, worn by soldiers and rulers hundreds of years ago. Here are the garments of state worn ages ago by kings and queens, and other so-called great people. Now, look through these great rooms and see tens of thousands of queer old pistols, carbines, muskets, rifles, ramrods, bayonets, knives, daggers, swords, spears, battle-axes, lances, helmets, breastplates, etc., all formed into various and curious shapes; like suns, flowers, crowns, birds, butterflies and ornaments. The walls and ceilings were frescoed with them. One place was fenced with swords, each picket was a sword, the handle being up. Bayonets and ramrods were curiously wrought together.

To add to the interest of these sights we were informed of the great age of many of the relics and who had worn and used them, and where they had been rent by arrow, spear, battle-axe or bullet, or stained with human blood. Crowds of people were here, also looking at these historical things and scenes. Outside were cannon brought up from the "Royal George," which went down into the sea with nearly a thousand men on board one fine day in 1782. When the port-holes were opened she rolled on one side into the water, and before the guns could be righted she went down, and this cannon was brought up from her wreck fifty-two years afterward.

We must leave London Tower, with its blood-soaked cobble-stones and carved prison walls, and its old beheading-block and axe; its guarded crowns and war relics; its red-coated soldiers, and kilted bag-pipers from Scottish highlands. We pass the strange looking, three-barrel cannon captured in 1706 of the Portuguese, and pass out over the draw-bridge and moat and find our way to a steamboat landing and embark on the Thames for Greenwich, a few miles down the river.

We stand on the deck of a long, low steamer and gaze out on some of London's great buildings, reared for worship, pleasure, business and commemoration. We see many narrow canal-boats loaded with coal, timber, brick, etc., being towed by tugs. There are great warehouses and factories, some of them bearing names well known in America.

Here cross railways into stations where hundreds of trains come and go daily—stations so extensive and manifold in their departments and offices that a stranger can do but little more than ask questions, and, at last finding the right platform, and right train, and right car, and right compartment, and seeing his

(10)

luggage safe at his feet or overhead in the car, hand the poor, patient porter a small "tip," say anywhere from two-pence to a shilling. Yonder in inland docks are acres of shipping.

The docks of London are now chiefly out of the city proper toward the sea, where room and water are more abundant. The London docks are, of course, very extensive, and in construction are much like those of Liverpool. Here goes a great ocean steamer, pushing out to sea, but among so many smaller ships and boats she must move cautiously. There are cattle and lumber boats. There is a great elevator, and there stands the "Lion Brewery," a large building. A shower comes up and we, or many of us, go down into the rather small and close cabin, among men and women, young and old, handsome and ugly, chatty and silent, while others almost drench their finery on deck under, or partially under, umbrellas rather than go below. After some miles of a ride, for which we paid three-pence, we arrive at Greenwich, near the celebrated Observatory which stands on an eminence in very pleasant grounds, some distance from the Thames. Here is the Greenwich Naval Academy, the Hospital, the Museum, the Painted Hall, etc. The buildings are large and handsome, surrounded by smooth and extensive walks and grounds. The buildings have forests of fine, tall columns in front of them, enough to stock a cemetery.

I always find myself admiring columns, and do not wonder that all great and beautiful buildings have columns. Sometimes in front, some on all sides, some a few stories up from the ground; but columns nowhere look grander to me than when, two hundred feet from the ground, forty or more of them encircle and bear up a great dome, for instance, like St. Paul's, London.

The "Painted Hall," whose walls and lofty ceiling show the fine paintings, which took an artist twenty-one years to do, is a very interesting place. The scenes are historical, and chiefly represent naval battles and naval heroes. These fine works of art must fire the energy and ambition of patriotic youths to deeds of daring.

If there is one man above another, that Great Britain honors, he is Lord Nelson. You find him up-reared on lofty and graceful columns and monuments in nearly all her cities, and his face and form well painted in all the art galleries and museums. Here he is the dominant genius, and we find him in many of the paintings, and in most of the battles he is the prominent figure, in the front and hottest of the fight. If artists have not misrepresented him, he was one of the most lion-hearted men the world has ever seen. They have nearly painted him a god in contending hand-to-hand against brave seamen in distant seas, where blood tinged the waves, and fire and smoke muffled the atmosphere, that shuddered with the thunder of artillery. Even after he lost his arm and an eye, he would not give up the resolve to cover his country with glory until he met his death at Trafalgar, October 21, 1805. He conquered sea and land, and crowned the "wooden walls" of "Old England" with the wealth and art of many lands, and his countrymen are determined that lasting glory shall crown his name. Here they display his garments worn in the battle of the Nile, and the blood-stained coat he wore when the fatal bullet struck him at Trafalgar. A cynic might ask was he working most for self or country. His genius prompted him to contend for mastery on rolling waves, and he was not disobedient to the glorious vision.

We saw many magnificent models of ships that have sailed for England's honor and wealth, during hundreds of years, past and present; but, as we wish to do Crystal Palace yet to-day, we must leave this interesting locality.

# CHAPTER XIII.

## CRYSTAL PALACE, WESTMINSTER ABBEY, THE QUEEN'S HORSES, ETC.

CRYSTAL PALACE; ITS FOUNTAINS, STATUES, PAINTINGS, AND ORIENTAL HALLS—SOUTH KENSINGTON, A CITY OF PALACES CROWDED WITH BEAUTIES AND WONDERS—THE QUEEN'S MONUMENT TO A LOVING HUSBAND—THE MUSEUM—THE FIRST STEAM ENGINE—NATURAL SCIENCE MUSEUM—BIRDS TALL AND SWIFT AS HORSES—FIVE THOUSAND HUMMING BIRDS—WHALES, ETC.—THE BRITISH MUSEUM—MADAM TOUSSAUD'S WAX KINGS, QUEENS, POETS, WARRIORS, AND MURDERERS—A WALK UNDER THE RIVER THAMES—SPURGEON, LONDON'S PREACHER—CITY TEMPLE—WESTMINSTER ABBEY, WHERE THE FAMOUS DEAD SLEEP FOR CENTURIES—SOLEMN PLACE, WHERE STONE FACES GAZE HEAVENWARD—STONE LACE FOR FRESCOING—MARBLE, GRANITE, BRASS AND BRONZE BLOSSOM INTO ANGELS AND BOUQUETS TO GLORIFY THE BELOVED DEAD—THE QUEEN'S STABLES—SIXTEEN PRINCELY HORSES, AND TWO GROOMS IN ONE BEDROOM—MOROCCO HARNESS, GOLD-BOUND—GILDED CHARIOTS.

Leaving Greenwich by steam railway, we went to Crystal Palace, which is at Sydenham, some miles out from London. On our way we passed Blackheath, where, in broad, green fields, we saw many young men in white and gay-colored suits, engaged in playing cricket and other athletic games.

The train stopped at the world-famous palace and we passed out and into it, all the time under roof. The building is beautiful and extensive, though built more than thirty years ago. It is of glass and iron and cost over seven millions of dollars. The columns, girders, braces, arches and rafters are iron, graceful in construction and covered with glass, through which the sunlight falls mellow and pleasant.

I would judge the building to be a thousand feet long at least, and say three hundred feet wide, and in the centre at least one hundred feet high, with a handsome tower at each end of about two hundred feet high, from the top of which fine views are had of the grounds and surrounding country. It stands in a fine park of two hundred acres. It would take a large book to mention and describe the handsome things seen here.

We passed in by flowers, shrubbery and plants of many rare varieties; by fountains, paintings, statues, fine show-cases, bazaars and thousands of well-dressed people. On the stage, opposite the great organ, a young lady was singing some sweet and pleasing song, to which a thousand or two listened and then heartily encored.

We greatly enjoyed ourselves among the many fine paintings done by painstaking children of genius. Here the romance of love, the glory of war, the beauty of home, the freshness of the country, religion's crosses and crowns, and the nobility of patriotism were all grandly represented. Now we come where genius has caused great and beautiful things to blossom out into pure white marble in the form of fish, birds, dogs, lions, horses, fountains, cupids, nymphs, angels, men and women.

Truly, we roam here "'mid pleasures and palaces," hanging gardens, crystal fountains, baths, aquariums, bazaars, grottoes, columns, arches, domes, oriental and marble-paved halls, full of melody, perfume and beauty. A military band furnished excellent music.

We passed through the Egyptian, Pompeian, Italian, Alhambra, Byzantine and Mediæval courts. We look out over the extensive grounds, beautiful with flowers, fountains, lakes, music-pagodas, thickets, bridges, terraces, etc.; all of which at night are brilliant with colored lights and fire-works. There, to one side, is the toboggan slide.

When we re-enter the palace we find it resplendent with tens of thousands of lights, shaded by colored glass; also electric lights and gas. The scene is really enchanting, especially to those of a romantic and poetic temperament.

South Kensington, adjoining Hyde Park, is a clean and delightful quarter of the city. You might say it is a city composed of palaces, full of beautiful, rare, valuable and ancient things from all the realms of nature and art. Here is the "Albert Memorial," the most elaborate and beautiful monument I have yet seen. It is as handsome as granite, marble, bronze, gold, and glittering stones, combined with beautiful images, can be. It bears the following inscription, "Queen Victoria and her people, to the memory of Prince Albert, Consort; as a tribute of their gratitude for a life devoted to the public good." The monument stands on a plateau approached by granite steps. A large, gilded, statue of the prince sits upon a high, broad pedestal, over which, upheld by four grand clustered columns, stands the tall and graceful monument. The whole structure is one hundred and seventy-five feet high, and cost about $600,000. On high pedestals, at each corner of the monument, stand most beautiful sculptured groups representing Europe, Asia, Africa and America. There are about three hundred life-size figures in and on the monument, representing poets, painters, musicians, soldiers, statesmen, sculptors, bishops, etc. Near this is the "Albert Hall," a large, circular building, devoted to art, music, instruction and amusement. The building is about one thousand feet in circumference, and six stories high. An elevator lifted us up to the picture gallery, where the whole circle is filled with paintings. The inner side of this great circle is divided into thirty arches, resting on handsome pillars, and as we look across the wide, deep arena, we see, under the circling arches, and between the handsome columns, large pictures composed of many fine paintings. It seats eight thousand people. In the evening about five thousand gas burners flash at once into blaze at the mystic touch of man-made lightning.

We also visited the Kensington museum, a large and handsome building, full of curious and beautiful things from the four quarters of the earth. The floors on which we trod were pictures; the windows were prize paintings; the furniture was carved and inlaid with fine substances; the walls, ceilings and columns were of porcelain, gracefully formed and artistically colored, speaking with characters plain and allegorical. Here were many pieces of sculpture, samples of tapestry, carvings, inlaying, pictures in bronze, models of rare old masters, coffers, urns, rare and ancient furniture, chandeliers, curtains, etc., glass stairway, gilded ceiling, grottoes, and hanging gardens on twisted columns of bronze upholding works of art.

In the machine department I saw what was labeled "Puffing Billy," "the oldest steam engine in existence;" completed in 1813, and was in operation till 1862. It was not large, and contained beams of oak which showed great age and wear. Also saw "The Rocket," an engine built by Stephenson & Co., in 1830, which was "the first to draw passenger trains, and took a prize of five hundred pounds in 1830." Here were the watch, rule, etc., of George Stephenson, the great machinist. Also, the "first and original reaping machine made in 1826, and used all the time to 1867." Also, "the first fire engine in which two cylinders and an air vessel were combined." The original engine for steamboat "Comet," the first advertised steamboat to carry passengers and goods on the Clyde in 1812; "made by John Robertson in 1812, and set up here by him in 1862, at the age of 81 years."

Here was a gilded royal state barge two hundred and seventy years old; sixty-three feet long.

The "Natural Science Museum" is in a large, neat and modern building, admirably adapted for its purpose. It is built of terra cotta blocks and is beautiful. Images of animals and monsters are seen on the cornices, window-sills, etc. Here the sightseer finds nearly everything in nature, animate and inanimate. Here were the skeletons and stuffed remains of animals, birds, fish and insects; humming birds of a half ounce weight, to the ostrich of seven and a half feet; swans, emus, cassowaries, etc.; whales, sharks and minnows; rare plants, and hundreds of cases of minerals and precious stones, bird's nests and their eggs; the skeleton of a whale fifty feet long; a bamboo cane, eight inches in diameter, eighty-one feet long; Gould's collection of humming birds, say one hundred six-sided glass cases, each containing fifty specimens of these tiny birds; a model of the largest nugget of gold ever found in Australia, the "Welcome Stranger," weight 2,280 ounces, etc. Here, sixty feet from the ground, we dine amid wonders of nature and beauties of art, served by modest, handsome and intelligent English girls.

We went to the British Museum, Great Russel street, a massive stone building surrounded by a forest of lofty columns. This is one of the favorite institutions of England's great ones, and it is embellished and enriched with rare and ancient things from all of earth's continents and every realm of science. The rows of Egyptian mummies, men and women—the thousands of rare, old and precious books, written and printed in many ways and bound in various materials, and things unearthed in holy and unholy lands, possessed the chief interest for me. The guide-books say the largest library in the world is here. It is a most wonderful place, calculated to overpower a brain of limited calibre.

We went to see Madame Toussaud's exhibition of wax-work. We saw scores of great people and royal families resplendent in bright wax and gay garments of silk, lace, velvets, coronets, etc. We could scarcely tell at first glance which was the spectator and which the one done in wax. If wax, like figures, won't lie, then the cemeteries of England contain many very handsome folks. Here was Napoleon's old carriage, "from which he saw the burning of Moscow;" here was the bed he died on; here the coronation robes of Josephine, etc. In the "Chamber of Horrors" were the ugly faces and forms and garments of hideous male and female villains, and the old gallows that had strangled many; and here was Lipski, the Polish Jew, who had been hanged in London only the day before.

We went down a circular stairway like going into a deep well, and walked through a seven-foot tube away under the famous river Thames, while ocean tides and steamboats floated far above us. It was much like a mine, and I breathed more freely when we again came to the great, roaring outside world. I did not admire the looks of the few people we met in the great tube or sub-way.

Sunday morning, August 21st, Henry and I walked across Holborn Circus, on, near Ludgate Hill, to Blackfriar's bridge, over the Thames, and thus on along the great, busy street, to the "Elephant and Castle," where stands Rev. C. H. Spurgeon's large and very plain tabernacle. It was ten minutes past ten, but already the people were going in. We went in and up to the second gallery, and sat in the aisle until about 10:45, when we were allowed to take seats in pews. There were say 5,000 people present. The preacher stood on a level with the floor of the first gallery, with listeners above and below him. The galleries, too, run all around the church, which is on the oval order. The pews are cushioned, but have no doors. The singing is congregational and good, led by one man; no instrument. The preacher read the first chapter of Ephesians, and made sharp telling comments on the same. His prayers were simple, pointed and powerful. He took for his text the 12th and 13th verses of the first chapter of Ephesians; subject, "The Predestinating Power of God." The sermon was plain, earnest, and calculated to be helpful in the every day life of an active worker and Christian. It was a good sermon, and showed much tact and ability. His manner is sincere, earnest, friendly, but not violent nor loud. He appeared to be about fifty-four years of age, and to weigh, say two hundred and ten pounds.

In the evening we went to the "City Temple" to hear Dr. Parker, but that eloquent man was on his way to Brooklyn, to preach in Beecher's pulpit. The minister was from Scotland, and as he prayed for Dr. Parker, he also prayed for "that great country" to which he was sailing.

Of course, I visited Westminster Abbey. This ancient burial-place and cathedral, stands opposite the House of Parliament, not far back from the Thames river, in a grand and historic portion of London. Its length is four hundred and sixteen feet, breadth at transept two hundred and three feet, height of western towers two hundred and twenty-five feet. The building dates back nearly a thousand years, and its architecture is much like the cathedrals of England, for here you have the grand, massive and lofty columns, the organ, the stained glass, and towers, and bells, and choirs, etc., but, we have more here for the place is crowded with fine, old and handsome monuments to dead heroes, poets, and others, and Henry the Seventh chapel is here, well guarded by locked doors and gates, which a small fee will open at certain hours of the day. I confess to being considerably impressed when shown the bronze and marble tombs, and images of kings and queens, of whom we have read and heard so often. Here lie King Henry VII and his queen, finely represented in marble, side by side, with rare and significant emblems all about them—emblems of power, wealth, intelligence and Christianity. Here are the straight, graceful forms of princes cut down by the tyrant Death before they had crowns set upon their heads. There they lie and rest while London roars like the sea, and centuries come, bringing railways and steamboats, and go leaving telegraphs, telephones, and palaces blazing with domesticated lightning. We can not do much more for our great ones than to cut their images in stone and lay them with their faces looking toward heaven, from whence cometh power and glory, and where the brave and good find lasting happiness. The ceiling over these famous monuments is of stone, cut like lace, most intricate and beautiful. It is said to be unequaled, and I believe it, for I never before saw stone so wonderfully chiseled. After all, it seems only consistent that granite, marble, brass and bronze should blossom into bouquets and burst into crowns and angels to honor their last resting-place, for they in life were busy beautifying the homes and graves of others, or moulding granite and metals into forms to protect and please those who already lived or should live.

Calling at the rooms of the American Legation, in Victoria street, not far from Westminster, Mr. Henry White, chief secretary for Minister Phelps, an affable and competent man, secured for me passes to view both Houses of Parliament, the Queen's Stables, and the Royal Arsenal at Woolwich. The stables where the royal carriages, harness and horses are kept are well guarded by soldiers, policemen, door-keepers and guides. They are open from 2 p. m. to 4 p. m. to those having tickets. The stables are of brick, solid, extensive and unpretentious. At the gate I met Mr. Bray, in neat uniform, who informed me he had been here thirty years, and when he knew I was from Pennsylvania he told me he had a son, a Presbyterian minister, at Edgehill, near Philadelphia. Mr. Blandy, a pleasant young man, accompanied me about the place. He showed me perhaps one hundred fine horses, bays, blacks and creams. The stables are clean, light, large and comfortable, and the horses stand in clean, white straw. The name of each horse is painted above his manger.

Mr. Blandy said: "The Queen is now at Balmoral, Scotland, and most of the princes have gone to Germany. She takes twenty-three horses to Balmoral and hires the others she needs there. In London she drives bays and when in the country she drives grays." Here are eight black and eight cream-colored stallions, magnificent horses, to be used on state occasions, when a guard walks at the head of each horse. This breed of unequaled cream-colored horses, with Roman nose and round, smooth forms, and stout, graceful limbs, and long, flowing tails, "came from Hanover and are bred here, and are not now found elsewhere." "They look handsome in harness and are driven when the Queen goes to open the House of Parliament." The blacks are also magnificent horses. Two men sleep here near these sixteen fine horses. I saw fine red and black Morocco harness, gold and silver-plated, enough to stock several stores and add interest to a state fair. Some sets were made of one piece of leather and elaborately ornamented with bright metals. Here were dozens of handsome saddles. I was also shown a number of handsome carriages and gilded chariots of state, brilliant with paint and gold-leaf, and ornamented with carvings, images, crowns, coats of arms, etc. Here was the queen's state carriage, one hundred and twenty-six years old, weighing four tons and heavily gilded. These things occupied many spacious apartments. The attendants are pleasant, agreeable men and are not permitted to take "tips" or fees from the visitors.

# CHAPTER XIV.

## SOME PEOPLE AND PLACES BEYOND THE SEA.

QUESTIONS ANSWERED—A FLOATING VOLCANO—WAR-HORSES WITH WHITE MANES—OCEAN ROBED IN CRIMSON, GREEN AND GOLD—PEOPLE AND CLOUDS SMILE—PLACES VISITED—THE LARGEST CITY—THE MOST BEAUTIFUL CITY—THE LARGEST SHIP—WHERE CANNON SHOOK PURPLE HEATHER—COUSINS MET IN ANCIENT AND FAMOUS CITIES—A WALK ON THE MOORS—TURF CAKES AND MILK—A POPULAR AUTHORESS—WITH EDWARD ON HIS LOCOMOTIVE—UNCLE JAMES'S BLESSING—KIND FRIENDS MENTIONED.

Many friends and readers since my return have asked me the following questions: "Did you have a good time?" "Where did you go?" "Did you find friends there?" This letter may answer these questions, and then I will go on to Paris.

Yes, I had a good time, a pleasant time, a grand time. For many years I had an intense longing to visit my father's native land—the land he left fifty-seven years ago last May.

On the 14th of July I went to New York and on the 16th of that month I sailed for England on board the "Servia," a magnificent ship of the famous Cunard line. This ship is so large that when you promenade around her once you walk one-fifth of a mile, and it takes five large locomotives to haul the coal she needs to cross the ocean once. It reminded me of a floating volcano. The firemen shovel two hundred and five tons of coal per day into her furnaces to keep her engines of ten thousand horse-power at work breasting the awful billows at the rate of a mile in three and a half minutes.

I have told you how pleasant I found it on the sea morning, noon and night, and how grand the ocean is when it lifts up its waves like dark war-horses with foaming nostrils and white manes. At the sight of these things multitudes trembled and turned deathly pale, and retreated to their swaying and restless couches. How great fish leaped above the waves and whales in the distance spouted columns of white water into the air, while the sun wedded sea and sky under a canopy of glorious light; and, when we came near Ireland, the white sea-birds circled above us and the sea turned a beautiful green, and in the evening the setting sun painted the old ocean a thing of beauty, in robes of crimson, green and gold. How pleasant, helpful and companionable were the officers, crew and passengers. How cool, fine and dry I found the weather in England—so fine that millions of men and women could not remember a similar summer; so fine that the wheat was harvested in August instead of September. How kind relatives and friends were, and of the many great exhibitions open this jubilee year.

I landed at Liverpool and went to Manchester, Leeds, York, Whitby, Scarborough, Hanmanby, Sheffield, Birmingham, Leamington, Warwick, Coventry, Stratford-on-Avon, Oxford, London, Canterbury, Dover, Calais, Amiens, Paris, Versailles, Rouen, Dieppe, New Haven, Cardiff, Gloucester, Leicester, Middlesborough, Durham, Berwick, Edinburgh, Queen's Ferry, Dunfermline, Sterling, Glasgow, Greenock, Paisley, Dumfries, Stranraer, Larne, Giant's Causeway, Portrush, Coleraine, Belfast, Dublin, Chester, etc. I saw the largest city, and the most handsome city, and the largest ship. I saw where kings, queens, princes, patriots, priests, poets, painters, soldiers and martyrs were born, died, chained, crowned, burned, beheaded or buried. Where battles were fought near walls and castles that were gray with age when Columbus was seeking America. Wide, lonely moorlands, where the roar of cannon had shaken the purple heather. Broad plains that had smiled with fields full of sheep and wheat for a thousand years. Where Josephine dined, and danced, and wept, and slept, and where the ashes of the great Napoleon are sealed in dark marble. Where the blood of hundreds of communists soaked deep into the pavement. Where Marshal Ney lies entombed without a stone. Where Abelard and Heloise, " unfortunate lovers," lie in effigies of marble, side by side, upon a high tomb, looking into the sky.

At ancient York, where the great, gray Minster stands on the gravelly plain, and the old city wall curves in beauty upon the smooth, green mound, and Roman coffins surround the ruins of St. Mary's Abbey and the " Multangular Tower," I found cousin

James, an excellent machinist, who gave me a cordial welcome.

At Sleight's, three miles from the sea, on the river Esk, I met cousin John, as station-master, on the Northeastern Railway. He succeeded his father here some years ago, and together they have filled the position more than fifty years. This pleasant village is in a cool, green valley, where two vales meet, and reminds me much of Huntington creek valley, from Waterton to Harveyville. John and I walked to "Falling Foss," a few miles over the high, ling-covered moor, to where a stream of water falls down a forty-two foot ledge into a shady and romantic glen. We saw the heather, or ling, in bloom, where the jock sheep and the grouse love to abide the year around.

We entered a house, and the good woman placed turf cakes and milk before us on a little, round table, and we enjoyed the simple repast much. We saw her baking the cakes in a covered frying-pan, a turf fire with smouldering turf also upon the lid. The cakes were nice, like a short cake, the size of a tea plate, and nearly an inch thick. I afterwards found that cousin had asked her to "surprise" us in this agreeable manner. The farmer's wife told us she had a deeper pan, or kettle, which they called a "hang-on-oven," in which bread and pies are baked.

We returned through woods, and groves, and gardens, along by stone walls, and through the breckons (brakes) where rabbits resort, and we went into the "Hermitage," a circular room cut in a large, gray rock; on by old alum mines, and on to where "John

Allen" had set up a great marble lion's head, through the mouth of which rushed clean, sweet water.

The following lines were copied from the metal panels:

> " Man made the trough, the water God bestows,
>   Then praise His name, from whom the blessing flows.
> " *Hempsyke, 1856.*                              JOHN ALLEN."

> " Weary stranger, here you see
>   An emblem of true charity;
>   Rightly my bounty I bestow,
>   Made by a kindly hand to flow:
>   And I have fresh supplies from Heaven
>   For every cup of water given.
> " *Hempsyke, 1858.*                              JOHN ALLEN."

> " The stream is pure as if from Heaven it ran,
>   And while I praise the Lord, I'll thank the man.
> " *1864.*                                             TRAMP."

At Whitby I met Miss Mary Linskill, daughter of my uncle, the late Thomas Linskill. She is a popular English authoress, widely known in England, and admired by many people in this country, who appreciate pure fiction of a high order. She is an able and very interesting writer, being one of the best lady writers England has ever produced. She and her mother reside in a neat little cottage in Stakesbyvale. When I was there she had recently returned from a tour through France, Switzerland, Germany and Italy, with which she was much pleased. I dined a number of times with her and her mother, and the occasions were indeed pleasant. Miss Linskill's great story this year is entitled, " In Exchange for a Soul," and is being published in the "Sunday Magazine," London, and is also reprinted in this country. There appears to be a very brilliant future before her.

Cousin Edward Linskill and his wife, and daughter, May, at West Cliff, Whitby, treated me with marked courtesy and kindness, and here were my headquarters while in and about Whitby, my father's native town. Edward is an engine-driver on the North-Eastern railway, where he has been employed more than thirty years. I might tell you how he took me up on his engine and how we dashed up the green valley of the Esk drawing the passenger train with almost the speed of the swallow; how we thundered over bridges and whizzed under viaducts; rolled along embankments and roared through cuts, with the breath of summer on one cheek and a chilly blast on the other, if you moved your face beyond the shield or side of the small cab. When a young boy he went to live in the country with the great engineer, George Stephenson, but he soon asked to be allowed to go into the machine shops at Newcastle-on-Tyne, when railroading was in its infancy, and how, when about nineteen years of age, he was given an engine to run on the "third railroad in England."

I have mentioned his bright and active wife and his daughter, May, clever in drawing, painting and in music on the piano and violin. I called on Uncle James Linskill, at Sandsend, a number of times. He was nearly eighty-one years old and was feeble in body, but bright in mind. He was expecting to depart this life every day, and he said I had "come only just in time." He wrote a few lines in my book at the request of my sister. He did it without glasses and the writing was very neat.

Before leaving Whitby Edward and I called upon Mr. John Stewart, a retired tailor, a kind and interesting old gentleman of eighty-two years, who lives in a pleasant place on West Cliff with his daughter and her husband, Captain Pearson, who has often sailed the blue seas in past years. This was a very pleasant family, and refreshments of various kinds were placed before us. But why mention this, for you can scarcely enter a house in Great Britain without being nearly forced to eat and drink. Cousin Anna Stainthrope, of Middlesborough, prepared five meals in the twenty-two hours I was there and then accused me of not eating.

At Whitby I also called upon the Thistles, Waddingtons, Bryans, Nicholsons, Gaskins, Ripleys, Laws and Watsons. I also met Messrs. Payne, Stroud, Jackson, Hardy, Purcival, Greenbury, Fisher, Robinson, Jonathan and others. At Fulsgrave, near Scarborough, I met Alfred Linskill as postmaster and dealer in stationery, confectionery and toys. At Leamington, one of the most beautiful cities in central England, I found cousin Emma Hodgman and husband and child. In London I found cousin John, a dealer in jet jewelry; cousin Henry, a jet-worker and carver, and cousin Thomas, a carpenter and builder. At Hanmanby I found a Thomas Linskill, a farm hand, but we could not trace a relationship. I mention these, for they are the people I met by my name. There are very few of the name in England.

One cousin said that he thought our name, centuries ago, had come from Norway.

At North Shields I found one of the chief streets labeled "Linskill Street." I asked Charles Jenkins if there were any of the people of the name in the place, and he said, "No, Captain William Linskill has removed to Cambridge to educate his son there. He was a captain in the army in India for many years. He is a grandee, a rich man, and married a titled lady. He was a son of Colonel Linskill. There is a 'Linskill Terrace' and a 'Linskill Place,' also in the city." "Where is his magnificent mansion?" "Oh, he took it down before he left. He did not want anyone else to live in it." I thought this too eccentric to be lovable. "Land Agent Jackson is his agent here."

At North Burton I met Stephen Pudsey, and his sister, and her family, who also treated me very kindly. Here is where my father learned his trade with the elder Pudsey, and passed some pleasant years of his early life. He is well remembered here yet, over a gap of nearly three score years. I heard of Rev. Mr. Linskill in Warwickshire, but did not meet him. In Paris I met a number of pleasant American tourists of both sexes. In Cardiff, Wales, I visited Edward Edwards and James Edwards, brothers of Geo. A. Edwards, of Wilkes-Barré. They made it very pleasant for me the twenty-six hours I was in the city.

While in Scotland I called on Alexander Bennett, senior and junior, on James Morgan and family, on Andrew Swan and family, and on George Sharp and family, to all of whom I was recommended by Charles

Graham, of Scranton, Superintendent of Motive Power for the Delaware, Lackawanna and Western Railroad, and by all of whom I was very kindly treated and entertained. And as I told you before, I was well all the time on sea and land; so now you know where I went, and why I had a pleasant time.

# CHAPTER XV.

FROM LONDON TO PARIS, VIA DOVER AND CALAIS.

A HIGHWAY UPHELD ON POLISHED GRANITE PILLARS—BARBERS AND THEIR WORK—MOVING OUT OF LONDON—HOPS IN KENT—NINE TUNNELS—MARY ANDERSON AND MOONLIGHT IN CANTERBURY'S GLORY—DOVER; ITS CHALK CLIFFS, ITS BARRACKS, ITS BOASTING CANNON—MARTIN'S PICTURE OF CUT WOODS—LEAVE ENGLAND BEFORE MIDNIGHT—"CAFFA" IN "CALLA" BEFORE STARTING FOR "PARRA"—HE KNEW THE STOMACH BETTER THAN THE TONGUE—LOCOMOTIVES BLACK, GREEN, YELLOW, BROWN—THE ENGINE SNORTED ABOVE A TEMPEST OF FRENCH WORDS—RUSHING THROUGH OATFIELDS AND WILLOWS, BY FLOCKS AND STILL WATERS, IN "SUNNY FRANCE"—THE SEA DIVORCED ENGLAND FROM FRANCE—AMIENS—TREES LIKE SOLDIERS—IN PARIS—LONESOME WITHOUT DINNER AND FRIENDS—THREE BOTTLES OF WINE—COOK & SON—MET A YANKEE IN "PLACE VENDOME"—OBELISK OF LUXOR—PLACE DE LA CONCORDE—ARC DE TRIOMPHE—CHAMPS ELYSÉES, ETC.

On the afternoon of August 26th, I bid "good bye" to cousins in London, and walked over to the Holborn street station, on the London, Chatham and Dover Railway, and bought a third-class ticket to

Paris for one sovereign and two shillings. This immense station is near the beautiful and grand "Holborn Viaduct" in great London. Did I tell you that Holborn, one of the busy, broad streets of London, formerly ran down into a hollow or vale near Snow Hill? and how the poor horses would slip and fall on their knees going up and down this hill with thousands of tons of goods and millions of passengers; that many horses fell down there to get up no more; and finally Christian Charity and Common Business met under the auspices of Royalty and Peasantry, and this great highway was lifted up out of the valley and set upon many mighty pillars of polished Scotch granite, and now traffic and travel roll over on a high, broad level, while busy Farringdon street runs below as usual on its way to Ludgate Circus and the Thames? The viaduct is fourteen hundred feet long and eighty feet wide.

Having an hour to wait, I went into the barber shop and was shaved. The charge for shaving in these kingdoms is from one penny to three-pence. This barber asked me a few questions, and I said "Yes" to one of them, and he put a very few drops of bay-rum on my chin and said, "Sixpence," (twelve cents). If I had said "Yes" again, I presume he would have charged me a shilling or more. I presume the reader knows that a penny is about equal to two cents, and a shilling is about twenty-four cents, and that a pound or sovereign is worth about five dollars.

Many places in England you can get shaved for a penny, but this is too cheap to be satisfactory. The chair is a common chair, or maybe a bar-room chair, with a narrow board running up the back to steady your head; the razor is dull, and the boy's thin hands are cold, and he is in a hurry, for he can not take much time for a penny; he cuts your chin, and you wash your own face, and pay a penny or two, and wish you were again in America, where you could find a comfortable barber chair, and be smoothly and easily shaved for ten cents. When I was nearly ready to leave London, I did find a place where the chairs were comfortable, and they shaved with keen, smooth razors, and the charge was only three-pence. The barbers of Whitby did pretty good work considering the ridiculously small price they charged. On the sea we paid a shilling for being shaved. In Dublin I found a good and busy barber shop. There were a dozen chairs, and all of them were engaged. The charge was three-pence.

An American in England visited a barber shop and the barber asked him some questions, and he kept on saying "Yes" until the barber had dressed the hair on his face and head, cleaned his ears, colored his whiskers, shampooed him and taken the tartar off his teeth, and the bill was "seven-and-six" (nearly two dollars), which he paid under protest and then called upon the burgess or some one in authority and wished his money back; but the judge could not help him, only to tell him he must ask the price of such services in future and book up his countrymen by telling them to make bargains before the work is done.

We average Americans will not forgive that fellow

for "giving us away," and we pronounce him a greater fool in the court than he was in the barber shop. Let him brighten up his own ears and teeth or pay for it. And the man who colors his hair—oh, pshaw! he isn't worth pen and ink; pack him off with the woman who paints. But, I presume I must tell you about prices and other things here at another time.

At 4:15 p. m. the train started for Paris via Dover and Calais. We run out of the city on the "high level." This road runs on a high, broad, brick wall, two, three or four stories from the ground, and as we look out we see thousands of acres of house-roofs covered with terra cotta chimney tops—all the way from ten to fifty on each house, for each fire-place where they burn soft coal needs a chimney and a chimney-sweep. Perhaps London will soon have a great "Valley of Hinnom" where she will burn all the coal, and fuel, and smoke, and filth, and lead in the light and warmth and power by pipe and wire, and thus leave vast, populous old London free from smoke and dust. She filters sewers and rivers, and why not filter the air by fire, water and other chemicals? This "high level" wall is arched and the vacant places under the railroad are occupied as places to store coal, lime, lumber, flour, feed, grain and nearly all kinds of merchandise.

After leaving "Herne Hill" we come into a green, pleasant country where stand rows of neat, cream-colored brick houses. At "Dulwick" it still looks city-like. Now we pass through a long tunnel. Englishmen would rather run through a mountain than around or over it. They would as soon cut a tunnel through rock as to cut a mountain of rock into arches, keystones and viaduct pillars. We roll on through towns and villages and farm land. A gentleman said, "Kent is one of the finest counties in England; Devon and Cornwall are also fine agricultural counties."

We pass through Rochester, Chatham and Canterbury. A gentleman pointed out a large, round temple on a distant hill, which he said the "Latter Day Saints" had started, but had fallen into bankruptcy before they had got it finished. At Canterbury we saw from the train the fine, old and picturesque cathedral. This famous cathedral is beloved by Mary Anderson, and she is said to be the only person who has been permitted to view it internally by moonlight. Here we pass through three or four tunnels. There are nine tunnels between London and Dover. Now we are among the hop-fields of Kent. There are hundreds of acres of hops standing straight and orderly like soldiers clad in green. These hops bring the largest price.

As we approach Dover the white chalk crops out here and there, and a farmer said, "We do not like it to be too near to the surface." There, near a wall by a railway station, is a stalk of Indian corn, the first I have seen since leaving America. In England wheat is called corn. As darkness settles down we enter old Dover, with her high, white cliffs of chalk standing on almost every side. I have two hours to wait for the boat to Calais; I leave my travelling bags at the cloak-room, and pay two-pence for each, that they may be taken care of, and then I go to find John Martin, Warden of the Convict Prison here, and hand him a letter which his brother Alfred in Plymouth, America, had sent by me. Mr. Martin was found, and welcomed me as his brother's friend. He is a pleasant man, and has been in the service of his country for thirty years. Mrs. Martin and a son were visiting in Cornwall. Mr. Martin showed me a handsome round table of his own make, for which he had received a prize at an exhibition. It was finely inlaid with 11,000 pieces of mahogany, satin wood, ebony, and other fine woods. After a few minutes visit he accompanied me to the station, and to the boat, and as we walked we talked, and I found that the long, straight row of lights there are the lamps along the Esplanade or water front; those lights there, as if a mountain had windows in it, are at the barracks where four regiments of soldiers are quartered, and this high hill is the South Cliff looming far above the old church tower and the railway station.

Yonder is where the old cannon stands menacing sunny, fun-loving France, and carved on its brazen side are these words of threatening and promise: "Sponge me out and keep me clean, and I'll carry a ball to Calais Green." As the distance is twenty-one miles across the channel, where two seas delight to meet, it is probably a "brazen, loud-mouthed lie." "Up that street lives John ———, the largest man in England; he weighs over forty stone, more than five hundred and sixty pounds! An ordinary man weighs say ten stone. He keeps a public house. Here we are on the boat." "Yes, leave the satchels there. Tell Alfred I would like to see him. Good night; a safe and pleasant journey. Try to stop when you return and see Dover by daylight!" "Thank you; good bye!"

At 10:10 p. m. our Channel boat "cuts loose" from old England and we "strike out" over the waves for France. I wrapped my garments about me, and while various specimens of humanity ran to and fro and reclined here and there, I drew myself behind a post to escape the cold, damp draft, and, half dozing, we reached Calais, France, at midnight and saw the revolving, and colored, and electric lights blazing all along the shores to guide us aright. The sea was quiet and I think we all escaped illness. We, or many of us, entered a railway station and reclined on hard cushioned benches, waiting for the train to start. About 4 a. m. a man came in and awoke us, and, as he spoke French, I did not know what was the programme, but presumed the train was about to go. But, when he came to me and said "caffa" two or three times, I concluded he meant, come to breakfast before starting for "Parry." Calais is pronounced "Cally." I arose to follow him and turned to look at my luggage, when he said something to a man in the room and by signs assured me it would be all right. I and some others followed him out around several lonely corners and I began to wish I was at the station with my bags. We entered a plain-looking place and soon a bowl of hot and excellent coffee and milk was placed before me. I enjoyed it much and paid a half franc or franc, I do not remember which. Yes, that neighbor in a foreign land knew what my American stomach needed at 4 o'clock in the morning before starting for "Parry," where we could not arrive until nearly noontide.

About 5 a. m. there was a hurrying to and fro, a rumble of trunks and boxes, a ringing of bells, a tempest of French words, and the iron horse snuffed the cool, morning air and rushed out with us, away from the sea toward distant Paris.

My last week's letter left me on my way to Paris, drawn by a black locomotive, the first I had seen since leaving America, for the locomotives in England are painted, some green, others brown, yellow and drab. Did I tell you that the locomotives in England have no cow-catchers? They are not needed, for England will not have anything on her railroads but engines and cars. Here the locomotives have head-lights, in England a small lantern at each side of the engine, on the front, answers the purpose.

Beg pardon, we are on the road to Paris. Perhaps I can do no better than to copy what I wrote in my memorandum book, as we rolled through France at the rate of forty or more miles an hour. "August 27th, at Calais, in France; somewhat cloudy; left for Paris at 5 a. m. Level country; oats harvest, many fields; hundreds of acres without trees, in this respect, unlike England. Cars in compartments, third-class have no cushions, seats flat, backs straight, and the car is not clean. The conductor walks on a narrow foot-board outside, holding on to an iron rod running along the side of the car. The houses have pitching roofs, covered with red tiles. Fields and fields of oats; in France, as in England, the harvester swings his scythe toward the standing grain and leaves the swath leaning against the uncut grain. Here is a man cradling or mowing, and a woman is binding.

Here men are hauling away wheat or barley, and yonder a woman loads the grain which a man pitches upon the wagon. The white chalk crops out of the banks here as in the south of England, all of which makes some people think that England and France were once united by land instead of divided by water. It is quite probable that the Atlantic and German Oceans wishing to embrace, dashed through the channel, and now not living harmoniously, their contending and foaming make myriads ill.

Here and there are wind-mills, and here is a stonequarry. Now we pass through a long cut of rock and sand. The French passengers, though unacquainted, chat pleasantly with each other. Now we come among some hills. A man rings a bell energetically, just before the train leaves a station, and active Frenchmen dressed in livery run this way and that, all the time, earnestly talking and calling out orders.

Here we roll along a high embankment. Over my head are painted the words, "Cinquante Places," which signifies that there is room for five passengers on each side, but as there are but three or four of us for ten seats, we are not crowded. Now we see the sea on our right, and soon we are at Bologne.

Going on, we run across low, flat land, thousands of acres, cows grazing near creeks and pools of still water. Yonder are thickets and rows of willows along creeks and fields; there are piles of peat, or turf. Here, in a wide meadow are say three hundred sheep, first I have seen. More meadows with rows of tall, slender trees between. Train rushes fifty miles an hour along a small river with banks willow-walled. Good vegetables in gardens on islands and among marshy places—a few poor apples seen—good road made of stone.

Here is old Amiens—a large place, grand cathedral, with tall spire; on through a region of vegetable gardens. Yonder are thousands of acres of land sloping off on to hills; no fences, no trees, no stone walls, yet, some hedges; no large barns. At last I see a low, wood-crowned mountain. Thousands of acres of wheat and oats in bundles, shocks and stacks. Country looks dry and brown.

This has been a dry summer for this portion of our globe. Now the fields are large, square and smooth; the trees on the hills stand straight and trim, like well-drilled soldiers. More potatoes and vegetables; hedges well-kept; the sun does not shine quite so brightly.

I see we are nearing great, gay Paris, for the engine seems to have imbibed a new life. We rush as if the happiness of families and nations, time and eternity, hung upon a few moments of time. We are in the suburbs of Paris and roll on in a long way until we stand still in a wide, busy, stone station in the heart of the city. I walk out with my satchels as if I was not a stranger; the porters do not annoy me. I pass on along grand streets and by fine buildings, looking for a friend, looking for dinner and wishing I could speak French, yes, almost wishing I had not come. If I had one lonely hour while I was absent, it was this first hour in Paris, before I had taken dinner and before I had found an English-speaking person.

In front of gay hotels and restaurants sat hundreds of handsome, well-dressed people around small round tables, which were covered with wine bottles and glasses and sandwiches, or some kind of luncheon. I entered a neat-looking place and after a while managed to make myself understood so well that the polite waiter brought me a sandwich and coffee. Then I asked for dessert, but the waiter looked perplexed; then I said, "tart, pie, etc.," when he went out and brought in three bottles of wine. I shook my head. A handsome, talkative woman at a table looked friendly and wise, and spoke to the waiter, and he said "Plum pudding?" and I thought it a good time to say "Yes," so I nodded "Yes," and in a short time he brought in three little round cakes iced in fine sugar. They were very rich and much like moist fruit cake. I dared to eat two of them and then paid my little bill, which, I think, was two francs and forty centimes, or forty-eight cents. Then I went out, gazed on as an object of interest, if not of pity.

Remembering Cook, that famous Englishman, who has an office in nearly every great city, to sell tickets and furnish guides to tourists, I essayed to find his place. After a good many questions and a walk of a mile or two through the grand streets of great Paris, I came to a busy centre, where a building was inscribed, "9 Rue Scribe, Thomas Cook & Son." Here the clerks spoke English, and sold me "Cook's Guide to Paris," and directed me to the Hotel St. Petersbourg, in that vicinity. They seemed kind and reliable, so I bought a ticket of them for a few days' board at the hotel mentioned, for which I paid at the rate of two dollars a day.

I went to the hotel and was shown a very pleasant room, and was informed that the dinner hour would be at half-past six, and breakfast anytime from eight to eleven; two meals a day, as we were expected to lunch somewhere "'mid pleasures and palaces," in or near the city. Then I sauntered out and soon found myself gazing up at the great column of cannon-metal in the "Place Vendome." While there I saw a man also quietly looking around, and I asked, "Do you speak English?" He replied, "Yes, sometimes; my name is Hiram Holt; I am from Maine, United States, and I make and sell a patent hay-knife. I left America, June 3d, and have been with my wife and daughter through Europe." This famous and tall column, bearing aloft a bronze statue, stands in a granite-paved square, smaller than Public Square, Wilkes-Barré, Pa.

Going on I found myself in a grand, and beautiful, and historic quarter. Here, near great and beautiful fountains, stands the obelisk of Luxor, from Egypt, sister to our Cleopatra Needle in Central Park, and one of the oldest and finest monuments on earth. Yes, this is the "Place de la Concorde." This fine, open place, full of fountains and statues and surrounded by columned and domed palaces, and temples, is one of the most historic and magnificent places in Europe.

Yonder is the Seine with its grand bridges, and graceful boats, and grove-lined banks; yonder the Madeleine Church with many vast columns, yonder the Louvre palace full of thousands of the finest paintings and other things of beauty. Here the garden of the Tuileries, and yonder, a mile and a quarter away, on a slight eminence, with the sky for a background, stands the immense, grand and sombre "Arc de Triomphe," spanning the magnificent Champs Elysées, perhaps the most beautiful street in the world, especially at night. It is near the dinner hour, and as my letter is quite long enough, I will close here.

# CHAPTER XVI.

PARIS: PLACES OF BEAUTY AND PLACES OF BLOOD.

PLACE DE LA CONCORDE—THE GLITTERING KNIFE—A LAKE OF BLOOD—PRANZINA BEHEADED—BAPTISM OF BLOOD—FOREIGN ARMIES—LIONS, BEARS, EAGLES, DRAGONS—GILDED DOMES TREMBLE—A NEEDLE WEIGHING TWO HUNDRED AND FORTY TONS—ASKING OTHERS TO DIE FOR US—CHAMPS ELYSÉES, A STREET UNEQUALED—A BALL-ROOM ONE AND A HALF MILES LONG, FLANKED BY TWO KINGDOMS, NATURE AND ART, FULL OF LIGHT, MUSIC, BEAUTY AND WINE—THE ARC DE TRIOMPHE, A GLORY TO UPHOLD GLORY—COST MILLIONS—PICTURES IN MARBLE AND BRONZE—TWELVE PROUD, GAY AVENUES BOW AT ITS FEET—IT SHOWS US A WIDE PANORAMA OF MAGNIFICENCE—AT DINNER—LINEN, SILVER, CRYSTAL, BROADCLOTH, SILK, LACE, SILVER HANDS, GOLD FINGERS, MIRRORS, WINE, FLOWERS AND FOUNTAINS—AN HOUR AND A HALF GOING FROM SOUP AND FISH TO WINE, GRAPES AND PEACHES.

At the close of last week's letter, the writer stood in the Place de la Concorde, near the Egyptian obelisk, where the Guillotine once stood in an awful lake of human blood; blood that had gushed from the headless bodies of men and women of high degree, in the revolutionary days, when fair, fickle, glory-loving France waded through blood to find something better than she had known. I fancied I heard the sobs of children, the groans of loving friends, the screams of victims as the keen and glittering knife fell with strokes more deadly than those of lightning.

For readers who have not seen a Guillotine, I will say, it is like two stout posts about eight feet high and two feet apart, between which slides up a broad, heavy knife, and when the victim or criminal is securely bound on the block, the cord is jerked and the knife falls, severing the head from the body.

Murderers are still executed in this manner, and when I was there, August 31st, Pranzina was Guillotined in front of the Prison de la Roquette at 5 o'clock in the morning. Here the day and hour of an execution is not announced, for it would attract too large a crowd. The condemned person is supplied with fine food, wine and cigars, but he does not know the hour he is to die until about two hours before the time. Many people waited around the old Prison de la Roquette for days and nights to see the ghastly spectacle—the beheading of a human being.

As I have been walking and writing, "'mid pleasures and palaces," castles, cathedrals, art galleries, and ruins, for weeks the reader may shrink from this baptism of blood, so I will not now point out the many places of blood in this grand city, but the reader may as well know that near where I stood that afternoon, thousands of human beings had met violent deaths;

many beheaded, others burned, hanged, stoned and trampeled.

On those broad, solid pavements, at different periods, foreign armies had encamped, with strange banners emblazoned with lions, bears, unicorns, eagles, vultures and dragons. Here the bright bayonets of foes, and the clang of scabbards worn by enemies, were seen and heard, while the tall columns, fine marble statues, and palaces, and gilded domes trembled as great dark-mouthed cannon from distant lands, wheeling into line, thundered the deep bass of the Empire's dirge. Yes, more than once had foreign foes here placed a strong, bloody hand on the fair, white throat of guilty France.

And here Frenchmen had rushed upon Frenchmen, in dark days, and communistic times, and glistening bayonets turned red, and cannon-belched iron balls, and fire, and smoke, and the murderous Mitrailleuse hurled its leaden hail, while curses, groans and shrieks, pierced the blue curtain that rolled above the cobble stones once more, cemented with human blood. Yonder, behind a cross-crowned altar, in that magnificently-pillared temple, hundreds of communists had been shot, stabbed, and crushed into hideous, bloody clay. Now, near this beautiful obelisk, which is a handsome tapering stone, seventy-six feet high, and weighing two hundred and forty tons, and standing on a block of granite weighing ninety-six tons, are two immense and fine fountains, throwing rivers of bright water into the air, which descending in beauty, seem striving to wash away the awful stains that have marred the place. Truly, sparkling water looks better in a place of Concord than thick, red blood.

The following lines from a guide-book are so interesting, that I make room for them here:

"Place de la Concorde, the finest place in Paris, and, indeed, in Europe. It is situated between the Garden of the Tuileries and the Champs Elysées. From the centre of the place, where stands the Obelisk of Luxor, sister monolith to Cleopatra's Needle, can be seen the Arc de Triomphe, the Madeleine, the Palace of the Louvre, the Corps Legislatif, or House of Commons, and many other fine public buildings. It was completed in its present form in 1854.

"This site has a tragic history. Originally a waste ground, it was reclaimed in 1748, after the peace of Aix la Chapelle, and a statue of Louis XV. was erected there by the municipal council of Paris. The place then received the name Place Louis XV.

"On the 30th May, 1770, at a display of fire-works to celebrate the marriage of the Dauphin, afterwards Louis XVI., with Marie Antoinette, a panic arose from some unexplained cause, which resulted in twelve hundred persons being crushed to death or suffocated and two thousand seriously injured.

"During the Reign of Terror in 1793, the Guillotine was erected on the spot where now stands the obelisk. Louis XVI. and Marie Antoinette were the first victims. Between January of that year and May, 1795, upwards of two thousand persons were here decapitated.

"In 1799 the square was named Place de la Concorde. It was afterwards renamed after Louis XV., and in 1826 after Louis XVI. In 1830 it was again christened Place de la Concorde, and the Luxor obelisk, given to Louis Phillippe, was erected where it now stands.

"The obelisk is a monolith, or solid piece of stone, seventy-six feet high and weighing two hundred and forty tons. The gray granite pedestal on which it stands, is a single block of ninety-six tons weight.

"The eight fine statues in the square represent the chief towns of France, viz., Lyons, Marseilles, Bordeaux, Nantes, Rouen, Brest, Lille and Strasburg (now German).

"Foreign armies have been encamped on the Place de la Concorde three times."

Let us hope that the world will very soon become so Christianized and civilized that nations shall find health without the violent letting of blood; that men and women may learn to be happy without going about asking others to die for them. It is high time that the practice of sacrificing human beings should "perish from the earth." This place at night is all aglitter with thousands of gas lights, and let us hope that scenes of blood may never again cause these fountains to blush and the lights to pale.

Yonder, a mile and a quarter away, stands the grand Arc de Triomphe, forming a blue arch above the horizon. After a walk of half an hour I arrived at its base, having passed along the famous Champs Elysées.

This magnificent boulevard, with its broad, smooth driveway and wide walks and rows of trees and fountains and easy seats and wine and concert groves, is more than eleven hundred feet wide, extending from the river Seine to a row of light stone palaces. At night it is like a fair; yes, like a fair and a ball-room and a concert, for all along, amid thousands of gay colored lights, are concerts within labyrinths and walls of shrubbery, where strains of strange, voluptuous music, instrumental and vocal, are heard; and, while colored wines flow in rushing, foamy streams, dancing of the wildest and most fantastic forms is going on.

Here fun, vanity and folly hold High Carnival and the devotees for a season seem to hope that pleasures have no sting.

Since my return, people unlearned and young, as well as many others, have assured me that they appreciate these letters from abroad, which they would not have done if they had not understood what I have written. Now, that all may understand what I think of the Champs Elysées (pronounced Shons E-lee-sa), the most beautiful place in Paris, let the reader imagine a ball-room a mile and a half long, in a beautiful grove more than one thousand feet wide; on one side a sparkling river, on the other side a row of marble palaces; at one end a grand granite arch one hundred and sixty feet high, at the other end a graceful, imported obelisk and two great fountains, backed by a number of fine, large statues, human and equine, and a delightful flower garden; smooth, broad ways through the middle for carriages and people on foot; and at night this all glittering with light and throbbing with exciting music and sparkling with flowing wine, bright eyes and fine dress, and this is like what the Champs Elysées appeared to me.

Walking up, inside, about two hundred and fifty steps of stone, I find myself upon the top of the Arc de Triomphe. This is claimed to be the finest triumphal arch on earth. It is one hundred and sixty feet high, one hundred and forty-six feet broad, and seventy-two feet deep. It is arched two ways, that is, two avenues cross beneath it at right angles. It was commenced in 1806, and not finished until 1836, and was designed to commemorate the success and glory of Napoleon the Great. It cost nearly two millions of dollars, and it bears upon its sides the most magnificent pictures carved in high relief—great events in the history of France and Napoleon.

It stands on a slight eminence in the "Star" where twelve handsome avenues centre at its base. What a panorama of glory and beauty is here spread out! Thousands of carriages and people are moving quietly over the smooth and wood-paved streets. The atmosphere is quite clear. What a contrast with London! Here we can look over the whole great city of two millions of laughing and suffering men and women.

Yonder is the gleaming Seine, and in at least three directions are seen mounts in the dim distance where fortifications and monuments, or great public buildings stand, or are being erected. Yonder, to the north, stretches the great, deep green forest of Bois de Boulogne, with its twenty-five thousand acres, containing towns, lakes, fountains and palaces. There is historic St. Cloud, where the great Napoleon once appeared in great splendor with his almost invincible army, bearing bright banners, and brilliant badges and scarfs.

Away there is the column of July, 1830, standing in the Place de la Bastile. There is the Pantheon with its vast dome, and there the two towers and spire of the great and ancient Notre Dame Cathedral, and nearer stands the Palace Louvre and the Luxembourg. Yonder is the lofty gilded dome of the Invalides, a fitting canopy for the dust of the ambitious Napoleon. There, fountain-guarded, stands the beautiful obelisk in the Place de la Concorde, and here to the right the beautiful and extensive Palace Trocadera rears its two lofty towers nearly three hundred feet above the waters of the Seine, looking down upon its broad, magnificent dome, and the great fountains in a wide garden of fragrant beauty. But it is time I descend from this enchanting eminence. I bought a book of Paris views from the handsome young lady who took charge of my umbrella while I admired the gorgeous scene.

I wish all my readers could see how beautiful it is to look down upon a broad boulevard in which stand four long rows of beautiful trees, while fine statues and fountains sit on diamonded thrones amid the sweetest and most brilliant angels of vegetation. The young lady smiled and looked somewhat puzzled as she wrote, in compliance with my request, her name and a short sentence in French in a note-book which I carry to supplement my memory. As I had walked quite enough, I took a street-car going toward the Hotel St. Petersbourg. The street-cars here are clean, handsome and neatly painted, and many passengers ride outside on top.

I told you that I put up at a hotel where the clerks and waiters, though French, spoke English. At 6:30 o'clock we entered the dining-saloon in a court, flanked by flowers and shrubbery. The canopy was splendid with chandeliers, flowers, angels and stars, and the walls were resplendent with mirrors and gay curtains held in exquisite forms by graceful hands of silk and metal.

But I must hasten; I cannot stay to tell you fully how an army of polite and finely-dressed young men quickly supplied the wants of the two hundred or more people who chatted in English around the three large tables; how wines, liquors and sodas of various colors flowed and foamed, while good, clear water filled half the goblets; how a dozen beautiful monogramed plates were placed before each guest from time to time as he helped himself from liberal waiters, passed at his left hand, and ate and conversed for more than an hour. Yes, the French are cooks; they could please me in this line greatly and easily.

We begin with soup, and passing through courses of fish, flesh, fowl and vegetables, we go on to puddings, etc., and finish with a cluster of grapes or a peach. Though for the first half hour at dinner you might remain hungry, that sensation would certainly depart before the close of the repast. The dinner hour is ended; it is nearly 8 o'clock; the city is brilliantly lighted up and thousands of visitors from various parts of the world are either walking and riding out, or still planning where they will pass the evening or greater part of the night.

# CHAPTER XVII.

PARIS: HER PAST, PRESENT; PALACES AND PRISON.

A CITY PEERLESS IN BEAUTY—BUILDINGS BOW TO WINNERS OF GLORY—EAGLE-MOUNTED BANNERS AND NUMIDIAN LIONS—CÆSAR IN A WOLF DEN—MANY PALACES, FEW HOMES—GOLDEN ARGOSIES WRECKED UNDER RAINBOWS—THE STRANGE WOMAN—WOE TO THE CITY—DYING ALONE—SUNDAY IN PARIS—WINE FLOWS—BUILDINGS GOING UP, ETC.—BOULEVARDS, COLUMNS, ARCHES, FOUNTAINS—AN ISLAND OF FLOWERS FLOATING THROUGH JET TO HONOR THE DEAD AND PLEASE THE LIVING—PLACE DE LA BASTILE—ANGRY MEN LET IN THE SUN-LIGHT AND BEHEAD THE KEEPERS—ON TOP OF A FLUTED, VIBRATING COLUMN OF BRONZE—THE TALL, GILDED ANGEL—RED LINES IN THE PAVEMENT.

I now stand in a well-lighted and grand thoroughfare in the gay capital of France, nearly four thousand miles from the little vale where I was born and where Mr. Bennett helped me to find "Paris" on a well-worn map. I think of the history of this great city in the heart of France. This city, peerless in beauty, where banners of love or banners of war are always unfurled; where cannon have boomed in battle and orchestras throbbed music for dancers; where captains, generals, kings, queens, emperors and presidents have paraded the streets with tossing plumes, while the buildings seemed to bow and the city shook with the roar of artillery and the swell of music. I thought of the time when the wolves howled where the great Louvre now stands, and of the later times, when the great Cæsar marched his mighty legions this way under the eagle-mounted banners of invincible Rome, with soldiers bronzed on deserts where roared Numidian lions and with helmeted Centurians who had commanded at cruel crucifixions in lands beyond the sea. Now it is a vast city of many palaces and few homes, where great buildings contain myriads of things beautiful, curious and ancient.

Surely, gods have walked along the Seine, or we should not here see such palaces and paintings. It is nearly 9 o'clock in the evening. There stands the Grand Hotel filling a square, and on the broad pavements around it are hundreds of men and women seated at small round tables drinking sparkling wine from fairy-like glasses, beautiful as the pink and pearl sea-shells on the emerald shore of Dream-land.

Yonder is the Grand Opera House, covering nearly three acres of ground. It cost many millions of francs and is considered the grandest opera on earth. I walked around it and took five hundred and sixty-three long steps in making the circle. It took thirteen years to build it. It is not open to-night and I do not gain admittance, but they showed me pictures and told me of its interior magnificence, which made me think of a green and purple isthmus where a royal fleet of golden argosies had wrecked among beautiful billows of marble on a silvery beach under rainbows that linked heaven and earth.

Many brilliant stores, shops and bazaars are seen in every direction, in some of which you see the words, "English spoken here." Many neat and beautiful street-cars, and 'busses, and cabs, are seen rolling along all the broad, smooth avenues. Here comes a street-car filled with people, inside and outside, drawn by three handsome gray horses hitched side by side, and as they trot they seem to keep step. Well dressed and orderly people are passing and re-passing.

In a short walk of half an hour along pavements bright with gas and electric lights, I hear and see things that I was sorry to witness, things that tell us plainly that this great city is awfully corrupt. For there is the "strange woman" with the "impudent face" to interrupt the stranger and young men who go straight on their way. Some said, "No!" with a scornful emphasis; but, alas, some went "as an ox goeth to the slaughter." Vice and crimes that I dare not mention are committed here every day and night. And any city thus wicked deserves to be wrecked with bombs, or swallowed by earthquakes, or purified by fire. I came where men, and women, and children, were standing before a show window, and looking in, I saw pictures and photographs at which decent people blush. I turned away, for I would not dare to describe them here. And male villains try to tempt strangers into the vilest dens.

Having seen evil enough of Paris by gas-light, on the pavements, I turned toward my hotel, where I might write a letter for the *Telephone*, or write down the incidents and sights of the day for use at a future time. Next morning at breakfast a Londoner, a young married man, told me how some people spend their nights in this glittering whirlpool of moral corruption. Of course, Christians, and gentlemen, and decent people must deprecate these "amusements"(?) and depart from, or rather keep from, such scenes. The whole truth need not be told now, but a portion of it may warn and do good. Strangers are often asked to buy packages of obscene pictures, on cards, by young men who show them slyly. I did not befoul my pockets with any of them. I would rather turn young people, who are not fixed in good habits, into the wilds of Africa, than to leave them unguarded in Paris. The French are, as a rule, handsome people, and the girls you see attending shops and places of business, are fine in face and form. If the reader should say these scenes of beauty and pleasure do not condemn vice, let him imagine the awful suffering, poverty, sorrow, chagrin, and disgrace, and despair of those who worship pride, pleasure, fashion, wine and vanity for such pleasures are only for a season; though we may dance and laugh in a crowd of friends we must weep alone—alone in a dark, chilly night, full of fears, and pains, and wants,—a night that has no joy awaiting it in the morning.

I walked out on Sunday morning. The streets were gay with travel and travelers. Though surrounded by temples, I heard no church bells. Here men were building a house; here painters were painting a building; here restaurants, and hotels, and gardens were full of gay wine drinkers and cigarette smokers; here men were paving the streets and here were others putting down pipe in deep trenches. The street-cars are well crowded going up and down. I noticed that many of the largest stores were closed; at least the great iron shutters that lay fold upon fold had been let down.

Street-cars passed me with "Madeleine" and "Place de la Bastile" painted thereon, so I concluded to walk the way to the Bastile. I walked the grand boulevard looking and learning. Streets would cross streets at angles, right, acute and obtuse. Here is a square and there a circle; here a statue and there a fountain; here an arch of victory and yonder a temple with pillars; here a hotel and there a gilded spire, and here is where a most gigantic bronze lion crouches at the foot of the monument in the Place de la Republique. This monument is grand and massive, but not lofty.

Here comes a funeral procession; see the two black horses, harness, hearse and driver, all decked in shining black! A few white tassels and rosettes enliven the hearse, which is a large, open one, and the casket is almost lost in banks of flowers. A man in black walks on each side, and about forty men and women, in sober black, slowly follow the steadily moving funeral-car, while eight fine barouches, well filled with mourning friends, bring up the rear. It is like a fragrant island of flowers floating amid graceful columns and arches of jet, and the whole scene seems to say, "What a quiet, pleasant, beautiful thing it is to go to a funeral in Paris, whether your arms are folded under flowers and glass in the glossy casket, or whether your hands are full of fragrant roses, as you walk by the handsome hearse, over asphalt pavements, between rows of gay palaces, where trees and fountains cool the air!"

At a later day we noticed the gay rosettes on the bridles of the horses, and they say, "There goes a wedding party." In Paris one must bow to the tyrant Fashion, whether living or dying.

Clear water runs in the gutters with which to scrub the streets. The streets are paved with stone, with wood, with asphalt, and with tar, sand and gravel. Now I arrive at the Place de la Bastile. Here is the place where the famously infamous old castle and prison "Bastile" once stood. I need not tell you about this old prison, for have you not read about it in your school books and in your cyclopædias? It was built about 1375 and was called the Castle of Paris, and here for ages had great people and men of learning been imprisoned until they were forgotten; until no man knew why they were shut up away from the free sunshine of heaven.

Well, in 1789 a great mob, or, rather, an army of revolutionists, armed with cannon and courage, came upon it and after a struggle took it and broke open the dusty and rusty doors, and let out the prisoners and cut off the heads of those in charge of it and scattered its stones in ruins—stones which have since been used in good bridges and public buildings.

Now, in the centre of the place stands a magnificent and stately fluted column of bronze thirteen feet in diameter and one hundred and fifty-four feet high, bearing upon its side the names of brave men who died while fighting for "public liberty" on the 27th, 28th and 29th of July, 1830. The base is white marble, and on top of the column stands an immense gilded figure on a great gilded ball. The figure represents the "Genius of Liberty" running, a bird in one hand and a broken chain in the other.

For a small piece of silver I am permitted to ascend the column on the inside. I go around and around a good many times in the darkness before I get to the top. Now we are on top just below the great ball and gilded figure. I will not attempt to describe what I saw—the spires, towers, domes, columns, statues, arches, fountains, distant hills, parks, groves, markets, etc. Soldiers, gentlemen and ladies are here and we almost jostle against each other there in the air, for our platform, or gallery, overhangs the great column. The wind blows strong and the column trembles and shudders, and a young lady also trembles and shudders as she shrinks back from the slender metal railing; but I trembled, too, somewhat, as I noticed the vibrations of the great metal column and gazed on the hard, white paving stones so far below. I would have felt safer had there been fewer people up and the day had not been Sunday. What is that red line in the pavements, running this way and that?

That shows where the old Bastile once stood. Now I breathe more freely; I am on the ground once more. See the centre of this wide boulevard! Four rows of trees, flowers and fountains! In the centre are men, women and children selling nearly all kinds of notions and articles, among which are second-hand articles, old clothing, old rusty keys and nameless things too numerous to mention, spread all over the pavement and ground. It is near dinner-time. I get upon the top of a street-car and ride toward the "Madeleine."

# CHAPTER XVIII.

PARIS: PLACES MAGNIFICENT AND GLORIOUS.

BREAKFAST—GUIDED THROUGH PALACES—AMERICANS MET—THE MADELEINE—A MARBLE SPLENDOR—THE DECALOGUE SWINGS IN BRONZE—TRUE ART CALLS FOR TEARS—THREE HUNDRED COMMUNISTS KILLED NEAR A PULPIT—TROCADÉRO PALACE AND GARDEN—LOOKING DOWN ON A CANOPY WHICH COVERS SEVEN THOUSAND SEATS IN RED VELVET—STEEL FINGERS TOWER A THOUSAND FEET WHERE LIGHTNING RULES—CATHEDRALS CUT IN ROCK AND LIGHTED BY RAINBOWS, AND FILLED WITH MUSIC OF SEAS, BIRDS, THUNDER, ETC.—PANORAMA OF REZONVILLE—A FROZEN BATTLE-FIELD—AMERICA'S MONUMENT AT YOSEMITE SMILING AMONG CLOUDS—NAPOLEON'S TOMB, GUARDED BY MARBLE HEROES, THREE HUNDRED AND FORTY FEET BELOW A GOLDEN HEMISPHERE.

Monday morning, August 29th, in Paris. At breakfast, between eight and nine o'clock—the beefsteak is tender and very finely broiled; the potato is sliced in slender pieces the length of your finger, and browned in butter; the bread is in delicate, brown, crescent-shaped rolls, not much larger than the handle of a table-knife; the butter is good and sweet, and is without salt; the coffee is fresh, hot, clear, and not too strong, in a silver pot; mixed with a liberal quantity of good, hot milk, and a tablet of loaf-sugar, it is unsurpassable. This breakfast pleased me so well that I left the thousand and one other things and asked it to be repeated each morning while I remained in the city. Other guests keep dropping into the dining-room, and breakfast will be served all the forenoon. I walk out, the morning is cool, and the atmosphere is clear and fine. Calling at Cook's office, 9 Rue Scribe, the clerk says, "Will you go with one of our four-in-hand excursions? In three days, this way, you will see nearly the whole city, only two dollars a day for each person." I paid the two dollars, or eight shillings, or ten francs, I do not remember which, and stepped up in the carriage drawn by four horses, and driven by a fat Frenchman, in blue broadcloth, gold-colored braid, and high, shining hat. Eighteen or twenty of us excursionists from America and England fill the five seats that run across the carriage. By my side is a young man from London; there is a young lady from Baltimore; there a married lady from Philadelphia; there Mr. S. and his daughter from New York; there a tall, old maid from Wisconsin; there a young man from Cincinnati, and here one from New Jersey, and others too numerous to mention, but not too numerous to be good company and have a good time all day, shown through palaces and parks by our good-natured and witty guide, Henry de Heerdt. Life-long friendships were doubtlessly formed on that and succeeding days. At 10 o'clock we start, our guide having two carriage loads to guide and instruct, and he rode with us. We drove along a grand boulevard by the Grand Opera House, and came to the Madeleine, or church of St. Mary Magdalene. This is a great building, and was many years in being erected. It reminds me much of Girard College, as it stands surrounded by many mighty columns, on a broad plateau of granite lying layer above layer. I counted fourteen columns in front, which I set down as six feet in diameter and sixty feet high. "The entire cost of the Madeleine was two millions six hundred and fifteen thousand and eight hundred dollars. It stands on a raised platform, three hundred and twenty-eight feet long, and one hundred and thirty-eight feet broad, and has at each end an approach consisting of twenty-eight steps the entire length of the façade. The architecture is Grecian. A colonnade of fifty-two Corinthian columns entirely surround the building, giving to it a grandeur of appearance which few structures in Europe attain. Between the columns there are niches, and a row of colossal statues stand in them."

The bronze doors are massive and magnificent, being thirty-six feet high and sixteen feet broad. The doors have ten panels, in each of which is a representation of one of the Ten Commandments. These are great and beautiful pictures in bronze. I have not the time nor the ability to describe the interior of this great and gorgeous temple; but let me assure you that it is resplendent with marbles of fine polish and various colors, gold, silver, altars, baptismal fonts, crucifixes, confessionals, pulpits, chapels, shrines, and fine and rare statues and paintings illustrating the birth, life, death and resurrection of Christ, and the history of saints and nations of later times. I sometimes think I would be almost happy if I could describe clearly to our readers these scenes of grandeur and glory, for more than once in the presence of great works of art and rare music did my soul melt and my eyes reveal the fact in glistening drops like dew, while I, in a figure, bowed one knee to the worker below and one knee to the Master above. Our guide said: "There, behind the pulpit, three hundred Communists were killed," and as we went out he showed us where balls and bullets had scarred the columns and walls during a struggle with Communists. As we drove by the Luxor obelisk, in the Place de la Concorde, he said: "There is where the Guillotine stood, and here is where foreign armies have encamped." And driving along the Champs Elysées we came to the Panorama of Rezonville, which is a representation of an awful battle between the French and Germans, in which nearly thirty-four thousand lives were lost. We enter a building, and, going through a dark passage, go up into a circular room which appears to be in the centre of a large and bloody battle-field; motion and noise are the only things lacking to make it appear entirely real. It is thrilling, awful and graphic, like a bloody battle-scene suddenly frozen or struck into silence and immovability by power superhuman. You see the sky and clouds above, the fields, woods and mountains near and many miles away. The smoke hangs over the cannon, the bombs are suspended in air. Thousands of soldiers and horses; some charging with banners, and many fallen, bleeding and dying. Here is the dusty road of midsummer, broken fences, wasted harvests, houses on fire, dust upon the weeds, gravel, and leaves of plants and trees, broken guns, wrecked wagons, torn horses, and men fearfully mangled. The scene was awfully real—quite real enough. The painters, Messrs. de Neuville and Detaille, are indeed great artists. We could not tell how near we were to the canvass or surface upon which these awful scenes were so vividly portrayed. Going on by the Arc de Triomphe, we arrive at the Trocadéro Palace and Gardens.

Here our party, or those who wished to pay a small fee, were hoisted by a grand hydraulic lift to the top of the great tower, nearly three hundred feet above the Seine, where is had one of the grandest views of the city. The morning is clear. The guide said: "We burn gas and charcoal, and that leaves our atmosphere clear. This circle below us is the largest dome on earth, and the festival hall beneath it contains seven thousand seats in red velvet." Underneath is a great aquarium, and there in front is the immense cascade which falls over eight plateaux. Yonder is the Pantheon, the Notre Dame, the Hotel des Invalides with its beautiful gilded dome rising three hundred and forty feet from the ground. Yes, here on every hand is beautiful Paris; flowers in full bloom, and fountains in full play; and our party, composed of people from distant lands, is jocular and joyous. There, just across the Seine, in a great, open space, where a world's fair was held in 1878, they are now erecting a vast steel tower.

This lofty tower is to surpass all the towers of the earth. It will eclipse the towers of the brick age, the granite age, and the golden age. Yes, this iron and steel age surpasses the age when nations chiseled cathedrals out of rocky mountains and windowed them with rainbows, and bribed Old Ocean, and thunder storms, and birds, and æolian harps to make music among their everlasting pillars. This daring structure is to be a thousand feet high. Think of it! Columns of steel lifting their glittering fingers, nearly a fourth of a mile into the heavens, where lightnings flash and rule; is it not audacious? For years, I have dreamed of a glass palace rearing its bright crown a thousand feet into the sky, but here I am confronted and cast down by a real one of cold steel. But, maybe an army of us "energetic and enterprising Americans," led by a romantic dreamer, will go westward on a crusade, and coming to the awful ledges of the Yosemite, smite with our steel chisels until we cut clear from the mountain a national monument two thousand feet high; and then with the mighty enginery of modern times we will roll it to the centre of Yosemite's vale, where it may forever smile down upon the little needles of Cleopatra.

Tomb of Napoleon: The ashes of Napoleon I. are enshrined in a massive sarcophagus, weighing tons, which is of beautiful, dark-red granite finely polished. It is in a circular crypt, thirty-six feet in diameter, and twenty feet deep, and is seen from the main floor, the circle being surrounded by a marble balustrade. The tomb is directly under the lofty, gilded dome of the Hotel des Invalides, which I have already mentioned. The floors are marble, the columns and walls are marble; fine statues stand around and the rarest paintings glorify the ceilings. Here are the magnificent tombs of his brothers, Joseph and Jerome Bonaparte, and other heroes, all standing amid splendors which are gazed upon by our party in almost breathless wonder and admiration. In fact, my London friend said, "I can hardly breathe in here." Then I laughed, for I perceived that I too had not been breathing for a moment. Yes, there were so many great and beautiful things to see, "all in one breath," that we looked rapidly and forgot for a brief period to breathe. Oh, see that beautiful altar on spiral columns of rare marble, where the light is mellowed into gold before it falls upon it! Now we are below, near the massive coffin. See the twelve heroic and beautiful statues facing the costly urn of glorified human dust! The church is one of much interest and beauty. Here are fine statues of famous heroes and great men, and many old banners forced from fierce warriors on distant and blood-red fields, in the days of triumph, when Glory showered bright crowns upon France and her daring and desperate sons.

## CHAPTER XIX.

### PARIS: CHURCHES, MARKET, CEMETERY.

NOTE-BOOK IN HAND—PALAIS ROYAL—DINE IN THE FAMOUS PLACE—MUSIC—RED WINE—CHURCH ST. EUSTACHE—CROWDED WITH BEAUTY AND GLORY—TWELVE HUNDRED CELLARS UNDER TWENTY-TWO ACRES OF GLASS-ROOFED MARKETS—PERE LA CHAISE—TWENTY-TWO THOUSAND ATTRACTIVE HOMES FOR THE DEAD—MIGHTY MEN SLEEPING IN MARBLE BEDS—ABELARD AND HELOISE, FAMOUS AND UNHAPPY LOVERS, IN MARBLE, SIDE BY SIDE, GAZING INTO THE HEAVENS—MARSHAL NEY'S GRASS-BLADE MONUMENT—A BEAUTIFUL PARK—THE LOUVRE PALACE—ART GALLERY ONE-FOURTH OF A MILE IN LENGTH—GREAT PAINTINGS—BRILLIANT ROOMS.

As the reader may begin to weary of gay, gorgeous Paris, I will cut short my voluminous notes taken in France, and thus get ready to go to mountainous Wales and "Bonny Scotland." When I left Wilkes-Barré, I provided myself with a note-book of sufficient size, I then thought, to contain the notes I would take while on my trip; but, when I returned to America the great, the bright "Queen of the West," enthroned on emerald, silver, jet and gold, between the two oceans, I was writing in note-book number eleven. I wrote at morning, noon and night, on sea and land; in the street, above the street, and under the street; walking, talking, and riding; in steam-cars, tram-cars, and 'buses. Thus the reader will see that I have still material for letters without drawing upon my fancy, imagination, memory or guide-books. One day's drive or walk in Paris gives matter for two or three lengthy letters.

After viewing Napoleon's magnificent tomb, our party drove to the Palais Royal, where we lunched at an expense of from two to three francs. It seemed somewhat strange to dine here, with gay, careless sight-seers, in this grand and famous old palace, or rather cluster of palaces, in form parallelogram, enclosing a most luxurious garden blooming with flowers, flashing with fountains, and musical with vibrations from instruments bound in wood, catgut, silver and brass.

Red Wine sat on the throne, and coffee and water obeyed her nod and beck. Here were finely decked tables, glittering chandeliers, graceful pillars, and walls, and ceilings, finely emblazoned in high art. The lunchers were cheerful, witty, loquacious, and banners of friendship and love seemed waving over them. Well, I rather see palaces crowded with feasters than filled with tyrants, prisoners, soldiers, or lonesome, longing pride.

Arriving at the Church St. Eustache, our guide said: "Ladies and gentlemen, if you wish to enter the church you must alight, for carriages are not admitted." This is one of the great churches of Paris, and is three hundred and forty-eight feet long and one hundred and eight feet high on the inside. The reader may imagine that it takes some splendor, color and art-work to transform so much height, length and breadth into a place of pleasing beauty. As I walked through the building I wrote in my note-book as follows: "One of the richest churches in Paris; stone columns in rows, gilded shrines, tombs, altars, candlesticks; paintings grand, stained glass beautiful."

Now we pass through the Central Market, Halles Centrales. Let the reader imagine a twenty-acre lot under a glass roof upheld by iron pillars, and under this canopy thousands of men, women and children exhibiting, buying and selling all kinds of things eatable and wearable. The garden, the field, the forest, the air, the rivers, and seas, and workshops have all been conscripted to lay their treasures here. Oh, what a wonderful place is a great market of a great city! Through its wider avenues horses and carts come and go with various products. The place is so interesting that I clip the following lines from a guide-book:

"The largest market in Paris, consisting of ten pavilions, intersected with covered streets, covering a space of twenty-two acres and erected at a cost of over ten million dollars. Underneath are twelve hundred cellars for the storage of goods, twelve feet high, and lighted with gas.

"To see the Halles at their best the visitor should go early in the morning, when the retail dealers are making their purchases for the day.

"The Halles stand on the sight of the old Marche des Innocents, to which they afford as strong a contrast as does the Farringdon Market to old Smithfield."

As we drove on by historic glories, that I have before mentioned, toward the famous cemetery of Pere la Chaise, our guide said: "Here is the Prison de la Roquette and there are the stones in the pavement in front of it where, in a few hours or days, the Guillotine will be brought out and set up to cut off the head of the murderer Pranzina, who is confined there. These people are waiting day and night to see the decapitation, for they know it will soon take place." The man was beheaded the next morning at five o'clock. Now, at last, we have reached the gates of Pere la Chaise, the old and populous cemetery of Paris. As we entered the grand and massive granite gateway our guide turned and addressed us in a somewhat subdued manner, as if to at least partially warn us to comport ourselves with the decorum proper for the place, and said: "The gentlemen will please not smoke while here, for the dead can't bear it."

This City of the Dead, on a hill overlooking Paris, seems with its many avenues lined with grand tombs, monuments, vaults and mausoleums, like a silent city of the living, except that the structures are small and nearly all cross-surmounted. Our guide said that soldiers had camped here in days long past when Paris was in peril and some of the monuments had been injured by shot and shell. There are twenty-two thousand tombs here. The place is beautified by fine walks, flowers, shrubs, trees, and fountains for purposes of irrigation.

We were shown the graves, vaults and monuments of many famous persons. This plain, solid tomb is Rothschild's; here is General Foy's tomb, the favorite of Napoleon; here lies the dust of Marshal Ney, the "bravest of the brave," according to his will he has no tombstone, only a little hedge enclosing grass and flowers. Here is the tomb of Visconti, the great architect who remodeled the grand church into a gorgeous tomb for Napoleon. Here is the tomb that all travelers and lovers wish to visit, that of "Abelard and Heloise." Our guide says, "These unfortunate but faithful lovers have been remembered for hundreds of years, and wept over by thousands; if you wish to know more of them you must read it, for I will not tell you." Their beautiful marble effigies lie side by side, looking toward Heaven. I took a few pebbles from the grave and put them into a labeled envelope, also a leaf or two from Marshal Ney's grave, as a memento of the place.

That the reader may see I have not used hyperbolical language, let me quote the words of the traveler and writer, Bartlett, who says, "I visited it, (Pere la Chaise) but once, and then came away displeased with its magnificence. * * It is distinguished for the size, costliness and grandeur of its monuments. * * There are temples, sepulchral chapels, mausoleums, pyramids, altars and urns. * * It is calculated that in forty years not less than one hundred millions of francs have been spent in the erection of monuments in Pere la Chaise."

Buttes Chaumont: This beautiful park is not far from Pere la Chaise. It is one of the most romantic spots I have ever seen. I will give the reader what I wrote hastily on the spot, and leave him to judge of the place. It covers about sixty-two acres; was once a stone quarry; was beautified by Napoleon III; high hills, trees, green lawns, flowers, lakes, cascades, grottoes, water-falls in caves, suspension bridges, ivy-grown rocks towering sixty feet high, white cliffs, high, rocky islands ascended by bridges and terraces; music, beer, wine, singing, dancing. A neat-looking woman with a child in her arms said, "Can you give me something?" I gave her sixty centimes. Our party are entering the carriage, and soon the whip cracks, dogs bark, and little boys run by our side, begging, the first we have seen here.

The Louvre: The Louvre is perhaps the largest and most interesting building in Paris, and all tourists are expected to see it. It is a great palace of art and curiosities. Its name is said to be derived from Louverie, or wolf resort. It is very extensive and surrounds an open court. I walked around it and found it to be two thousand two hundred and seventy-five yards in circumference, or a little over a mile and a quarter. It is of gray stone, substantially built, but not brilliant on the outside. Statues of men, horses, etc., stand in niches, in and along its outer walls. I entered the building, but what shall I say, when it requires large books to contain a list of the curious and beautiful things. A month would not suffice to see it, and I went through it in less than three hours. Oh, the beautiful statues of marble and bronze on rare pedestals of variegated marble! Here are thousands of paintings, many of them large and fine. Here is one gallery a quarter of a mile long, in which I counted nearly ten hundred paintings; a guide-book says there are over one thousand four hundred. Think of it! A room big enough to show so many hundred pictures, and some of them nearly, or quite, 20x40 feet in size! Oh, the power and glory that is in a great painting! What romance! What history! What valor, what love, and what suffering! Here is a grand painting of women and babes staying an awful battle in a street, in olden times. See the strong, fierce men with helmets, swords, shields, spears, and war-horses, in pride and strength, prancing down through gorgeous streets, over dead and dying men! The brave, strong women showing their charms and their courage, and their lovely and innocent offspring! Now see the waves of war stand still, and then sullenly retire! Indeed, what can be more inspiring than the courageous action of lovely women? Men every day, everywhere, dare death for such. Oh, see this great painting of Christ at the wedding in Cana! How grand is the court surrounded and filled by columns, galleries, verandas, towers, domes, fruits, flowers, wines, pigeons, dogs, monkeys, clowns, musicians, colored servants, tables, food, guests, richly-clad men, women, and children, and Christ! Of course, I believe Cana was a plain and poor village, and the wedding quite humble and informal, still I have but partially described the painting. Lack of wine illy accords with a place and with people so grand.

What grand, smooth oak floors! What frescoing! Some of the ceilings are as beautiful as "pictures of silver" full of oranges and apples of gold. Here are rooms finished off with oak, wonderfully carved and full of vases of fine china, and cases of rare stones, pearls and diamonds in delicate and costly caskets. Here is a room brilliant with gold crowns and great N's, "where Napoleon contracted his second marriage;" and here a room where King Henry IV. died after being stabbed in the street. Here are large, grand rooms full of rare and ancient things from distant lands. Time and space wave their silver wands toward me, spelling in mystic characters the word "Halt!"

# CHAPTER XX.

### PARIS: NOTRE DAME, PANTHEON, ST. CLOUD.

BANKS OF THE SEINE—GODS DISTILLING WATER—BRIDGES—HOW I ASKED QUESTIONS—NOTRE DAME—IMPRESSIVE BUILDING—A MARBLE MOUNTAIN WITH PEARLS AND SHELLS FOR WINDOWS—SHRINES—RELICS—A CATHEDRAL'S USE—TOWER SAINT JACQUES—THE PANTHEON—ARTISTS ON SCAFFOLDS FOR YEARS—MONUMENT TO HEROES AND ARTISTS—THE GREAT CROWN—ENROUTE TO ST. CLOUD—PARC MONCEAU—BOIS DE BOULOGNE—GRAND AVENUE—FINE VISTAS—ROTHSCHILD'S HOME—ST. CLOUD, WHERE THE GREAT NAPOLEON WAVED HIS SWORD AND VAST ARMIES SHOUTED AND MARCHED TO MAKE MILLIONS MOURN—ANGELS FLY HEAVENWARD—THE RUINED PALACE—THE ZULU-SLAIN PRINCE, ETC.

When I look over my note-books I find it no easy task to tear myself away from Paris. It is with this as with other great and beautiful stories—one finds himself constantly longing to tell it. Here are so many wide gardens resplendent with flowers; so many parks abounding with enchanting resting places, groves, lakes, swans and statues; so many squares and courts full of trees, columns and fountains—fountains throwing sparkling water up where it must fall in glittering streams down over plateau after plateau until it finds a home in the historic Seine. Here on the banks of the Seine, on a tall column, stands a gilded angel, but perhaps if it were not gilded it would be a brass devil, for it is a unique image with wings, and crowns are in its outstretched hands. A score or more of grotesque monsters at its base pour water from their throats. There are dragons, fish, mermaids, sea-lions, nymphs, sphinxes, frogs, lions, etc. See the glitter of the fountains and hear the rush and dash of the waters! The Genius of the place seems to cry, "Let everything that hath a mouth spout water!" Let us liken it to the laboratory where the gods distill seas of water. Yonder, at the end of a great stone building, a torrent of water rolls out and comes pouring down from basin to basin, from step to step.

The Seine is of a greenish tint, not muddy; I wonder how it is kept so clear. Many handsome bridges span the Seine, which appears to be four or five hundred feet broad. Fine high walls of cut stone line the river on each side, and rows of trees stand on its banks between the walls and the water, and here and there are neat stone steps leading down to the boat landings. The steamers are numerous, narrow, graceful, and glide rapidly, almost without noise. Men and boys are fishing, but I see no fish. Yonder is a long, high island in the river covered with trees, shrubbery and flowers. It is so smooth and uniform I think it must be a work of art.

My experience is, that if one asks a question in English of a Frenchman who can not speak English, he will not answer, but pass on, as much as to say: "I will not give myself away; learn French or hire a guide." I afterward learned to open my guide-book and point to the name of the building or place I wished to find, and then show it to a policeman or other gentleman, and if he could not tell me in English he would point the way and give me a little avalanche of French words. Then I would take my watch and he would point on its face to show how many minutes it would take me to walk to the place. If it were too many minutes, I would take a street car, so much inside, so much outside and so much on top. I was fond of riding on top of the neat cars, where I might see all that we passed. So, you see, I was trying to do Paris under difficulties, all of which induced me to go afterward with a carriage load of cheerful sightseers in charge of Cook & Son's guides.

Here are two good looking ladies, so much, in dress and feature and form, like English people that I addressed them in English, asking the way to the Notre Dame, but they laughed heartily because I had mistaken them for English ladies, still they pointed out the way to the grand and ancient cathedral of Notre Dame. This cathedral dates back to 1163. It has, of course, been greatly altered and improved since then. Now we stand in front of it, and two lofty towers, say two hundred and thirty feet high, stand one at each side, and a very tall and graceful spire rises from the centre and is seen between the towers. Three great arched doorways are in front, where many statues, or images in bold relief, look down upon us.

I counted about three hundred of these figures carved in the stone-work in the front of the edifice. Above the centre doorway is an immense and very beautiful rose window. This is one of the oldest, richest and largest Catholic cathedrals in Europe. It will hold twenty thousand people. These walls have a gray and ancient look, and the tooth of Time is slowly gnawing away the fine carving in the hard stone; but resolutely these solid old walls stand and fight for centuries the attacks of Time and the friction of rolling ages. Things of great beauty, things of vast worth and things of great age are always interesting even to the unlearned; what, then, are they to the heads and hearts crowded and matured with the classic stores of all times? Yes, education is a sword, a pen, an engine of mighty power. A thing of true beauty, it finds beauty and worth everywhere and is a joy forever. This is one of the most impressive buildings I have seen; I mean chiefly in its interior appearance and influences. It reminds me much of the gray solemnity of York Minster and its sacred dust and relics called up the memories of Westminster Abbey. I bought a few simple souvenirs from a girl at the door and gave a small sum to a poor man who stood in a begging posture, just inside, and passed in among the fine and lofty columns that stand in long rows.

Now look up one hundred and ten feet, where the nave arches are above us! See the many fine colored windows on all sides and above! The glass, fine and ancient, does not let in much light, and the place has a solemn and impressive aspect. I counted nearly, or quite, eighty majestic columns of white stone, and I thought it all looked as if it had been cut out of a great mountain of marble and made translucent in places by inserting pearls, stones and shells of bright color and pleasing contour; or a garden of stately trees, which, while in bloom, had been roofed over and then changed into marble. The organ is a great and powerful one. The carved woodwork in and around the choir is intricate and costly. The shrines are many and magnificent, where candles, crosses, crowns, crucifixes, fonts, paintings and relics abound. Many canonized saints are remembered in the construction of these sacred shrines, where many worshipers come for confession. Here are many costly and elaborate monuments to the memory of archbishops and divines of high degree. I went with a party of French people, led by a verger, or priest, into the treasury where many old doors, drawers, and fine cases were unlocked and their contents shown, consisting of ancient vestments, and crowns, and crosses, and chalices, and caskets, all representing the paraphernalia of church and state for many ages. Robes, and crowns, and swords, worn by those great in war and those high in ecclesiastical walks. I could not understand the guide, but I learned that the things were considered very valuable, very ancient, and very sacred. It is claimed by some that you can here see pieces of Christ's cross, and crown of thorns, and a nail from the cross. I cannot ask the reader to believe all these to be genuine.

The music was almost heavenly. Notre Dame

displays much wealth, magnificence and antiquity, and is, indeed, an interesting place. I never knew what a cathedral filled with a forest of lofty and massive stone columns was best fitted for until I heard the music, vocal and instrumental, rolling through hewn rocks in York Minster. When the uniformed choir chanted the Great Prayer, and choice selections of Holy Writ were sung, and the mezzo-soprano tones of the sweet singer rolled out and above the great volume of music, tears fell in the solemn old cathedral, while some who came to idly gaze bent low their heads to wonder and pray. Yes, that voice was almost superearthly, and appeared like the sweep of an angel's wing among fair clouds of the evening.

Here is the tower St. Jacques, a tower of singular appearance, tall, angular and very unique, standing in a garden among trees, flowers and fountains, where men, women and children, by the hundred, come to rest, read, talk, work, nurse and play. To me it seemed like a parlor and nursery out of doors, where mothers and maids knit, and sewed, and stitched, while dimpled infants laughed, and played, and slept on all sides. This was one of the most quiet, orderly and homelike places I saw in France. Gaudy pride, military show and barbaric splendor held themselves aloof from this quaint locality. Being in a central place, its observatory gives a good view of the city.

Here is the Pantheon, one of the grandest structures in Paris. It stands on high ground at the head of a broad street, and with its mighty columns below, and its lordly columns above, bearing up a dome of great extent and rare symmetry, it forms a striking picture. You enter, and its lofty ceiling flames with painted glory one hundred and eighty feet above you, where the white fingers and pale temples of true-born artists clung for years to immortalize themselves and make pictures of such beauty as to strike pity, and peace, and gentleness into the rude breasts of vandals. Look on its walls and see paintings worth kingdoms, illustrating the great eras of nations, and perpetuating the daring deeds of eagle-eyed and lion-hearted men. A mighty monument of art, it stands as a mausoleum for some of France's great sons, long dead. Now I am in the great boulevard leading to the Grand Opera House, that chiseled, gilded and velvet-lined glory, which bears aloft on its roof the largest crown ever constructed. I clip the following lines relating to the Grand Opera House, from a guide-book:

"Grand Opera, the largest theatre in the world, which covers an area of nearly three acres, although it contains less seats than the theatres of La Scala, Milan, and San Carlo, Naples.

"Between four and five hundred houses were demolished to provide the site, which cost £420,000.

"The building was commenced in 1861, from the designs of Garnier, and finished in 1874 at a cost of nearly a million and a half pounds sterling. Nearly every country in Europe has contributed materials for this magnificent construction, which may be studied to advantage externally by the electric light."

It is 9:30 a. m., Tuesday, August 30th. In front of Cooks' office, 9 Rue Scribe, Paris, the carriages are standing, while travelers from America, England, Australia and other parts of our little earth are climbing into them, each one having purchased a ticket for the day or for three days.  The guides (one guide for two carriages) take their places and soon we are rolling over fine, smooth streets among bright palaces, calling at this hotel and that boarding place for others, to make our load complete.  Here is Mr. Walmsley, a head clerk from London; there is Mr. Seymour and daughter, from New York; there is James H. Hamilton, from Cincinnati; there a pleasant lady from New Jersey, and here is Mrs. Benn, from Philadelphia, and there a lady and gentleman from Bristol, England, and here is Miss Mollie J. Barton, from Baltimore.  We drove through the beautiful Parc Monceau, a pleasant park in the heart of Paris.  We drove rapidly through the park, but we saw some of its beauties, which consist of green slopes by bright serpentine waters, graceful columns by a cool pool; hearts, crowns, crosses, anchors, diamonds and pyramids of flowers; fine old trees forming vistas, through which are seen shrubbery, fountains, pavilions and statues.  These grounds were laid out in the last century by Philip of Orleans, and they have witnessed some gorgeous pegeants.

Bois de Boulogne:  This fine avenue leads from the Arc de Triomphe, into and through the "Bois," a beautiful green forest covering two thousand, two hundred and fifty acres.  The avenue above named I counted to be about four hundred feet broad, with rows of beautiful trees on each side, and wide sidewalks. This grand forest park is diversified by lakes, meadows, avenues, cascades, fountains, mounds and arches. Now we roll under a stone viaduct, gray with age, and upon it is growing a large tree. The guide said: "These trees do not equal your great trees in America, but if your forests had been destroyed as often by war as this one, you could not boast as you now may.

"Here is the Grand Cascade, forty-five feet high. These falls beat Niagara, for we can stop these but you can not stop Niagara, and they are not as noisy, and we could have them come down somewhere else." Now we pass the race-course of Longchamps, where there is a track one and a half miles long, where each June races are held and thousands of dollars, of course, are at stake. I was told that there were races here nearly every Sunday.

Yonder on a hill is the Citadel of Mont Valerian, the largest and strongest fort defending Paris. Here, in a seventy-acre forest, is the residence of Baron Rothschild, surrounded by lakes, lodges, fountains, fine trees, lawns, etc. It looks like a great painting of green and silver. Here, near the banks of the Seine, is the historic town of St. Cloud.

This was a favorite place of Napoleon I., and from this point he marched out with his mighty army to cover himself and France with glory. I sometimes imagine I can see this iron-browed, compactly-built man, with dark eyes that glitter like those of a basilisk, his form erect and steady, as he sits upon a proud iron-gray war-horse, his brain flashing with more than lightning rapidity, his breast throbs and swells with resolution, revenge and Lucifer-like ambition—ambition incarnate. When he waved his sword great marshals spurred their steeds, loud trumpets pealed, fair banners waved, long lines of bright bayonets began to move with a steady undulation; long columns of brave men advanced upon prancing horses, while hundreds of iron and brass cannon—deadly engines of war—rolled forward, their wide, black mouths threatening destruction to millions. As he marched into distant lands, kings bent their ears to the earth to hear his awful footfalls, and, rising, exclaimed: "To arms! to arms! He comes! he comes!" Then the plowman leaves his field; the mechanic his work-shop; the shepherd his little flock on the mountain side; the son embraces his mother, the father caresses his children, and pale lovers, with trembling hearts and kisses, promise to be true; and, while gazing at each other through tears, the lines of battle form near the fair city, where the stern gods of war contend with loud roar and clamor until the dew of evening falls upon three-score thousand cold, white, bloodless brows, and sorrow sits on a hundred thousand hearthstones and sad angels slowly and silently fly heavenward.

This was also a summer resort for Napoleon III. In 1870 the grand palace was destroyed by war and it still lies in ruins, speaking apparently of the evils of war and the vanity of earthly ambition. A small piece of this once proud palace found its way into my trunk. The guide said: "Here is where Napoleon became emperor, and here is where he lived with Josephine; it was her favorite home. Here the prince

(15)

was born, Eugenia's son, who was killed by Zulus in far-off Africa. See where shot and shell have scarred steps, columns and walls." Fountains, statues, forests and green lawns abound.

# CHAPTER XXI.

VERSAILLES: FROM PARIS TO LONDON.

FOREST VILLE D' AVRAY—BOULEVARD DE LA REINE—VERSAILLES—A PALACE A FOURTH OF A MILE LONG—MAGNIFICENCE BRILLIANT WITH GLORIES—COST ONE HUNDRED AND TWENTY-SEVEN MILLION FRANCS—KINGS AND QUEENS—PILLARS OF SILVER AMID RAINBOWS, BEARING UP CANOPIES OF GOLD—SEVRES' CHINA PALACE—SHAKE HANDS—ANGELIC GUIDES—THE WONDERFUL ROAD, THIRTY-FIVE HUNDRED MILES LONG, RUNNING THROUGH EMPIRES OF WEALTH, LANDS OF MILK AND HONEY, AND KINGDOMS OF BEAUTY AND WONDER—THE UNITED STATES GREAT IN CITIES AND RAILWAYS—NO TATTERED BEGGARS—RUSHING THROUGH FRANCE BY MOONLIGHT—ROUEN SLEEPING—DIEPPE BY THE SEA—THE SEA DANCES IN GREEN AND WHITE—SEA SICKNESS—WHITE CLIFFS OF ENGLAND SEEN THROUGH MIST—RUSHING THROUGH WOODS, ROCKS, MEADOWS AND TOWNS TO LONDON.

The Forest of Ville d' Avray is a beautiful and extensive forest. The guide said: "Here is where Gambetta died. Here a battle was fought and five thousand men were killed. Here passes the great military road, eight hundred miles long, running from

Normandy to Italy, kept in good order all the way. Yonder is the Prussian cemetery, and there is the monument erected to the Prussian officers killed in the late war."

Now we drive on along shady avenues; the scene is changing every moment, lakes, grottoes, arches, avenues, green fields; now we see through long avenues into sunny open places in the form of squares, circles, crosses, stars, parallelograms, etc. Now, for a mile or two, we pass along the Boulevard de la Reine. On each side the trees are trimmed in the form of a smooth, true arch all the way, and on top they are cut off level, and it appears like green masonry on graceful gray pillars, and when you cross other streets they show the same beautiful arches stretching away on both sides. Some places the trees are trimmed like graceful mounds, and again, with pillars and arches below and spires above. Here is a large market under the thick foilage of well-trimmed trees. Thus, amid much wonder and pleasure, and many exclamations of admiration and delight, we arrive at beautiful Versailles.

Our guide said: "This is a city of forty-five thousand inhabitants, in a forest of twenty-five thousand acres in extent, with one thousand, six hundred and thirty fountains, which cost twenty thousand dollars to make them play for four hours." We did not see them playing, for they only play the first and third Sundays of each month, from 3 to 5 o'clock p. m. Here is the great and beautiful palace of Versailles, showing a front one-fourth of a mile long. It was twenty years in building, and cost four million francs to restore it. Our guide said: "This is the largest palace in the world, except St. Peter's in Rome. There have been expended here one hundred and twenty-seven million francs."

If I had a half-day's time, and say four columns more space, I might try to escort the reader up the broad, white stone steps, in through great columned and arched doorways, from hall to hall, from grand room to grand room, from magnificent gallery to glittering parlor, and from marble stairs to brilliant bedrooms. See the bright oak floors, waxed like glass! See the walls resplendent with paintings of French kings, queens, lords, marshals, painters, poets, architects and great battles! Now we pass through a hall, for hundreds of feet, full of fine statues. Here are thirty-two great war paintings, 15x30 feet, in a hall five hundred feet long. Here a great painting of Louis Philip, 20x40 feet, on horseback, surrounded by hundreds of his friends; a gay scene! We are shown rooms where kings and queens were crowned and married, and where princes were born, and where queens slept. Here is a grand painting of Washington and Lafayette at Yorktown.

Here is the crowning scene of Napoleon and Josephine. Here is a gorgeous room all resplendent with marble arches, pillars and statues; ceilings of green and silver, and crimson, purple and lavender, shining in gold; but I must not attempt to picture this solid, shining and painted magnificence, for it is like pillars of silver upholding clouds of gold amid rainbows that span bright lakes and blooming gardens. In the court stands a massive and grand equestrian statue of Louis XIV., termed Louis the Great. Now we pass through the garden and see fountains, flowers, lakes, statues, terraces and avenues of beauty, and walled gardens, as if in basements.

On our return to the city we stopped at Sevres, an old town in the neighborhood of the city, where fine porcelain wares have been manufactured for ages. We entered the exhibition rooms and saw many fine and beautiful specimens of their handiwork. We came on by the walls of Paris, which are thirty-three feet high and circled by a deep moat. They extend around the older part of the city and cost $25,000,000. Then, on by the "Viaduct of Anteuil," a very graceful railway bridge one and a fourth of a mile in length.

Now our carriage halts near the Grand Hotel, and as we shake hands we ask each other if we shall meet in a land of everlasting sunshine, amid splendors and glories eternal and indescribable, and be escorted for ages by guides angelic—winged guides of wonderful intelligence and unspeakable loveliness, whose feet are miracles of sculpture, whose hands are blessings from which emanate perennial health, whose breath is the rarest perfume, whose hair circles in crowns or falls in festoons of silver, whose eyes are like liquid diamonds, whose cheeks lend beauty to spring mornings, and whose heart is a thing of triumphant joy and undying beauty.

I have mentioned that we dined at half-past six each day. We were at the Hotel St. Petersbourg, in a spacious and elegant dining hall surrounded by flowers. There were, perhaps, two hundred English-speaking people seated at the tables: young men and elderly men, young ladies and their parents, husbands and wives, etc.; some water drinkers and many wine drinkers. A young man from London, just across the table, said to me, "Mr. L., what did you think of the great highway, eight hundred miles long, which we were on to-day, and which is kept in such good order all the way? You have nothing like that in America, have you?" My attention, my imagination, and my national pride were appealed to and aroused, and I replied, "Oh, yes, we have a road more than thirty-five hundred miles long, which passes through a city of a million and a half inhabitants; the Atlantic throws shells upon it in the east, and the Pacific bathes its bright pebbles on the west; it passes by factories where labor of hand and machinery thunder together in rolling out buttons and locomotives, pins and bayonets, pop-guns and great cannon; on by private residences worth more than a million dollars each; on through dark and wide forests of pine, oak and walnut; on through vast groves of apples, peaches, grapes, oranges and lemons, across fields white with snow, and others white with cotton; on by the mighty cataract where a hundred Seines fall straight down with an awful roar one hundred and sixty feet; on by great tideless seas of fresh water, where float the world's largest grain boats; on across a valley twelve hundred miles wide, where, in fields miles long, wave millions of acres of golden wheat, and corn with tassels of silver and emerald banners and streamers; over the largest rivers on earth, on through prairies where Indians yell and buffaloes bellow, and where glorious Indian summer manufactures her veil of blue; on over mountains that cool their white brows more than three perpendicular miles above the bright sands of the sounding sea; on under ledges of rock which wave pine-tree-plumes three thousand feet overhead; on where fiery-hearted monsters throw from the depths of earth lofty columns of boiling water; on where great, solemn and awful trees rear their lordly heads four hundred feet into the sky; on through sunny valleys where the river floors sparkle with silver and glitter with gold, and coming to the 'Golden Gate,' where Columbia bids 'good evening' to the sun, it is lulled to slumber by the everlasting murmur of the vast, motherly Pacific."

My friend gazed at me and forgot to eat, and when I finished he exclaimed: "Is it possible! Is that so?" I replied, "Yes, sir; and more, too." After dinner a pleasant elderly gentleman said to me: "From your remarks, you seem to be an American." "Yes, sir; I am from Wilkes-Barré, Pennsylvania." His name was John L. Lawson, of Philadelphia, and he knew a number of prominent people in various portions of the state. He saw that I was a lover of America, her cities, railroads, etc., and he told me some things which I will briefly mention in his own words: "There are 120,000 miles of railroads in the United States. The Pennsylvania Railroad Company control 12,000 miles of railroads. The Reading Railroad Company has 900 miles of railroads underground. Philadelphia has two times as many houses as Paris, and as many houses as New York, Brooklyn and Boston, she having two hundred and ten thousand houses. Fifth avenue, New York, is a street of palaces, and there for miles scarcely a house rents for less than $4,000 per year. Philadelphia has a street built up all the way for seven miles, and New York has a street nine miles long."

I, as well as many others, noticed the almost entire absence of beggars, tatter-de-malions, old hags and wrinkled sinners in the streets of Paris, and I still am at loss to account for it, as I was not there long enough to find out where they stay or are kept, for they must have many old and poor people in so large a city. My experience is that the French people will not sell cheaply nor work cheaply. Their ideas are grand, and it requires much money to float pride upon grandeur.

At 11 p. m. I entered a great stone railway station near the centre of the city. Here are guards and policemen, and soldiers with guns; iron gates and granite doorways, all looking like stern business. A long train backs in, I enter a compartment, but when I read on the door "Femmes," I see it is for ladies only, so I find another place. A great crowd of people are entering the cars with boxes, bags, shawls, rugs, coats, canes, umbrellas, etc., and I notice that some of them are bound for England and America after "doing the continent." A gentleman said to me, "Are you going direct to London?" "Yes, sir." "Will you please look after my son?" "Yes, sir." Then a bright, active boy of sixteen came into the compartment, and then two ladies with bandboxes and handbags entered, and soon we began to roll out of the great city.

It was moonlight, and I shall not soon forget the pleasant ride through France, along the Seine, to the sea at Dieppe. There runs the silvery Seine for miles between rows of graceful poplars. Here are quiet, green meadows where cattle lie at rest, here are quiet farm-houses, and smoke ascends from a chimney here and there. Now we rush through quietly sleeping hamlets and towns which are still and lonely—nature, animate and inanimate, is recuperating. Now we see long streets all lit up and guarded for miles by street lamps, but we see no one stirring. This is Rouen, at three o'clock in the morning, a great city of France, sleeping. A gentleman said, "Women are not allowed on the streets of Rouen after 8 o'clock in the evening." What a contrast this is to Paris!

Now, in the gray morning, we approach Dieppe, by the sea, where sixty-four miles of wild billows clap their hands, and shake their white heads, and shout, ha! ha! before we can reach the quiet town of New Haven, in the south of queenly old England. A young woman comes upon the boat and sells us fine, mellow pears, which proved to be just what some of us seemed to wish. At 7:20 a. m. we sail down the river, passing a high cross standing on the wharf, where, time out of mind, the wives and daughters of sailors and fishermen have come to kneel and pray for the safety and success of dear ones. Now fearful eyes look out to sea and see Old Ocean dancing in green and white. We had been out upon the short, broken billows but a few minutes before my young friend and the two ladies were taken very ill with seasickness, as well as many others, and it was difficult to keep from laughing at the ludicrous figures and faces made, but later when the faces of friends had assumed the color of death, and they lay stretched out on all sides, scarcely able to breathe, then we began to pity, and every half hour I went around to see if they were still breathing, and learn if there was anything I could do for them. But at last the smooth, white cliffs of England were seen through the mist and salt spray which almost constantly dashed over our sidewheel steamer.

Now we enter the harbor of New Haven and I look to see if the sick ones have strength to walk ashore. Yes, they all, with but little help, gain terra firma and begin to be grateful. My young friend said: "I am always deathly ill when I cross the channel. I was certain I would be sick." Now I wish to see Wales, and they say you must go by the way of London. We enter a train and soon the horse with steel sinews and a red-hot heart snorts steam from his nostrils and rushes with us through towns and meadows, over rivers and highways, through rocks and trees, through hills and dales till we again see Crystal Palace, near great and smoky London.

# CHAPTER XXII.

### FROM LONDON TO CARDIFF, WALES.

PROUD ENGLAND BY MOONLIGHT—SHREWSBURY STATION—COFFEE, DOGS AND BABIES AT MIDNIGHT—WELSH NAMES—HILLS AND VALES—WATER LEAPING INTO GREEN VALLEYS—OLD MINES—CARDIFF—A LETTER FINDS A FRIEND AMONG HEAPS OF GOLD—CARDIFF CASTLE—BUTE DOCKS—THE ARCADE—NAMES FROM ALL EUROPE—GRAPES UNDER GLASS—A KIND FAMILY—PENARTH AND HOSPITALITY—A POPULAR MAN—THE ESPLANADE—QUEENLY CITIES LULLED TO SLEEP—CARRIAGES ROLL AND SHIPS ROCK—GUARDIAN SPIRITS ARE ANXIOUS WHERE MEN AND WOMEN MEET DESTINY—GREAT PRINTING PRESS—A BUSY CITY—FAREWELL.

At 4:15, on a rainy and gloomy afternoon, we arrived at London Bridge Station, where I was informed that if I wished to go on at once to Cardiff, Wales, I must go to Euston Station, so I raised a finger and soon a cabman rushed up, and in a moment I, with my baggage, was rapidly rolling through the busy streets of London, and, after a few miles' ride along streets crowded with lofty buildings, we came where great columns and arches told us we had reached the entrance of the massive and extensive Euston Station, where I was told a train would start for Cardiff about 10 o'clock p. m. Soon after 10 o'clock I find myself on a train rushing out through the cool, green country, and, the moon coming out, revealed many pleasing landscapes and quiet hamlets and towns. After a run of about three hours we ran into Shrewsbury, where many stately houses stood among fine trees. A net-work of railroads covered the ground, while the air above was woven full of wires, and signal-boards rose and fell as the rods and levers clicked under the skillful touch of the watchful signal-worker, and the steel rails locked and unlocked at either end of the great station, which was about two hundred yards long and through which ran say ten railway tracks. Here we leave the train and enter a refreshment room, where young women are setting out coffee, tea, beer, sandwiches, scones, meat-pies, biscuits, etc., to a great crowd of people. Then we go into a general waiting-room, where men were nursing dogs, and women were nursing babies, and one poor man, stretched out on a seat with his head on his bag, was nursing a terrible cough.

We passed through Shrewsbury and Hereford, and changed cars and stopped so often before we reached Wales that I began to wonder what awful thing I had done, that I should be so harassed here and there for eleven hours going to Wales' metropolis. I probably traveled a hundred miles farther than was really necessary that night, all of which proves that it pays to get started right.

When morning came we gazed out upon Abergavenny Junction, and go on to Brynmar Junction and Nantwich, on through Rhymney, Pontlollyn, Tirphil, George Inn, Bargoed, Pengam, Hengoed, Ystrad, Pwllyphant, Caerphilly, Llanishan, and arrive at Cardiff.

On the way I saw some of the most picturesque landscapes that I ever saw, small green valleys into which rushed many streams of water from high hills, some of which were smooth, some rocky, some wooded, and some that were covered with the debris of mines that had been worked generations ago. Cattle and sheep grazed in many green vales. Now we pass through old mining villages on mountains, where stone houses stand in long rows, and where coal and iron are shipped to distant markets. The varied forms and colors of the mountains make a pleasing picture, for some are green, some brown, and others yellow or black; some smooth, some jagged, some pyramidical, some oval, some conic, some serrated, and others with straight brows.

Cardiff: Soon after reaching Cardiff, the chief seaport and largest city of Wales, I found my way to the office of the Taff Vale Railway, where I met Mr. Edward Edwards, brother of Mr. George A. Edwards, of Wilkes-Barré. Mr. Edwards was preparing to pay the employees of the railways, but the letter which I bore from his brother in far-away Wilkes-Barré took me in where thousands of gold sovereigns were being counted and parcelled out. The written word of a distant, but respected brother, caused me to be received with respect, friendship and confidence. Mr.

Edwards went with me through the old city and pointed out places of interest.

There is Cardiff Castle, the residence of the wealthy and powerful Marquis of Bute. Here are the tramways running to different parts of the city. Here is the Arcade, where nearly all kinds of goods are sold. Here is the old, commercial part of the city, where names from the north of Europe and the west of Europe—names from the snow-banks of Norway, the lemon groves of Italy and the vineyards of Spain, are painted over the doorways. Here in the great docks may be seen the sailing and steam craft of the world, loading and unloading, while sailors with unknown tongues and singular costumes pass here and there, or assemble in small companies.

About noon I went with Mr. Edwards to his very pleasant residence at 37, The Walk, in a quiet beautiful street. Mr. Edwards has a kind and interesting family, of wife, sons and daughters. He took me into his greenhouse, where fine grapes of different species hung ripe, in large, luscious clusters, some of which bowed low to honor our presence.

If England and Wales wish good grapes, they must ripen them under glass, or import them from climes more sunny.

In the evening we went across the bay to Penarth, where Mr. James Edwards and his family live.

Penarth is a handsome and enterprising town on a promontory just across the Cardiff bay. Here many pleasant residences crown the heights and command good views of land and sea, city and ships. Mr.

James Edwards, brother of the Edwards mentioned above, is Collector of Harbor Dues, and is a man having authority. He is a handsome, portly, good-natured man, having a pleasant family and many friends. His "admiring friends" had recently presented him with a magnificent silver waiter and set, valued at five hundred dollars. Lodges and other institutions were named after him, all of which show that he is much respected. He was building for his own use a spacious and commodious house in a desirable part of the town.

We took a walk down through romantic gateways, bowers, terraces and ravines, until we came to the "Esplanade," where the sounding sea sent salt spray to the feet of thousands of people who promenade there in search of health, peace, love, fame, knowledge, wealth and pleasure. Oh, ye esplanades, ye sands and strands of earth, where queenly cities sit by the heaving sea, where mighty waves dash against proud lands, where lights flash over dark waters, where carriages roll on one side and ships toss on the other side, where men and women smile and frown, and where souls meet destiny! Ye are places of much interest for guardian spirits! Ye are drawn in bright colors on Eternity's atlas!

I went with Mr. E. Edwards through the Cardiff *Times* printing office, belonging to the Duncans, where they kindly showed us through the establishment. We were shown a printing machine of great capacity, said to print and fold twenty-four thousand large papers in an hour. Young Mr. Duncan was just about ready to sail for the United States, to take a hasty view of some of the wonders of the New World.

The following morning William Edwards, son of Edward, went with me down along the docks, where great and small ships were discharging the world's various commodities. Here we saw the great granite-bound dock of the Marquis of Bute, which had lately been opened with much pomp. This dock covers thirty-seven acres. The docks of Cardiff cover one hundred and thirty-four acres.

Cardiff, after Liverpool, London and Glasgow, is perhaps the chief seaport of the British Isles. The population of the city is estimated as high as one hundred and twenty thousand. I noticed many pleasant residences and fine stores in the place; also a goodly number of churches and institutions of learning and of benevolence. I was surprised to hear nearly every one speaking English, and I am sure I have heard more Welsh spoken in Plymouth, Pa., in a given time than I heard in Cardiff. As we passed along Mr. Edwards said: "Here is the spot where a few days ago Lady Walker, sister of Lord Tredegar, was so injured in a runaway that she died yesterday."

There is thirty-two feet difference between high tide and low tide here. The Taff Vale Railroad is ninety-four miles in extent and is chiefly for transporting coal, of which about nine million tons are carried every year, and it pays a large dividend. I was pleased with the kindly greetings and the business habits of Cardiff, and though cordially urged by the Edwardses to remain over Sunday there, lack of time impelled me to leave them about Saturday noon, bound for fair Leamington, in one of the midland counties of England. I shall probably never forget the kind and friendly hospitality extended to me by the Edwardses in Cardiff and Penarth.

# CHAPTER XXIII.

## FROM WALES TO SCOTLAND, VIA ENGLAND.

TRAVELING IN LONDON — RAILWAYS FLOODED — GOLDEN APPLES — LEAVING WALES — OLD CASTLE BLOOD-CEMENTED — "CAN WE SMOKE?" — WRITING ON WHEELS RAPIDLY ROLLING — TOWNS, CASTLES, FARMS, RIVERS, MOUNTAINS — BIRMINGHAM — LEAMINGTON, WARWICKSHIRE — GOING TO MIDDLESBOROUGH — HILLS AND DALES — PURPLE SNOW — KIND COUSINS IN AN IRON CITY VISITED BY SHIPS — PARKS, ETC. — STATUES FOR BRAINS AND ENTERPRISING WEALTH — ENROUTE TO EDINBURGH — DURHAM — THE CATHEDRAL — POWERFUL NEWCASTLE — TWENTY-FIVE THOUSAND MEN MAKING GREAT GUNS, SHIPS, CHAINS, ENGINES AND CARS — JUBILEE EXHIBITION — A BIG GUN — THOUSANDS OF MODEST GIRLS SERVING — OFF FOR EDINBURGH.

A respected and aged man, of Kingston, Pa., told me recently that he had followed me on his atlas through all the countries and cities I had mentioned. And as further evidence that he had been interested in these letters, he said, "I noticed that you called a cabman to drive you from London Bridge station to Euston station; how far was it, and how much did you pay?" I could not tell him then, so I will mention it here. The distance is about two and a half miles, and

I paid one shilling and six-pence, or thirty-six cents. In the central portion of London you pay a cabman for yourself and baggage that goes inside the cab, six-pence a mile, (twelve cents) baggage that goes outside in care of the driver costs extra. You cannot, however, hire a cab for less than a shilling, (twenty-four cents,) thus a half a mile will cost you as much as two miles. Outside of the four-mile circle from Charing Cross, the cabmen charge you one shilling a mile. In old London proper, tram-cars (street-cars) are not allowed, but omnibuses and cabs are there in great numbers.

London is a cluster of old and large towns. The tramways and railways are very numerous, and the Metropolitan railway runs underground and in a circle about eleven miles, and carries millions of people at a very low fare; two-pence pays for a number of miles. The Underground, or Metropolitan railway, mentioned above, runs in an oval circle under the city, and thus carries one to the near vicinity of many places in the great city, and you thus travel rapidly and quietly through the darkness under many miles of streets that are clashing and roaring with business and travel.

Did I tell you that on the night of the terrible thunder storm, when we saw Buffalo Bill with his braves and wilds performing in a powerful rain, while electricity flashed from engines on earth and from black clouds in the heavens, these underground railways were flooded with the great rush of water that was suddenly finding its way from the lakes in the clouds to an earthly home in the muddy Thames, and travel underground was impeded for hours?

Oh, how much of life can be seen while traveling in railways in London! Lawyers, merchants, mechanics, teachers, sewing-girls, beggars and tourists; some going to work, some to dinner, some going shopping, some returning; some with game, some with fruit, some with bread, some with clothing. There is a woman with a small basket of poor, green apples, for which she paid four cents a pound, and here one with a pound of tomatoes, not large, for which she paid eighteen cents. All the apple orchards I saw in England would not equal a good New York state orchard. When you see large, red and golden apples in England you may know they crossed Atlantic's billows from warm, generous America, the most queenly daughter of Mother Earth. However, plums, gages, pears, currants, etc., do well in England.

Before leaving Wales, perhaps I should mention the old castle at Caerphilly. This old, extensive and picturesque castle, which is in ruins, stands a few miles from Cardiff. The old round tower, which leans so much, still stands as it has stood for generations. This leaning was caused, I was told, by an explosion, but, as the cement which holds the stones together "was mixed in blood," it will not fall. I presume rather the cement was mixed by blood—good blood in strong arms and brave breasts. When I visit Wales again I shall probably remain there more than twenty-eight hours.

I left Cardiff, South Wales, about half-past twelve; five men in the compartment with me. They seemed rather "jolly" Englishmen of the middle or farming class. They asked me if they might smoke. I said: "Yes; I am from America; I like liberty." One said: "Do not take any bad notes back about England or this party." If the word "Smoking" had been painted on the car door they need not have asked me if they could smoke.

Here are some words as I wrote them in my notebook as we rushed say forty miles an hour: "On Great Western Railway; level, green country; most too swampy; romantic country road, winding through groves, thickets and hedges. Newport—pleasant seaport; mountains a few miles to the north, and sea on the south; pleasant green city; woods, hill, mountains in distance; hedge on top of cut each side of railroad; green, cultivated mountain side to the northwest; turnip and potato fields; rock-cut on a curve, fifty feet deep and a thousand feet long, ivy-grown; now fifty feet of a fill across a green vale. Chepstow—beautiful place; tide comes up along high, rugged cliff, in small bay; great ivy-grown castle among trees and hills; can not see whether it is in ruins or not; green fields, sloping hills; the Severn or Cardigan bay on the other side; looks like a forest beyond the Severn; dash by stations so fast can not read the names. Lydney—small, pleasant place; fine bridge over the Severn, iron pillars and spans. Newnham—village; apple orchards; fruit small and not much of it. Grange Court—pleasant farm region; run through cuts, red, green, white, yellow and black; men plowing with four horses tandem. Gloucester—fine old city; saw the fine; large cathedral.

"Change here to Midland Railway for Birmingham; pleasant gardens, mulberry trees, brick walls; fine farm country. Cheltenham—fine farm country; mountains in distance, quite fine, high, green. Worcester—'Union Hotel,' read the sign, 'patronized by H. R. H. the Duke of Cambridge, etc., quiet, comfortable and moderate; Mrs. Mirgfield, Proprietress;' fine, green country, full of shade trees. Droitwich—farm country. Bromsgrove—Barnet—green country, rainbow; oats and beans in shock. King's Norton—fine country, stone spire above stone tower. Gardens near Birmingham, fine, small, all hedged, green, full of vegetables, and fill the small vale. Five Views—now we enter Birmingham."

As we run in by brick yards, coal yards, gas works, and through acres of cars and locomotives, the passengers begin to gather up their canes, umbrellas, baskets, coats and traveling bags, and I close my notebook and begin to get ready to contend with great, busy Birmingham. Here is a monster station, where the great arching roof spans the many trains rushing in and out to all parts of England. Hundreds of people are walking the high bridges above locomotives and cars trying to find the right platform and the right train, but many uniformed employees are hurrying here and there, and are ready to answer questions relating to time, trains, places, etc.

I arrived at Leamington, in Warwickshire, about 6 o'clock in the evening, where I remained over Sunday with cousins. The reader will remember the notes given above were taken as the train rushed forty or more miles an hour, and I might go on thus transcribing from my note-book until we come to Edinburgh, "Bonny Scotland," but time does not admit of this now, neither can I write, at present, of the interesting visits made to Leamington, Warwick, Coventry and Stratford-on-Avon. Having returned to quaint, old Whitby, and visited friends there and at North Burton, Scarborough, Sleights and Sandsend, I bid good-bye to relatives and kind friends at Whitby and start for Liverpool, going away around through Scotland and Ireland.

On my way to Middlesborough, going north, I might ride along on the cliffs and gaze on the sea, but I decided to go up the dales and wind along creeks among the moorland hills. The day was rainy, and yet the trip was an enjoyable one. As I passed the stations I wrote their names in my note-book, and a few words hastily. "Sleights—Egeton—Glaisedale—a beautiful little valley up a branch of the Esk; green, uneven hills on each side, which undulate away to the 'dry, dark wolds,' or moors. Lealholm—small hamlet; stacks, moors in distance. I like the scene much; high, dark hills beyond, through hill-gaps, fine. Grain still out, (Sept. 13th.) Danby—stone village, roofs of red tiles and slate; more moors; village on green hill near the moor. Castleton—high, dark mountain in distance, one nearly covered with heather and breckon;

moorland comes nearly down to the railroad. Commondale—small hamlet; now the purple heather comes down to the railroad. Oh, the purple-clad hills! smooth, barren, dark; as if covered with purple snow. Kildale—hamlet; bold, dark promontory stands out against the rainy sky, now wider valley. Battersby Junction—green plain; change here for Middlesborough; yonder, on a high hill, stands Captain Cook's (the circumnavigator's) monument, granite, about fifty feet high. Great Ayton—'Roseberry toppin;' this is a high, conical mountain, running into the valley, very bold, 'wonderful view from its top.' Munthorpe—farm country. Ormsby—small place. Martin—fine town, graceful spires and a dome, and stately, clean roofs above fine trees. Here is Middlesborough."

On Tuesday afternoon, Sept. 13, I arrived by train at Middlesborough, in the north of England, and soon found Mr. Richard Stainthrope, who was at the station awaiting my arrival. This kind friend was my cousin Anna's husband. He is a ship carpenter and has sailed wintry seas, where icy mountains float slowly through billows of cold, salt water, and again through sunny seas, where spicy islands breathed fragrant blessings on all around, and where cool waves foamed on the burning sands of India; but, now he is settled upon land in this city. He and Mrs. Stainthrope and a number of interesting children made my one day's visit here very pleasant.

This city of sixty thousand inhabitants has come up in the present generation, and is a remarkable sample of enterprise, business and growth. In its size, appearance and business, it reminds me much of Scranton, Pa. The production of iron, and things made of iron, have made it a large and important city in comparatively a few years. We walked through the city and saw the fine town-hall, market square, iron, steel and salt works, docks, the stores, post-offices, churches, etc. We passed through Albert Park, fine, large, public grounds, which, though new, are beautiful, with lakes, fountains, shrubbery, trees, statues, swans, band stands, walks, drives, seats, flowers, arches, etc. In a few years it probably will be a very delightful retreat.

I was shown statues of Mr. Vaughn and Mr. Bolckow, who were the founders of the city. One having furnished money and the other brains and enterprise, they began to turn the mountain of iron ore into wealth and life and beauty, and now their heroic forms stand in solid marble on great pedestals in the crowded squares of the city.

My cousin pointed out twenty-seven blast furnaces and a number of salt wells. In the docks we saw many ships loading and unloading, while on the piers were piled thousands of tons of railroad iron—rails, chairs and ties. Some go to Egypt, some to India and some to Canada. The rails used on railways in England are double; that is, same on both sides, and when one side is worn out the other side is turned uppermost.

Mr. S. said: "All these people here came up from nothing. There are a good many Jews here and we think well of them." He said, "Rossvalley, the converted Jew, is here. Shall we go and hear him to-night?" "No, thank you; I heard him in Wilkes-Barré some years ago."

In the park I was shown an oak tree, or a piece of one, five feet in diameter and weighing nine tons, nearly black as ebony, which had been taken up out of the bottom of the river Tees, where it had lain maybe for centuries. At 3:15 on Wednesday I bade good-bye to my kind cousins and went on toward Scotland.

I passed through Stockton-on-Tees, a busy, smoky iron city, and went on through the county of Durham. Here is Eagle's Cliff, a small place in a level, green country; no hills in sight; did not seem to be rich soil. Passing Dinsdale, a small town, I came to Darlington, where there is a fine double station, say a thousand feet long. Here we change trains for Durham and Newcastle-upon-Tyne. Darlington, large, smoky town, say fifty thousand inhabitants. Go on through beautiful meadows full of sheep and cows. Now we pass Ferry Hill Station and arrive at Durham.

Durham lies in a hollow, and also runs up the sides and over the top of two or three hills. The railway runs over a high viaduct, and you look down on a large portion of the old city. Yonder is the grand, old cathedral, the most striking object within the range of vision, barring the sun and the earth. There, on an eminence, are Durham castle and public buildings, grand, massive, and substantial. Aside from these objects the city did not present to a flying view anything of special interest. Durham is on the river Wear. We ran through a green vale full of meadows, sheep and stacks of grain, and now look into a ravine full of woods where is seen a castle. Now we enter Gateshead on the Tyne, opposite Newcastle.

Now our train runs across the high bridge over the Tyne and we enter Newcastle, a powerful and enterprising city, noted for coals and the construction of ships and cannon. The gray stone station is solid and spacious, the churches, the old castle, the cathedral, the banks, the hotels, the post-office and the stores are all rich, substantial buildings. The city wears an air of modern enterprise, business and solidity, which are very observable. Population about one hundred and fifty thousand. Gateshead opposite, has about eighty thousand people, supported chiefly by iron works. A chain works there employs a thousand men; iron bridges are also built there, also glass and chemical works, and the railway shops of the North Eastern Railway employing three thousand men; also marine boiler works employing six hundred men. The high bridge mentioned above, which for forty years has been a valuable landmark, is about one hundred and twenty feet high, and is one-fourth of a mile long and has three tracks upon it. A carriage road runs across under the railway tracks.

This enterprising city is talking of making a circular underground railway under the city. While I was there a grand jubilee exhibition was going on, which was attended by thousands each day. A large volume could scarcely contain the things to be seen here. Machinery, paintings, statuary, minerals, mines, bazaars, cannon, engines, cars, china, glass, terra cotta, curiosities, printing, models of ships, etc. Here was a model of one of Armstrong's great guns. These words were displayed on it: "Length, 524 inches; weight, 110½ tons; shot, 1800 pounds; powder for charge, 960 pounds; velocity, 2148 feet per second; penetration, 33.7 inches." I understood that this tremendous engine of destruction could hurl nearly a ton of metal through more than thirty-three inches of iron plates. Here are Sir William Armstrong & Co.'s great works, where they employ more than twelve thousand men in making cannon and ships. These works are said to run along the river a distance of one and three-fourths miles.

While at Newcastle I put up at the Crown Hotel, Clayton street. It was substantial, neat, quiet, and the clerks and waiters were young ladies. I may here say I saw thousands of handsome, well-dressed and modest young women serving in shops, restaurants, hotels, bakeries, confectioneries, etc., in the British Isles, and almost without an exception they conducted themselves like real ladies. The place impressed me as being busy, substantial, sensible.

I went as far as North Shields along the river; returning, purchased a third-class ticket to Edinburgh for ten shillings and four-pence, which is one hundred and twenty-four pence, showing the distance to be one hundred and twenty-four miles. The train left Newcastle-on-Tyne at 5 p. m. and at about 8 p. m. rolled into fair Edinburgh, but the things I saw and thought on the way must form a portion of next week's letter.

# CHAPTER XXIV.

## EDINBURGH, SCOTLAND.

HEALTH—FINE WEATHER—KINDNESS—PLACES PASSED THROUGH—THINGS NOTED—EDINBURGH—A QUEENLY CITY—GOSPEL HYMNS IN THE STREET—ARTHUR'S SEAT—CASTLE HILL—CALTON HILL—A SLOUGH TURNED INTO A FLOWERY VALE FULL OF LOCOMOTIVES AND BUSINESS—THE OLD CANNON-CROWNED CASTLE—SIR WALTER SCOTT'S FINE MONUMENT—THE MOUND—GRANITE CITY—SPIRES, MONUMENTS, ETC.—HOLYROOD PALACE—BIRD'S-EYE VIEW—BAGPIPES AND ARTILLERY—PLAIDED AND PLUMED SOLDIERS, ETC.

I am assured by words spoken and written that many readers have followed quite closely all the way gone over by these letters, and now, as we enter the north country, I trust my humble account may not be unworthy of "Bonny Scotland," nor uninteresting to our readers. I often wish that I could describe the landscapes, cities and people more vividly, so that the reader might perhaps see them with a more discerning and intelligent eye than the writer possesses. It is true that, being well all the time and blessed with the finest weather possible to these regions, and permitted to roam in and around places long since seen in atlases or read of in school books or histories, was a pleasure so great as to banish care, loneliness and home-sickness. Of course, for various reasons, I dare not promise everyone so enjoyable a time should they go there.

In one of my note-books I find these words written: "The sea smiled to please me and frowned to awe and teach me. The bright, open heavens beamed with good weather. Epidemics did not rage; mobs did not roar, and steam was not rebellious. Strangers received me courteously and we parted lasting friends. Relatives rejoiced at my coming, and when I departed we shook hands amid falling tears." I bring in this apparent digression to show that while absent I was thoughtful, grateful and active, and that I also wish to claim the reader's attention for some of the very interesting objects and places seen in Scotland and Ireland, and also in the return voyage on the waves of the sea.

As I have mentioned, the train left Newcastle at 5 p. m. and arrived at Edinburgh, one hundred and twenty-four miles away, between 8 and 9 p. m. I took the train at the Central Station in Newcastle. This station is a grand, large, solid stone structure, say three hundred by five hundred feet, with glass roofs.

September 16th, the weather is May-like. We ran out northward through a green, level country and saw many fields of wheat and oats still out. Our train is an express and stops seldom—not much time for stops when they go from London to Edinburgh, four hundred miles, in eight hours. I will mention some of the places we ran through: Killingworth, Anitsford, Gramilton, Plessey, Netherton, Morpeth,

Warkworth, Christobank, Fallcon, Chathill, Newham, Belford, Beal, Screnerston, Spital, Tweedmouth, Berwick-on-Tweed (and also on a cliff overlooking the sea—about fifteen thousand inhabitants, six or eight nice spires; Berwick is here pronounced Berick; the "w" is silent), Bournmouth, Dunbar, Drem. Now it is dark. While traveling on trains I wrote nearly all the time of what I saw from the car windows, and this habit no doubt had much to do in keeping me from loneliness and weariness, for I could rest all day on a train, but at night found it very tiresome riding in cars. For say an hour as we rushed along I noted some things I saw, and this is the result: Bridges run under, 35; sheep in many fields, 3,200; cows and other cattle, 250; stacks of grain, etc., 155; fields of wheat still out, 34; oats, 15; turnips, 37; beans, 7. After running an hour or more after dark, we run into a tunnel and soon the train stands still in the deep heart of great and beautiful Edinburgh, a city of two hundred and fifty thousand inhabitants.

I looked up and saw a castle-like building on a ledge, and was told that it was the jail. Leaving the train, I walk up a hundred or more stone steps and enter a broad, beautiful, busy street. This is Prince's street, the finest in the city, and lined with fine, tall buildings on one side and monuments on the other. I went to the Waverly Hotel, but it was full, so I went over and up into High street and was cared for at Buchannan's Temperance Hotel. At the corner, near the hotel, a large company of people were singing familiar hymns, such as are heard at camp-meetings

(17)

in America. I was told that it was a "Mission Band" that sing, talk and pray in the street every evening in the year. It sounded much like home. Those gospel hymns are encircling this little world, and "when crowns and kingdoms in the dust are laid," they will still be young, vigorous and powerful.

Edinburgh, (always here and in England pronounced Edinboro,) is considered one of the most beautiful cities on earth, for nature and art have done much to beautify the spot, while antiquity, romance, and war, also throw a charmed halo around it.

The city is situated on two hills and in one valley, and on two plains, while a blue arm of the sea, (the Frith of Forth) stretches along to the north, about two miles away, and to the east and south stand guard a number of bold, picturesque crags and hills, most conspicuous of which are Salsbury Crag and Arthur's Seat. Arthur's Seat, a mount which rises abruptly to the height of eight hundred and twenty-two feet, in the distance, somewhat resembles the form of a lion crouching, and from this eminence can be seen nearly all of the city and a portion, at least, of a number of counties, or shires, as they are here called.

As the atmosphere was not clear the days I was there, I did not go to the top of Arthur's Seat, but was content with ascending Castle Hill, Calton Hill, Sir Walter Scott's Monument, and other eminences. The two high hills, Castle and Calton, upon which important portions of Edinburgh are built, remind me of two lions lying, one looking to the east and the other to the west, while a narrow valley lies between. It is perhaps but a mile from the old Castle on the hill facing westward to Nelson's monument on the hill looking eastward.

Years ago a lake, or unsightly slough, lay in this vale in the centre of the city; now this valley roars with the trade and travel of kingdoms, while gardens, flowers, shrubs, and trees, also abound here, presenting beauty and exhaling fragrance, while tall and handsome buildings, public and private, cover the sides and tops of the hills. Great engines and trains are almost constantly rolling along the steel grooves in this narrow valley, over which fine, strong bridges stand to carry multitudes of people and vehicles.

A busy and interesting scene presents itself in the great railway stations in this vale. Trains rushing in and out—acres of depots and markets under glass roofs—hundreds of people seeking the right train,—many draymen with great, ponderous horses and carts, coming and going with immense packages of merchandise, and as you see the letters, "North British Railway," on the harness, and carts, and engines, and warehouses, you are considerably impressed with the solidity and importance of this company. I think I never saw a vale in which so much business and beauty clustered as in this. Where once an unwholesome marsh held sway, now great railway trains rush along under viaducts and temples, and almost under the lofty, cannon-crowned castle which clings to the abrupt rock hundreds of feet above. Yes, it was an interesting sight to see the locomotive, the modern giant, rushing along under the walls of a castle more than a thousand years old, built before the discovery of gunpowder, and when brave men dressed in brass and steel as they went out to battle. Now, our armor to be efficient must be several feet in thickness of iron or steel, and can only be worn by great fortresses on land and sea. Now, since nations go to war with the clamor and force of thunder storms; yes, armed with lightning, wars must become less frequent.

Here is Sir Walter Scott's magnificent memorial. This is one of the three most beautiful monuments I have seen. It stands on the south side of Prince's street, nearly opposite McGregor's Royal Hotel. A guide standing near said: "This monument cost seventeen thousand pounds; foundation walls laid (52 feet deep) in 1840, and monument finished in 1845. It is two hundred feet and six inches high, and two hundred and eighty-seven steps take you to the top of the fourth gallery, one hundred and eighty feet from the pavement. The sitting statue of Sir Walter, which sits in a raised position at the centre of the monument and in plain view, cost two thousand pounds." The monment is of stone, finely carved, and full of niches containing statues. It stands upon eight handsome clustered pillars, and is so graceful in its proportions that it is almost impossible for one to believe it to be two hundred feet high, until he ascends it. I paid two-pence and ascended. After winding around and around, up through a narrow stairway in cut rock, you come out upon the first gallery and commence to look down upon the city, but you must go on to the fourth gallery before you see the real height and beauty of the place and its surroundings. This monument is very graceful and elaborate, and in form is much like the Albert Memorial in London.

Now let us look down and around the city. At our feet are beautiful gardens full of flowers, containing statues of eminent persons; and just beyond us is the deep ravine through which run the railways above mentioned, and there on the Mound stand two massive columned buildings, the Museum of Antiquities and the National Gallery of Art. The Mound is a pleasing feature of the scene; it is a work of man, and is a broad embankment thrown across and filling up the valley to the level of Prince's street. On this Mound are the fine buildings mentioned, while the railways run through tunnels at the base of the Mound and along at the base of the Castle Crag they run through pleasant groves carpeted with grass.

The buildings of Edinburgh are of gray stone. I did not see one of wood or one wholly of brick. Let us look again; there to the right is the old castle with its walls running around the edge of the precipice. Yonder on the left is the Calton Hill, where stand Nelson's fine monument, the Royal Observatory, the unfinished and picturesque National monument, and a number of other graceful monuments. Churches, colleges, cathedrals and monuments and public buildings are seen in nearly every direction.

Yonder, nearly a mile away, in a narrow valley, near the foot of Salsbury Crag, is the extensive and very handsome Holyrood Palace, where royalty lodge when they visit Edinburgh. The place is ancient, and thrilling romances and tragedies have had origin here. The very elegant fountain there is much praised, while the ruins of the chapel are extensive and very interesting. Yonder to the south are Salsbury Crag and Arthur's Seat, and away to the west are the Pentland Hills, and there to the north is Leith (along the Frith of Forth), the harbor for Edinburgh. Now look along the street, somewhat more than a mile long, from Holyrood Palace on the plain to the top of Castle Hill, a gradual incline, up which runs a famous old street built up all the way and containing many old buildings made famous in history by the acts and lives of good, bad, wise and great people.

There on the level sits great, historic Holyrood, full of wealth, beauty and art, and yonder, more than four hundred feet above the level, is the old castle which was the residence and stronghold of mighty chiefs and kings many ages ago. The bagpipes are still heard there mingling with the roar of artillery as the tall and graceful soldiers march to and fro in the gay plaids and picturesque costume of centuries past. Here below and in broad, gay Prince's street are seen the multitudes on foot, and in carriages and tram-cars, going here and there on the various errands of business and traveling life, while the clash and roar of the city roll up to us, wave above wave.

# CHAPTER XXV.

## EDINBURGH, SCOTLAND.

ANCIENT BANNERS WAVED OVER THE BIRTH OF KINGS AND QUEENS—HER BEAUTY AND GLORY—A GRAND RIDE—TALL BUILDINGS ON LEDGES—HIGH STREET—KNOX'S HOUSE—THE OLD CASTLE—FIVE HUNDRED FEET ABOVE THE SEA—SOLDIERS IN RED COATS, AND IN KILTS, WITH SWORDS, SKEAN DHUS AND SPORRANS—A GREAT CITY DRESSED IN GRAY STONE—GRASS MARKET—ST. MARGARET'S CHAPEL—MON'S MEG—STONE CANNON-BALLS — CROWN JEWELS — QUEEN MARY'S BED-ROOM — A CANNON ROARS AT ONE O'CLOCK, TOUCHED BY FINGERS FOUR HUNDRED MILES LONG—WHAT IS MAN — CALTON HILL — NELSON'S MONUMENT—TWELVE COLUMNS; SCOTLAND'S "PRIDE AND SHAME"—A TEMPLE DESERTED ITS PORTICO.

The history of Edinburgh goes back to early in the Christian era, and it has been a place of importance for say a thousand years. Yes, it is allowable to call that place important where castles were built, and defended by soldiers; where armies fought and encamped; where chieftains, princes and kings upreared glittering banners, and brave men gathered around swearing to be true to their master and their country; where kings and queens were born, lived and died;

where temples were reared for worship and for learning.

Poets have sung of the beauty and romance of the place, and I will not try to surpass nor try to equal them. With its high, bold hills crowned with castles, cathedrals, pillared temples, monuments, arches, columns and domes; and its plains crowded with stores, colleges, parks, residences, public buildings, and churches with tall spires, and broad streets full of statues; and its vales full of railways, markets and gardens; and all its high places gazing away to the blue sea on the other side, it has been called the "Modern Athens."

Sir David Wilkie says: "What the tour of Europe was necessary to see elsewhere, I now find congregated in this one city. Here are alike the beauties of Prague and of Salsburg; here are the romantic sites of Orvieto and Tivoli, of Genoa and Naples; here, indeed, to the poet's fancy, may be realized the Roman Capitol and Grecian Acropolis."

I mounted to the top of the street-car and for a very few pence was carried around four or five miles on the circular railway. I can not tell of the hospitals, universities, museums, churches, etc., that we passed; but it was a very enjoyable ride. Yonder, on the left, are bold, rugged Salsbury Crag and Arthur's Seat, and on the right are "The Meadows," beautiful, public grounds, surrounded by pleasant and handsome residences. Now we come out where fine stone mansions line both sides of the street. Here reside many of the people of wealth. High, solid stone walls and iron gates cut off the view and make it somewhat difficult to see the fountains, flowers, statues, etc., which adorn these ivy-grown residences and walls; but my elevated position, the second story of a street-car, gives me a good opportunity to see how these people live, or rather what they live in. Now we pass three handsome stone churches and come into West Prince's street. I have already attempted to speak of the beauty of this stately street. You have heard of the tall buildings of Edinburgh. A few of the buildings are ten and others eleven stories high, and many of them six, seven or eight stories. They might average six stories throughout the business portion of the city. But at night, when one looks up to Castle Hill and counts the lights, he might almost think he saw buildings of eighteen or twenty stories in height, for there buildings stand on ledges above buildings. Now let us go to the Old Castle.

Here is High street. There is "John Knox's house." The street is smooth, of medium width and lined with good buildings, and ascends gradually until we are now in the broad esplanade leading up to the castle. Here are monuments to some of Scotland's great soldiers and others. Here is the old drawbridge, which is ancient and ponderous, with walls nearly twenty feet thick. Here are guides waiting to escort us; here are cabs awaiting the return of sightseers; here are soldiers in red coats and others in plaids, and kilts, and scarfs; in caps and bonnets; with guns, swords, bayonets, sporrans, skean dhus and bagpipes.

This castle on a rock, nearly five hundred feet above

the sea, covers about eleven acres, and runs back into history, I was told, to A. D. 320. Now we wind around among walls and the various buildings of the castle until we stand at the top surrounded by walls, cannon, soldiers and many sight-seers. Now we look down upon fair Edinburgh. I do not expect to see a more beautiful sight on earth. A great city dressed in gray stone finely cut and skillfully laid up.

Yonder is graceful Calton Hill crowned with domes, columns and arches, all clear-cut against the background of the sky; and on the south-west here, far below us, is the Grass Market, a pleasant, open place where farmers bring produce and sell to the shopkeepers and others. On the other side, far below us also, and beyond the vale and railways, are Prince's and other grand streets. To confine our attention to the castle: here is St. Margaret's Chapel, which dates back to 1093. This is called the oldest building in Edinburgh and the smallest chapel in Scotland. The small windows are of fine colored glass, and the place wears an ancient and sombre aspect. Here is "Mons Meg," an old cannon four hundred and one years old, and weighs six tons, and near it are several stone cannon balls about fifteen inches in diameter. Large marbles, boys; but they would roll down hill grandly. This old gun is of wrought-iron, with heavy bands wrapped around and around it. Of course it is useless now, except as a relic or as old iron. I went in and saw the crown jewels of Scotland; i. e., the crown, sceptre, etc., and the heavy oak chest in which they were preserved so long. I also went into Queen

Mary's bedroom, where James I. of England and VI. of Scotland was born.

Now it is nearly 1 o'clock, and there is a long row of cannon. Cannon No. 6 was charged and rolled to the port-hole and the electric wire attached to it, and as I stood there on the castle-crowned rock in Edinburgh of the North, with watch in hand, the cannon boomed over the city and the great ball rose and fell on the top of Nelson's monument on Calton Hill. The gun was discharged from Greenwich, four hundred miles away. This gives London time to Scotland every day at 1 o'clock. Though the pendulum swings in Greenwich, the clock strikes in Edinburgh. Truly, man has sought out many inventions. Three thousand years ago the poet David asked: "What is man?" I wonder how he would express it now if he could ask the question again. I'll warrant you there would be a long line of interrogation and exclamation points. The guide has matters of interest to tell of almost every doorway, window and room, but time fails at present, so I will go down from the castle and find my way to Calton Hill.

This sightly hill commands a view of Holyrood Palace, of Leith, of the Frith of Forth, and a large part of the city. Nelson's monument, a tall, handsome, round, stone tower, attracts the chief attention. Its size and position show how that great, lion-hearted naval officer is appreciated by Scotland's brave and honest sons. Here are also monuments to Robert Burns and other eminent Scotchmen, the Royal Observatory, and the unfinished National Monument.

This is called by some "Scotland's Pride and Shame." Some years ago they began the erection of a building, which was to imitate the Pantheon at Rome, but lack of interest or funds led to its abandonment, and now we see twelve large columns, say forty feet tall, standing there, with masonry binding them together on top. An architect would call this masonry on top of the columns the entablature. These columns are said to have cost five thousand dollars each. They form an interesting feature of the landscape and remind you of the portico of some mighty temple of the hoary past. This unfinished structure of twelve massive columns caused me to think of things pre-historic and seemed to speak of a vast and ancient temple that had been ground to dust by the revolving wheels of Time.

# CHAPTER XXVI.

### EDINBURGH AND DUNFERMLINE, SCOTLAND.

EDINBURGH—LIKE HOME—SOBER PEOPLE—MAGNIFICENT SQUARES—OASES IN CHISELED ROCK—FIVE STORIES CUT IN GRANITE—GIANT BREAKING FROM GLASS FETTERS—ON THE WAY TO DUNFERMLINE—STEEL SPANNING SEA WAVES—THROUGH A MOUNTAIN BY INVERKEITHING — SCOTLAND'S OLD CAPITAL — RUINS— ELECTRICITY FLASHES GREETINGS—METALIC HORSES —LINEN FACTORIES—WHEELS THUNDER AND SHUTTLES FLASH—THIRTEEN THOUSAND WOMEN—KIND FRIENDS—GOODS PICTURED FOR COLUMBIA—A WALK —STEEL COLUMNS ABOVE BLUE HILLS — ANDREW CARNEGIE—PRINCELY GIVER—SCOTCH HOSPITALITY — OLD PALACE RUINS INTERESTING — FINE OLD CHURCH—DECEPTIVE PILLARS—PICTURES IN GLASS— TOMBS OF KINGS—CURFEW RINGS HERE—THE LOOMS BATTLE — WORKING IN FACTORIES — PARENTS OF FRIENDS—HOSPITALITY MAKES ANGELS.

Now, as I get ready to depart from stately Edinburgh, her beauty, and peace, and order, and her spirit of sober industry appeal to my admiration and love all the stronger. Like a blessing, we do not know how sweet, cheering and ennobling it was until it leaves us.

I find these words in my note-book, written while on the top of a street-car returning from Leith: "More people looked at me friendly and kindly, as if they knew me in Edinburgh, than in any other place." Ladies and others look, dress and speak about the same here as they do in Wilkes-Barré, Pa. I do not remember to have seen a drunken man in Scotland, and I think I did not see five drunken persons in my travels beyond the sea. I did see men and women sleeping on the stones of London Bridge late at night, and others on the pavements in Liverpool at 4 o'clock in the morning, but they were poor, homeless people, and perhaps harmless, for policemen did not molest them. I remembered the great One who had slept in a stone cradle, and of one who, on a stone pillow, dreamed of a ladder reaching into the realms of eternal sunshine, comfort and glory. I heard very little profanity. I saw but little poverty and suffering, and little or nothing of criminals. I did not seek vulgarity and vice, and I did not see them. I looked for beauty and art and things glorious, and saw them. Yes, we find what we seek heartily.

I walked up by St. Andrew Square, on an eminence, from which you can look from the heart of the great, busy city, away out on the bright, blue sea, which is always a thing of beauty, glory and health. This square is cool with trees, flowers, fountains and grass, arranged in forms to please the eye, cheer the heart and rest the body. It looks like an oasis in a region of chiseled rock, as indeed it is. I walked through George street, which is about three-fourths of a mile long and one hundred and twenty-five feet wide, between the buildings, nearly all of which are residences five stories high. I saw not a tree in this street. There were say six handsome statues sitting on great pedestals in the middle of the street, among which were those of George IV., William Pitt and Dr. Chalmers. The street, which was clean, was rock-paved, and it all looked so solid, like a five story channel cut in granite.

Now I come around where a lofty and massive viaduct of stone upholds a great street as it runs over another street which leads down into the railway-crowded vale, where great steel bands stretch away to the north, south and west, to form a safe highway for nations.

Here is a crowd in the street. I also look and see that a chemist's boy had broken a large glass bottle of some powerful acid, and smoke is ascending from the paper wrapper on the stone pavement. A pungent exhalation assails eyes and throat. I congratulated him that it did not scatter over his clothing and person. I then thought of the corrosive, withering, blasting, deadening and destructive power of acids, alcohol, opium, dynamite and powder—good servants, but remorseless masters. They are worse than Shylock, for they need not account to man nor their Creator, and so they claim and take the "pound of flesh."

On the morning of September 17th, I went down to the great Waverly station and at 7:15 we started for Queen's Ferry. Our train ran out under the Mound through the pleasant gardens already mentioned, along and almost under the frowning rocks of Castle Hill, then in under the city for say half a mile, and now we emerge into the fresh, green country, galloping towards the Frith of Forth, while the Pentland hills appear away to the left. I saw hundreds of stacks of grain and hundreds of sheep. Of course, the barns are not large enough to hold all the produce, and the hay and grain are stacked near the barn or barns and look like a village of conical houses, well built and well thatched.

We ran by Ratho, Kirkliston, and came to South Queen's Ferry, on the Frith of Forth, where a most stupendous cantilever bridge is being erected, which shall be mentioned later. We went on around, another mile, to Port Edgar and took passage on ferry-boat "John Beaumont" for North Queen's Ferry, in Fifeshire.

Now we take the train for Dunfermline, running under a mountain, along by rocks, through ravines, groves and fields of oats, potatoes and turnips. The potato fields are very green yet. We passed Inverkeithing, a very old and quaint town or village. Yonder, on higher ground, are seen spires, and towers, and roofs, partially veiled in smoke, which I am told is Dunfermline, after reaching which, I inquired the way to the home of Mr. Alexander Bennett, Sr., and son, to whom I was recommended by Mr. Charles Graham, of Scranton. I remained over Sunday with these hospitable people in this ancient and very interesting city.

Dunfermline, now a city of about twenty thousand

inhabitants, is one of the oldest places in Scotland, in fact, it was the ancient capital of Scotland. It is known in history for nearly a thousand years, but previous to that time it is veiled in the mists of oblivion. Here are interesting and picturesque ruins of palaces and temples where centuries ago crowned heads had fought, lived and worshiped, and sought safety within thick walls of rock and ponderous gates, where hardy soldiers armed with swords, battle-axes, spears and bows and arrows, stood guard night and day, while storms of thunder and storms of war shook the fair, fertile isles of Britain. Now electricity flashes friendly greetings from the Lowlands to the Highlands, and Aberdeen, Balmoral, Dunfermline, Edinburgh and Glasgow salute London, Birmingham, York, Cardiff and Dublin before breakfast, while ten thousand bright, metalic horses, far more fleet and powerful than Job's war-horse, take up and bear away burdens, and soon their voices are heard on the hills and in the crowded marts of trade, shouting, "Ha! ha! I am here, and still you rest!"

Dunfermline is situated on elevated ground, a few miles north of the Frith of Forth, in Fifeshire. It is noted chiefly for the manufacture of linen fabrics, such as table-cloths, towels, napkins, etc. There are ten of these factories here. Beverege's is the most extensive, and they employ about one thousand persons, nearly all of whom are girls and women.

Mr. Bennett said, "Of the twenty thousand people here about two-thirds of them are women." Many employees come from villages and towns at some distance around. I have already mentioned that I carried letters to Mr. Alexander Bennett, from Mr. Charles Graham, of Scranton. They were old friends, having learned their trade in the same shops, in Dunfermline. Mr. Bennett and his son live in Foundry street.

These people were pleased to see me and treated me with much hospitality during the two days I could remain with them. They have a foundry and machine shop in which is some good machinery, and they were quite busy in turning out and putting up work in towns about. Mr. Bennett took me to Steele's linen factory and Mr. Davison, the foreman, kindly showed us through the works, in which were three hundred and thirty looms and about three hundred employees, nearly all females. The looms and machinery clicked and roared almost like thunder, and the flashing of the shuttles as they played back and forth was like lightning. We saw the work in various stages, but the most interesting to me was to see how the machinery followed the intricate maze of the pattern to produce figures and pictures and words upon the fabrics.

It was a curious sight to see those looms in a foreign land weaving in the mottoes, the banners, the coat of arms and the portraits of the United States into goods which, of course, were being made for American merchants. I asked, "How much do these workers earn?" and was told: "We pay them once a fortnight and they earn from sixteen to forty shillings."

As mentioned, this is one of the oldest towns in

Scotland, and while some of the residences are quite modern, others are very ancient looking. I noticed many places where the entrance to the stone buildings was through a passage-way at one side, or between buildings, and in the rear there were courts or closes with entrances into the buildings, and in many instances a flight of stone steps, running same way as the pavement, would lead up say five feet to the door-way of the houses. In a city where there is so much to think of and say in so brief a space, one hardly knows what to write and what to leave out, so I will leave my notes and write chiefly from memory, almost haphazard.

Miss Bennett kindly piloted me about the town one afternoon. We came to an eminence in the park from which we could overlook the country for miles around. The country was still green and fresh, and there, six miles away, could be seen the mighty steel columns, towering above high hills, which are to bear up the great bridge over the Frith of Forth. When you can see a work of man so plainly at such a distance, overcoming the sea, the delicate blue veil of smoke, and rugged, tree-crowned hills, you may know it is a majestic work. We saw the churches and the public buildings, and the extensive works and warehouses of the Beverege Bros. The Bevereges are wealthy and live in palaces in pleasant places. If men are diligent and prudent in their own business they may stand before kings, if they should happen to care to do so.

Here is the little house where the famous Andrew Carnegie was born. You have heard of Carnegie, the brilliant Scotchman who has made so much money at Pittsburg, and given so much to Edinburgh and to Dunfermline, his native town. He was in those places when I was there and the papers were full of his praise. His father was a hand-loom weaver. His mother was mentioned as a woman of powerful characteristics and fine qualities. She was the daughter of Robert Morrison, a celebrated Chartist.

The Carnegies were poor when Andrew was a boy, and when they came to America they borrowed the money to come with of a lady who is living still, I understand, and who is remembered substantially by Mr. Carnegie. Carnegie has given thousands of pounds to Dunfermline to build and endow baths, libraries, etc. I think I noticed that Dunfermline people did not quite relish his giving the two hundred and fifty thousand dollars to Edinburgh for a library, and some intimated that the money expended in Dunfermline might have been laid out to more advantage to the people. These probably thought his largest gifts should have been to his native town.

We called on Mrs. Henderson, aunt of Miss Bennett, and were cordially received. Scotland, of course, is famous for hospitality. You hardly can get seated in a Scottish house before food and drink are set before you, especially drink. Yes, the traveler will have his temperance qualities tried when he finds Scotland. When I remembered how dangerous and unpleasant it is to refuse to smoke the pipe with an American Indian, it somewhat modified my conduct in Scotland. It is a remarkable fact that the same kind of food and drink appear to taste differently and affect one differently in the British Isles from what they do in America.

Now we have come to the ruins of a once grand and extensive palace, and those of a monastery. Here is a high and thick wall running along a rock on the brow of an eminence, which looks down into a deep, shady ravine, where flows a brook. Great trees grow on either side of this old wall, through which are openings where doors, windows, closets and fireplaces once were. Yes, large trees stand there, on ground which for ages was covered and enclosed by halls and dining, dancing, sitting and sleeping-rooms, where crowned heads, princes and lords resided, visited and feasted; where they planned, suffered and died like other poor people. Neil Paton, a half-uncle of the famous painter, Noel Paton, had charge of these old ruins and escorted us around. He told us that the palace was founded by Malcom Canmore in 1071, and rebuilt or enlarged by James IV. in the sixteenth century.

"Up there," he said, "where you see that old fireplace, Charles I. was born. Here was the royal kitchen, there the scullery, and here the wine cellar, where flows a fine spring of water. There is the subterranean passage running to the monastery. Queen Margaret walked up and down that glen."

These ruins, which I have not time to describe, impressed me as much as any that I saw. Near this point is the old church, and with the new part, which was built sixty years ago, is a large and imposing building. Its appearance is cathedral-like; heavy stone walls, towers, lofty columns and fine stained glass windows, which show forth in beauty of form and colors many great things of church and state. Andrew Carnegie has recently placed large and magnificent stained-glass windows in a portion of this church. Hours may be passed in gazing, in pleasure, on the fine pictures in glass. Here are those pillars in this old church that, viewed from a certain standpoint, look as if they were standing small end downward, like a cone on its point, but seen from another point they are seen to taper upward. This is a mechanical illusion caused by V-shaped lines cut in the pillars.

"King Robert the Bruce" is buried under the pulpit in this church, and a number of kings and queens and lordly persons are buried here, and some fine statues in marble stand to perpetuate their fame and glory. I attended church here with Mr. Bennett, and after the services we walked through the pleasant grounds of the churchyard, and he pointed out the resting place of Mr. Charles Graham's parents.

On Saturday evening the principal streets were lively and cheerful with a great crowd of happy, peaceful people, out on the many errands and pleasures of civilized life. There is the fine new municipal building, which cost £25,000. Its lofty clock is illuminated, the gas being turned on and off by the clock machinery. Curfew is still rung here at 8 o'clock in this quaint and ancient city, and it is the only place I found where this old-time custom is observed.

Here comes a glittering engine on wheels. Is it a steam fire engine? No, it is a potato roaster or steamer, and the man halts here and there and sells hot potatoes for, I think, a penny apiece. This place used to be celebrated generations ago for hand-loom weaving. I presume hundreds of houses had looms in them at work, and there are still a few hand-looms in use, but when steam-driven looms came they waged a sure, cruel war against the hand-looms, and some of the incidents of patience, toil, and bravery and suffering would do no discredit to the heroism of blood-red battle-fields.

Now the factories begin to hum at 6 a. m. and run till 9 o'clock, at which time the employees go to breakfast. At 10 work starts again, and at 2 p. m. they stop for another hour and then work from 3 to 6 o'clock, making ten hours' work. Many fine walks and drives are found all around the city, some leading to the mountains, some to villages and some through groves to the Forth river.

In Maygate street stands the old Abbot's house, with this curious motto cut above the door:

> "Sen · Vord · is · thrall
> And · thocht · is · fre;
> Keep · veill · thy · tonge,
> I · coinsell · the."

While here I met William Fotheringham and Andrew Buchanan and their families, and found them to be friendly, frank and hearty people, glad to see one who knew their sons in Wilkes-Barré, a city in the distant and great "land of the free." (Their sons, P. H. Fotheringham and James Buchanan, I had met in charge of a store in Wilkes-Barré, Pa.) They had places of business in different streets of the city and appeared to be industrious people moving surely toward success. It is comforting, cheering, refining and ennobling to be treated so well by strangers in a far-off land. I can almost see how the entertainment might change ordinary strangers into angels. Let us not be unmindful of such matters. While here I met Mr. James Morgan, of Crossford; but Crossford and the great bridge must receive attention in another chapter.

# CHAPTER XXVII.

### SCOTLAND: A WONDERFUL BRIDGE, ETC.

SEA-WAVES CROUCH BEFORE RULERS OF KINGDOMS AND COMMERCE—FROM EDINBURGH TO DUNFERMLINE—SOUTH QUEEN'S FERRY — PORT EDGAR — NORTH QUEEN'S FERRY—TOWERS OF GRANITE AND STEEL PLANTED IN WATER—A HIGHWAY FOR THE PASSAGE OF FIERY CHARIOTS, BALANCED ON CIRCULAR TOWERS FORTY STORIES HIGH—MACHINE SHOPS SUSPENDED IN AIR—THIRTY-ONE MEN KILLED—FOUR THOUSAND MEN RIVETING FORTY-TWO THOUSAND TONS OF STEEL —HALCYON DAYS—THE SUN KISSES THE WATER BY A RUINED CASTLE—PLEASANT DRIVE—THE LOVERS WALK — QUIET, QUAINT, OLD CROSSFORD — KIND HEARTS—WALKING TOWARD THE LIGHTS OF DUNFERMLINE.

When crowned heads, and kingdoms, and commanders, and commerce, wish a thoroughfare or a great work, it generally comes to pass that the sea crouches and bathes the feet of nations, rivers flow smoothly to be spanned and mountains stand still to be perforated and terraced, while granite, and iron, and steel, and marble, stand in the strength and beauty which were decreed to them "in the beginning." Few of our readers have seen so great a work of man as this mighty bridge which spans the Frith of Forth, an arm of the sea between Edinburgh and Dunfermline.

One pleasant morning in September, as our train ran out from under old Edinburgh, into the fields toward the Frith of Forth, we saw the green meadows and the very green fields of potatoes and turnips. Here were fields of oats and beans still out; here a score or two of wheat, oats and hay-stacks, neat, symmetrical and well thatched, surrounded the barns, while cattle and sheep grazed in many fields. Here great flocks of crows and starlings are seen flying before and away from the train, and yonder are the Pentland Hills, looming up faintly through the mist as our good train rushes toward the north. I thought of Wyoming, Luzerne and Lehman, for I had seen similar days there.

Now our train halts at South Queen's Ferry, and then runs on around one mile to Port Edgar, where a ferry steamer awaits to carry us to North Queen's Ferry, in Fifeshire, beyond the Forth.

While on this boat we look away to the right and see the great stone piers on the land, and the steel colums from the water, looming up. In the distance the columns look to be about one hundred and fifty feet high, and say four feet in diameter, but when we go there, as I did in company with A. Bennett, Sr., and A. Bennett, Jr., and Mrs. A. Bennett, Jr., and Mr. James Morgan, I found the half had not been told.

This point is but a few miles north of Edinburgh, on the railway lines to the cities in the north of Scotland; and travel and commerce had grown weary of halting the trains on the shore of the Forth, and embarking on the steamers, and again taking the trains on the north side, so they resolved to build a bridge over this arm of the sea, and it was also necessary to get it high enough to allow the masts of ships to pass under, and at the same time do away with tunnelling the hills on the north side.

David Harris, a foreman at the bridge, kindly showed us around, and I certainly saw things to wonder at. I tell you, these Scotchmen know how to turn iron and steel into vast ships and mighty bridges.

I wish the reader to know that this is a great work, which will cost millions of money and interest millions of people. That the reader may form some idea of its magnitude, I will try to describe it. It is nearly a mile and a-half long, about one mile of it being over the water where the tides of the sea roll in and out. See the stone piers on each side, a dozen or more, about one hundred and fifty feet high. Now look at the great steel columns, fourteen of them, which lift their round, symmetrical forms into the air three hundred and sixty-five feet above high water-mark. This is, or it will be, for it is not nearly completed yet, the greatest cantilever bridge in the world. The vast columns mentioned above are twelve feet in diameter, four of them near one shore and four of them near the other side, while six of them loom up on a rock in the middle of the Forth. These pillars are made of great plates riveted together like boilers, and are firmly braced inside. They stand on ponderous masses of Aberdeen granite, and while they are one hundred and twenty feet apart at the base, they taper in to thirty-three feet at the top. The braces which help hold the vast pillars in position are eight feet in diameter and cross each other in various directions.

I walked with Mr. Harris up two hundred and twenty-one steps until I came to where the railway tracks will be laid one hundred and sixty-five feet above the water. "Come on," he said, but I told him I was high enough, for two hundred feet of iron and steel and ropes and chains and ladders and elevators and braces still loomed above us and caused at least some dizziness to look either up or down. These massive columns of steel, reaching out their arms for hundreds of feet over the water, impressed me with their greatness as being daring and almost awful. Think of it! These pillars have to stretch out their arms and uphold thousands of tons of iron and steel over one thousand, seven hundred and ten feet of water on one side and one thousand seven hundred and ten feet of water on the other side—more than two-thirds of a mile with but one resting-place. Those vast columns of metal, towering up there in the middle of the Forth, reach down their great arms to uphold a mighty bridge one hundred and sixty-five feet above the sea-waves, while ponderous engines roll across drawing passengers and merchandise, and while clouds float above and ships and sea-gulls below. Why, I imagined these fourteen great columns to be castles or barracks, forty stories high, in which fourteen regiments of soldiers might lodge comfortably, and when you consider also the great tubular braces eight feet in diameter, then you might lodge easily a hundred thousand men there within safe walls of steel.

"Mr. Harris, I understand you have an accident now and then?" "Yes; two men were killed a few days ago. Thirty-one men have been killed on the work since it began seven years ago. The distance is so great that when even a spike, or a bolt, or a burr, or a small tool falls it is about certain to kill some one, for we have six hundred and fifty men working on this one abutment. There are four thousand men in all employed on the bridge. The bridge is calculated to cost at least ten millions of dollars. It will weigh about forty-two thousand tons. The engineers are Sir John Fowler and B. Baker. The contractors are Tancred, Arrol & Co., London." As above mentioned, the bridge was commenced seven years ago and probably three years must go by yet before it is finished. Consider how much one strong man can do in one day, but this great work would employ the strength of one man for at least thirty thousand years to build. The bridge will have two tracks. Mechanical man is so correct in his plans and designs that when this becomes a thoroughfare the engines and cars made in the most distant part of Britain may roll easily and safely over it on their way to the Highlands.

Now, as the sun is setting at the close of a delightful day, we step into our wagonette and are driven along the Forth, by hedges, cuts, walls, groves, fields and mansions; up and down gentle declivities, and along smooth roads lined with shade trees. Now, across the waters, the bright, golden track of the sun is seen through a vista of trees, and beyond a green meadow, surrounded by water and black rocks, stand the remains of an old castle. Oh, the evening and the surroundings are pleasant! Halcyon days, those in Scotland, cannopied by clear skies and surrounded by humble, honest and kind hearts! The "good night" of the sun as he kisses water, meadow, hill and cloud, is indescribably sweet. The sun must reside in a rich and beautiful place or he could not give so much beauty and comfort to earth.

Now, as we approach Crossford, we begin to meet pairs of lovers from Crossford and Dunfermline, walking out to enjoy the twilight hour. Yes, there are many romantic walks in this region; but, why mention it? For I sometimes think there are few who know what romance is. Yes, the life of most of us is awfully tame, for we cannot be really happy without loving with the whole heart—willing to do or die in the right, for the one beloved.

It is dark as we enter the little, old-fashioned village of Crossford. Here we enter the hospitable cottage of Mr. and Mrs. James Morgan, and are kindly greeted by Mrs. Morgan and their hearty, rosy-cheeked daughters. Soon we are asked to sit by the table and partake of tea, scones, cheese, bread, butter, meat, etc. The food is clean, fresh, simple, cordially given and gratefully received, and partaken of heartily. The furniture, the fire, the faces, the china and all were appetizing. In this house my friend Charles Graham spent his days of childhood. He is a brother of Mrs.

Morgan. Mr. Morgan is a remarkably kind-hearted, friendly man. He told me of his fine, large garden full of fruits and vegetables, and of the old village. I somewhat regretted that I did not see it by daylight. We kindly bade each other good night, hoping to meet again in health and peace, and walked out of Crossford toward Dunfermline in company with A. Bennett, Sr., and his daughter, and Mr. Couper. Now the lights of Dunfermline appear in irregular lines ahead of us, and we enter the city not far from the old church and soon arrive at 18, Foundry street.

# CHAPTER XXVIII.

## SCOTLAND: STERLING AND GLASGOW.

FROM DUNFERMLINE TO STERLING—MOUNTAINS LIKE LIONS, SHINING LIKE VELVET—STERLING—GOING UP BY FAMOUS OBJECTS TO ROCKS MARBLE-DECKED AND CASTLE-CROWNED—CANNON ROAR BETWEEN THE CLOUDS AND THE WINDING FORTH—BRIDGE OF ALLAN—ABBEY CRAIG—A PLAIN DECKED WITH ROCKS, RIVERS, SHEEP, ETC.—A CEMETERY CLAD IN MARBLE, GRANITE, GLASS AND ROSES—OLD CHURCHES—RELICS OF KINGS, QUEENS AND KNOX—SCOTLAND'S STANDARDS—BEN-LOMOND—WATER LOOPED IN DOUBLE S'S IN MEADOWS FIVE HUNDRED FEET BELOW—SOLDIERS—HIGHLANDERS—SINGING WITCH—BANNOCKBURN—CURIOUS MONUMENT—ON TO GLASGOW—THIRTY-SIX HUNDRED GROUSE—WINAN'S DEER PARK—SIX HUNDRED THOUSAND BUSY PEOPLE—A CHIMNEY BREATHES FOUR HUNDRED AND THIRTY-FIVE FEET ABOVE THE PAVEMENTS—A GREAT ROAD WALLED EIGHT STORIES HIGH—GREAT BUILDINGS—GLASGOW NAMES—ST. ENOCH'S ROARING STATION.

At 9:20 a. m., September 19th, 1887, I parted with my kind friends, the Bennetts and Mr. Morgan, at the station in Dunfermline and took the train for Sterling. The railway runs through a picturesque country abounding with farms, hedges, groves, hills, vales, villages, towns, with mountain peaks in the distance. The mountains, still and solemn, make me think of lions crouching one beyond another. Yonder stand the Lochiel Hills, fine, high, rounding, pyramidical, and in the sunshine look as if they were robed in blue and brown velvet.

We pass through East Grange, Bogside, Kincardine and Kennet, Clark-Manning, Alloa Junction and Cambus. Here is a bold, rocky mountain where the dark rocks rise almost perpendicularly five hundred feet. Now our train runs along near the Forth and on our right is Abbey Craig, upon which stands a massive and lofty monument to Wallace, one of the most successful warriors Scotland ever produced.

Sterling is one of the oldest and most famous places in Scotland. In my note-book I find these words: "Wonderful Sterling! The most beautiful scenery I ever saw!" It is a pleasant day in September. I alight from the train in a spacious station; walk up a flight of steps and cross a bridge over the railway tracks, and walked out into the town and began to ascend the street, for I saw from the railway that Sterling Castle was on a high, bold rock.

I passed up by all kinds of shops and stores; up by banks, residences, public buildings, churches, ivy-grown ruins, cemeteries and monuments, and pass up and under great walls and archways into the courtyard of the old castle. I pass along by the row of black cannon, where balls are piled in pyramids and stand upon the wall. Above are the heavens, below are the city, the plain, the winding Forth, farms, flocks and hamlets.

Yonder is Bridge of Allan, a most beautiful and healthful watering place, nestling in woods along the base of a mountain.

Yonder is the romantic Abbey Craig, on which stands the fine Wallace monument. "King Robert the Bruce" also has a fine monument there. Let the reader imagine a wide, winding valley, on nearly every side surrounded by mountains, and through this valley winds a river, the Forth, and here and there rise rocks from the plain. These rocks are very extensive, and are covered with earth and vegetation on all sides except one. Sterling is built chiefly on one of these declivities or wedges, and the castle occupies the high and rocky part, and its walls almost overhang the valley.

I cannot take time to describe this old castle, and the handsome cemetery near and only a little below it, where many rocks, trees, monuments, statues and flowers are seen, and there are the old East and West Churches and Guild Hall, buildings which have been famous and gray for hundreds of years; where showcases, chests and safes contain precious things once belonging to kings, queens, lords, bishops, soldiers, poets, reformers, etc. I was shown the chair where kings and queens were crowned; the bible, and pulpit where Knox preached King James' coronation sermon. I was also shown the old standard yard-stick of Scotland, forty-five inches long, also old standard weights and measures.

Yes, here on the top of this rocky eminence, nearly five hundred feet above the plain, are the castle, the cemetery, the churches, and other works of past centuries; while to the northwest may be seen scores of peaks of mountains, away in the highlands, standing still and silent like an emblem of eternity. That blue, gloomy peak is Ben-Lomond, three thousand one hundred and ninety-two feet high, and that is Ben-Ledi, two thousand eight hundred and seventy-five feet high. Now look down to the valley and follow the "windings of the Forth." No, it is so crooked, so like a number of double S's, that I can not trace its course without help. See where it gleams among fields, groves, villages, and near Abbey Craig, and old Cambuskenneth Abbey, and away to smoky Alloa.

A young man said: "By carriage road to Alloa is seven miles, but if you go by water it is twenty-two miles," so the reader may know that the Forth is indeed winding—crooked as a truant's pathway to school. I understand the tide rolls up about to Sterling. Sterling is nearly thirty-six miles from Edinburgh, but, I was told, in clear weather the human eye could see portions of Edinburgh from here. There is "Lady Rock" in the cemetery, which commands so fine a view. A lady sits there now gazing around.

Here is the "Back Walk," a romantic pathway leading down along the rocks under the castle walls through trees and flowers to the valley, where shocks of grain, and sheep and cattle and houses and stacks dot the plain.

Here are soldiers, English and Scottish, clad in many colors and various uniforms, some drilling, some wheeling blankets, etc., up through passages cut or built in solid rock. The walls and moat are being improved.

Now we hear the bagpipes. Down there on the esplanade an old woman is singing a quaint and curious old song in very peculiar tone and with many repetitions. She is begging, but the soldiers do not seem to relish her presence and soon she was seen to depart. She was weird and old, but she danced and laughed in a peculiar manner. How strange! But Sterling Castle would not have been complete without the cannon, the bagpipes, the red coats, the bonneted and plaided Highlanders, the moat, the gateway, the walls, the rocks and the old woman with her song of past generations. Yes, certain surroundings always demand and secure other certain concomitants.

Now we gaze down upon the great and decisive battle-fields of Bannockburn and Sterling. It is nearly 1 o'clock, so I take a last look around on the historic and enchanting scene and go down through a little valley between the castle and the cemetery, where, among trees and rocks and shrubbery, stands a pyramid of cut stone about thirty feet high, called "The Rock of Ages." I do not remember the name of the man who had it erected to the honor of the old Covenanters. It is nearly covered with carvings of Bibles, crowns, crosses and symbols of science and art. It is a real monument to Christianity. At 1:15 p. m. I took the train for Glasgow.

Our good express train thunders and screeches along through cuts and fields, and over streams and under viaducts of rock. We pass Bannockburn, Larbert, Green Hill, Cumberland, Glenboig, Cartcosh, Cænkirk and Steps Road. I met a pleasant old gentleman who had come down via Killiecrankie from the Highlands, and when he knew of my being from America, he spoke of Winans' great deer park, where so many deer are kept and hunted among the mountains. He said on one gentleman's estate eighteen hundred brace of grouse had been killed during the season. Now our train runs into the old, wooden station in Glasgow. It is ancient, extensive, busy and rough-looking. I think it is the only wooden structure of the kind I have seen while abroad. It is probably the first station built here, and most likely it must soon give way to one more permanent.

Glasgow is a powerful and busy city of about six hundred thousand inhabitants. It stands on both sides of the Clyde, and fine bridges span the river. I found it crowded and much like New York. The buildings are massive, solid and granite, stamped with the dust and smoke of stern, unromantic business. Oh, see the lofty chimneys breathing their black breath into the clouds! How high is that chimney, please? "Four hundred and thirty-five feet." Is it possible! Four hundred and thirty-five feet, why that is high as a mountain, and it requires an effort to look to the top of it.

Here comes a tram-car, and I run to the top of it and go out the Great Western Road, lined with solid buildings of stone from four to eight stories high. Now we pass some fine churches with tall and slender spires of cut stone. Now we cross the Kelvin river and see many fine residences lining the broad thoroughfare.

Yonder is Glasgow University, an extensive building, with six acres of floors. A new spire is being built upon its lofty tower which pierces the heavens two hundred and eighty feet above the pavement. Yonder, on the hill, is the asylum, a neat, solid and large building. Yonder they are preparing buildings for the exhibition of 1888.

Passing along the streets of Glasgow, I saw so many familiar names that I wrote down a few as follows: Weir, McCulloch, Graham, MacFarlane, Hutchison, Dick, Kerr, French, Grant, Gilchrist, Cameron, Ferguson, Easton, Stuart, Taggart, Machell, Campbell, Black, Hillard, Wilson, Buchannan, Allen, etc.

Glasgow claims to be next in importance to London in the British Isles, in business and population. I went to St. Enoch's great stone station, where ponderous trains of merchandise and passengers were coming and going, while the tumultuous roar of nations rolls up on every hand. Ambition, competition, pride and poverty are mighty levers to keep men and nations from stagnation. Having some time to wait here, I found a somewhat quiet corner and wrote a letter to the *Telephone*. Now the train is nearly ready to start for Greenock. Twenty-four miles for nine pence! There is the work of competition. In an hour I am in old Greenock, in company with A. Swan, Jr.

# CHAPTER XXIX.

## SCOTLAND: GREENOCK AND PAISLEY.

GREENOCK—SHIPS AND SUGAR—THE CLYDE—A MORNING WALK — MOUNTAIN PEAKS—FAIRY LANDS — LOOKING DOWN ON GREENOCK—SCENE UNSURPASSED—AJAX—THE LARGEST SHIP—THE LYLE ROAD—ESPLANADE—HIGHLAND MARY'S GRAVE—WATT'S SCIENTIFIC LIBRARY—TELEGRAPHY IN 1753—THE SHIP YARDS—PAISLEY—SHAWLS AND THREAD—SCHOOL CHILDREN—TANNAHILL—WILSON—KILBARCHAN—MOVING TOWARD DUMFRIES.

Greenock is on the Clyde, in Scotland, about twenty-two miles west from Glasgow. Its population is about eighty thousand, and it is noted for ship building and sugar refining. The Clyde is an arm of the sea which winds among the mountains, making many bays, lakes, or lagoons, as they are variously called, or, rather, lochs here. The mountains are abrupt, rugged and irregular, and the sea winds in and around their base, where here and there a village or town claims a foothold between the waters and the hills, all of which gives a picturesque and romantic aspect.

As above mentioned, Greenock is located on the Clyde, where there is a comparatively level place, but the city has stretched out upon and up the surrounding hillsides.

Having a letter from Superintendent Charles Graham, of Scranton, to Mr. Andrew Swan, I called upon the Swans and remained with them all night, and on the following morning Mr. A. Swan, Jr., went with me for a walk. We ascended a high hill near the city, where we could look down upon Greenock and the harbor, the winding Clyde and the great maze of mountain peaks beyond, which is known as the "Duke of Argyle's Bowling Green."

It is early in the morning. The sun and atmosphere and city are clear. The waters and towns are bright, and we have one of the finest scenes around, above and below unfolded to our view. I have never, I think, seen anything quite so picturesque.

Among those misty and clustered peaks in the distance you might imagine you saw Youth-land, Hope-land, Fairy-land, Dream-land, Love-land and lakes, cities and gardens, guarded by tall, everlasting, rock-founded hills.

We walked up the Lyle road to the top of the Craig, and now stand at the foot of the flag-staff on the rock, four hundred and ten feet above sea-level. The sun is still clear to us; but see! a cloud already hangs over Greenock—a cloud which seems to rest on many pillars of black smoke which go up from the tall chimneys. The track of the sun on the Clyde looks like a broad pathway of copper. At our feet on the Clyde, below Greenock, lies Gourock, a pleasant and busy little town which will be a suburb of

Greenock when the railway is completed between the two points. The railway will run nearly all the way under the hills, for as we came up we saw the shafts, at the foot of which the thoroughfare is being made.

Now we are joined by Capt. Wm. Orr, an athletic little man of four score years, who comes up here for a walk each morning. His mind is still clear and active. He had been a sailor and followed the seas for many years. He said, "This scene is unsurpassed in the world. When I was a boy Greenock had about twenty thousand population, and nearly all of the people were employed on the sea or in seafaring business."

Ships, steamers and boats of nearly all kinds and sizes are coming and going. Here come a number of sidewheel steamers from various points down the Clyde, from Ardrassan, Stranrær, Larne, etc., bringing tourists and business people up to Greenock, Port Glasgow and Glasgow.

See that dark monster with six tall masts near the middle of the Clyde, beyond "Ajax," the guard-ship! That is the Great Eastern, the largest vessel on all the seas; six hundred and eighty feet long. Think of it! a vessel more than one-eighth of a mile long guided by men on the boundless and chainless sea! But she is too large to be profitable, and so she is lying here on exhibition.

We passed on around and down the fine Lyle road. Oh, what a drive! from the waves of the sea and the busy city streets up over the rocks almost to the clouds, by an easy grade! Thank you, Mr. Lyle! I say Mr., for I do not remember whether he is a captain, a general, a knight, or a lord, but I would knight him for making so grand a highway, which is used chiefly for pleasure and exercise.

Now we are on the broad esplanade, where walls of cut-stone for two or three miles keep the sea-waves in place, while business and travel move to and fro before fine residences. Now we come to the docks, and steamers land for a short time, and crowds disembark. Now we are nearer to the Great Eastern, and her size is still more impressive as we compare her with other vessels.

See the "Ajax," the grim war-ship, anchored out there! she is a floating fortress, and arsenal, and barracks, and drilling-room, for the sons of Great Britain. She carries two immense guns, and many smaller ones. Her full force is four hundred and fifty men, learning to serve their country on ocean-waves in various parts of the world. Yes, they go down to the sea in ships and do important business on great waters. I was about to say that war was exacting, stern and pitiless, but so is business, so is life, yes, so is even love, for if we do not assimilate, become on friendly, frictionless terms with our environments we are ground to powder fine enough for cosmetics, and the roar of the mills, run by the gods, drowns alike both curses and groans. Loving summer and joyous autumn will give us no roses and fruits if we do not sow and plant.

Here in a busy part of the city is the old "West Kirk." We went into the church-yard and saw many quaint and curious tombs and monuments standing near the gray and ivy-clad church, and surrounded by trees and flowers. Early as it was, the old sexton showed us "Highland Mary's" grave. You know Mary Campbell was Robert Burns' first love, but she died, and he wrote most touching and beautiful verses about "Mary in Heaven," etc. I took some elm leaves that waved against her neat monument, but the sexton, his name was John Rowan, gave me a flower from her grave and said, "I wish all were as careful as you." I asked, "Do many visitors come?" He replied, "Yes, and they are mostly Americans." Of course, I put some silver in his hand. After breakfast I walked down with A. Swan, Sr., and we stopped at a fine building labeled, "Watt's Scientific Library." I was introduced to the librarian, Allen Park Paton, a pleasant, intelligent man. They have there thirty thousand volumes. We saw a fine sitting statue of James Watt by Sir Francis Chantrey. Watt was a native of Greenock, and is considered the perfecter of the steam engine. Here is also a memorial of Charles Morrison, who knew something of electric telegraphy in 1753.

The genuine autographs of Byron, Burns, Scott, Dickens, Jennie Lind, and many famous writers of England, Ireland and Scotland were seen at this library and they form an interesting study.

Mr. Swan said there were thousands of tons of sugar refined here. I did not have time to visit the great ship-yards that almost line the Clyde from here to Glasgow, and which make the Clyde so famous, wherever ships sail. They build ships of iron, steel and good wood; great ships to carry soldiers and cannon, ladies and gentlemen, herds, oil, fuel, lumber, and all kinds of merchandise over sunny seas and icy seas.

Mr. Swan is an active, intelligent man who, when a boy, had traveled quite extensively in the United States, and he retains a vivid recollection of many of our busy and beautiful places in America. Bidding my kind friends good-bye, I took the train for Paisley.

I remained here but a short time and found it a busy and dusty city of say sixty thousand inhabitants. There were some large and substantial buildings, both public and private. Here are great shawl and thread factories, and some one said there were thousands of women employed in the works here. It is noon and the streets are full of little boys and girls with books, slates, school-bags, etc., talking, laughing, "tagging" and disputing, same as in America. In the dress and surroundings of one little boy I could see the care and labor of a kind, thoughtful, poverty-menaced mother, whose loving spirit encircled her child, there in the street, like a guardian angel. He was a pale, thoughtful child with a cheap muffler about his throat, and his clean clothes were neatly patched. I presume, if we could see clearly we should discern more spirits than bodies in this world.

Paisley is the birth-place of the poet Tannahill and of the ornithologist Wilson. A gentleman said: "Two miles over that way is Kilbarchan, one of the most primitive places in Scotland. The houses are still thatched with straw there, and hand-loom weaving is still in vogue, and there is where a celebrated piper was born, mentioned by Burns." Paisley has a fine museum.

Now I am at Glasgow again, waiting for a train to Dumfries. In my last letter I mentioned the stone bridges over the Clyde at Glasgow, but I did not mention the handsome suspension bridge which also spans the river here. At St. Enoch's station I purchase a ticket for Dumfries for six shillings and ten pence, which shows the distance to be eighty-two miles. At 2:30 p. m. our train runs out of Glasgow toward the south of Scotland.

# CHAPTER XXX.

### SCOTLAND: DUMFRIES.

BY TRAIN FROM GLASGOW TO DUMFRIES—THINGS SEEN—DUMFRIES—HISTORY—LOCATION—CHURCHES—WALK WITH MR. SHARP—FAMOUS NAMES—ROBERT BURNS; HIS DWELLING, HIS ALE HOUSE, HIS STATUE, HIS CHURCH, HIS ARM-CHAIR, HIS MAUSOLEUM, HIS POETRY, HIS ADMIRERS—CLYDESDALE HORSES—OLD CHURCHES—BRIDGE SIX HUNDRED YEARS OLD—FINE RAILWAY STATION—VIADUCT OVER RAILWAYS, ETC.

At 2:30 p. m. I left Glasgow for Dumfries, which is in the lowlands of Scotland, not many miles north of Carlisle, England. We crossed the Clyde and ran by great stone buildings and tall chimneys and now we are out in the country, rushing through fields and villages, through cuts in rock and cuts in sand, over creeks and viaducts, through meadows and groves, and run among the hills.

We stop but seldom, and rush with such speed as scarcely allows us to read the names of the stations. At 2:45 we pass a large stone building; girls, girded and bare-headed, are returning from dinner to their work. The factory hands have dinner between 2 and 3 p. m. and breakfast between 9 and 10 a. m., as I have already mentioned.

Here is Kilmarnock, a large town by a big creek; fine cemetery, nice farm country around. Boys from school enter my compartment. They are good-looking and well-dressed, but full of mischief, noise and romp. Here is Mauchline, not a large town, only middling farming country, full of groves and trees; run over a high bridge and look down into a deep glen full of rocks and trees. One high, square, perpendicular rock covered with trees, in the centre of the dark ravine, looks like a hanging garden.

Now, 3 o'clock; must do something, so I will count what I see for an hour. We passed eighty-nine fields of oats, fourteen pieces of woodland, seventy fields containing cows and other cattle, nineteen fields containing sheep, run under thirty-one viaducts and over eight bridges, through one tunnel and by five towns, passed six stations, run through eighteen sand cuts and four rock cuts.

Now we see high lands and low, green meadows. Now we sweep down a little valley along a small, blue river with smooth, green banks. Yonder are fine, green woods, and, away above, see those high and beautiful mountains, clad in brown and silver, motionless, silent, solemn, smooth yet irregular, resembling the backs of great camels and elephants.

We halt at Thornhill and nine big, good-natured farmers enter the compartment, and, of course, I am not alone; in fact, I hardly have elbow room to write. I nearly always managed to get a seat by the glass door or window so I could easily look out upon the country through which the trains ran. I asked, "Has there been a fair here?" and was answered: "No; it is show day." "What kind of a show?" I asked, and was told "A cattle show." Now our good train runs rapidly, and soon we halt in the old town of Dumfries.

Having letters to George Sharp and Charles Lennon, friends of Charles Graham, of Scranton, Pa., I called on Mr. Sharp at his office, near the fine, large station, where he is engaged as Superintendent of Locomotives on the Glasgow and South Western Railway. Mr. Sharp is a middle-aged man, of excellent habits, and is active in body and mind. He resides in a pleasant cottage on an eminence near and overlooking the railway, the viaduct, the station, and a considerable portion of the town. He has a pleasant family of wife, daughter and sons. His daughter, Miss Marion Elizabeth, rendered good, cheering music for us on the piano, and also some sweet old Scotch airs on the harmonium. The courteous treatment and careful hospitality received at the hands of this kind family was "like good news from a far country."

Dumfries and Maxwelltown, which closely adjoin, contain about twenty-three thousand inhabitants. It is also an ancient place, and is noted in history as the scene of some desperate struggles between the English and Scots. It is also noted as the seat of some dark tragedies, and brave deeds of religious reformers. It is pleasantly located on the river Nith. It contains a few fine old churches and a number of educational and benevolent institutions.

I took a walk with Mr. Sharp and he pointed out near his own residence, on a pleasant eminence, the house where resides the widow Aitken, a sister of the famous writer, Thomas Carlyle.

Sir James Anderson, of telegraph fame, did live here and has a sister here still. Miss Brown, the great-grand-daughter of Robert Burns, lives here.

Robert Burns, the famous poet, passed his last years in this town, and his remains lie in a mausoleum in St. Michael's church cemetery.

The station on the Glasgow and South-Western Railway here is a good, large and convenient stone station. It is double, having ticket-offices, waiting-rooms, cloak-rooms, lunch-rooms, etc., on each side of the tracks, and overhead are bridges for passengers to pass from one side to the other above the tracks and trains. Just below the station there is a broad, lengthy and handsome cut-stone viaduct, which carries the old turnpike on a level over all the tracks. In High street we see Burns' statue. It is a fine one and on the pedestal we see inscribed favorite lines from his best poems.

Now we come to the Sands, an open or public place by the river Nith, where horse fairs and shows are held. There was a fair to be held there the next week, and already the merry-go-rounds in the form of beasts, birds and fishes, accompanied by steam-power and music and other features of out-door show life, had been set up and the place was gay and noisy as a carnival. Near this point is the old stone bridge over the Nith, which has stood, they say, about six hundred years. It is used now only by foot passengers.

We went and saw the modest little two-story house

where the poet Burns lived and died, having acquired a name which now encircles the globe as one of nature's own true poets. He died in his thirty-seventh year, comparatively a young man. His wife, Jean Burns, outlived him thirty-eight years and died in the same house in 1834. We also visited the public house which he frequented, perhaps too much, and were shown the old arm chair in which he sat and sipped and smoked. The chair is locked in a small closet in the corner of the room, but I was permitted to sit in it. We were also shown his punch bowl, snuff box, etc. These relics of Burns are visited by hundreds of people every year.

The respect paid to the memory of Burns and things pertaining to him here is remarkable and almost amounts to worship. He is looked upon as one of Nature's poets, priests and kings, and Nature is almost, if not quite, worshiped through him by many. He seems ever to have stood for the freedom of speech and for the needy and oppressed. We also went into St. Michael's churchyard and entered, with the sexton, Burns' mausoleum and stood over his dust and saw the fine marble statue where the muse throws over him a mantle as he pauses by his plow. His sons and wife also are interred here. I handed the sexton a shilling, and the six-pence he gave me in change I still keep as a relic of Burns' burial-place. We entered the fine old church and were shown where Burns sat when at church. In the cemetery we were shown the tomb of the martyrs who lost their lives for religious liberty.

In one portion we were shown where four hundred and twenty victims of Asiatic cholera were buried, who died in 1832, from the 15th of September to the 27th of November. Forty-four died in one day. This was when the town was yet quite small. In our walk we passed through Kennedy & Co.'s greenhouses and flower gardens, and saw many varieties of lovely flowers arranged in beautiful and pleasing forms. I met Mr. Charles Lennon, who was also in the employ of the railway company. Here, as well as at Glasgow and Greenock, I noticed that the draft horses were large, well-formed and powerful, not so heavy as the Liverpool horses, yet I was told they were more hardy and solid, which, however, is a question in my mind. These are the Clydesdale horses, which have a great reputation in Scotland, as they also have in Canada and the United States, where many of them are taken.

We entered St. Michael's church, and found it a spacious, convenient and handsome edifice, with windows beautiful with pictures in stained glass. This church was built in 1178, by "William the Lion," and rebuilt in 1746. On a large tablet we saw the names of all the ministers from 1562 to the present. Rev. Mr. Paton is pastor now. In the churchyard already mentioned are hundreds of handsome and interesting monuments, ancient and modern. I noticed three fine church edifices, St. Mary's, St. Michael's, and Greyfriars, belonging to the church of Scotland, also a fine Catholic church, with schools and benevolent institutions connected.

Dumfries I found to be a pleasant and interesting place, finely located near a beautiful little river spanned by a very ancient, gray-stone bridge, with ranges of picturesque mountains in the background. The people were kind, industrious, orderly and neighborly, and fairly enterprising.

# CHAPTER XXXI.

## FROM SCOTLAND TO IRELAND.

LEAVING DUMFRIES—RIDING OVER MOUNTAINS, AMONG LAKES AND MEADOWS—MOUNTAINS DECKED WITH PURPLE HEATHER, WHITE GRANITE AND SHEEP—OLD STRANRAER—HOME-LIKE HOTEL—LEAVING STRANRAER—LOCH RYAN—SHIPS, SEA-BIRDS AND GREEN HILLS—LOCOMOTIVES RUSH DOWN TO THE SHIPS—THE IRISH SEA "LIKE A LAKE"—SHIPS LIKE SPIRITS ON ETERNITY'S OCEAN—MRS. SCOTT SIDDONS—AT LARNE, IRELAND.

I had intended while in Scotland to visit Dundee, Balmoral and Aberdeen, but time did not admit of these doubtless pleasant visits and I left Dumfries at 2:48 p. m., enroute for Ireland via Stranraer. I have a clear recollection of the trip, but I can perhaps do no better at this time than to copy from my note-book what I wrote as the train rushed through a wild, romantic country.

We ran out of Dumfries, along the river, through a rock cut, then over a high viaduct, and look down upon a fine cottage in a green vale full of gardens of flowers and vegetables and small lakes in which float white ducks; through another deep rock-cut and pass up a ravine with green mountains on each side—fine scenery—flocks of white sea-birds and crows in plowed field; on the other side a bold, bare mountain. Pass Killywhan, a rural place. Large flock of sheep and large drove of cattle. Some of the cattle were yellow and wild-looking, with long, sharp horns. Fields black with crows and white with sea-gulls. Now on highlands; mountains all around; men building bridge over creek; marshy; turnips; breckons are brown; stonewalls. Here is Dalbeattie, quite a town; scenery like Dallas and Jackson, Pa. Going on through rugged scenery we came to Castle Douglas, an interesting and picturesque old town on high ground. The hills and farms and stonewalls in the neighborhood make me think of Jackson township in Pennsylvania. By the way, this is where our friend Monighan came from, the superintendent of the Conyngham farms at Trucksville.

Going on we see a tall monument on a distant hill, but did not learn whose it is. Now we run for miles through a green valley among highlands, where many lakes are chained amid meadows, and arrive at Parton. Proceeding we find ourselves on brown, rough highlands; lake, clear river, flocks of sheep; bald mountains dotted with gray granite, brown breckon (brakes) and white sheep. Here is lake Scallan, barren mountains all around—few houses to be seen in this region. Brown, boggy meadow runs to and over high smooth hill, while granite mountains stand on the other hand. What scenery! barren for miles and miles, like traveling among Penobscot peaks. Now the mountains are smooth, beautiful and clad in purple heather. We see hundreds of sheep on the high mountain sides, looking like flakes of snow and they are also in the vale by the creek and they scamper away as the train rushes by. There broad waters gleam on the left and we see boats and ships; this is Wigton bay. We pass Creeton and run through a low, green country and come to Newton Stewart which is quite a town. We run on through meadows, turnip fields, moorlands and where many cords of peat are piled up.

Here is Kirkgowan, a village; more stonewalls, sheep, marshes, stacks of peat and low stone houses thatched, cattle and sheep. Man and boy in cart drawn by one horse. Here come two ladies dressed in black apparently been at a funeral. Here is Glen Luce, a quaint old town, chimneys smoking where suppers are being prepared, for it is 5:20 p. m.; Bay of Luce is in view. Pleasant evening, atmosphere like Indian summer in America. Now we reach Dunragit, a village, where we see many thatched stacks. I was told this is a great dairy district and there is a creamery here where butter is made on the "Danish System." Here is Castle Kennedy, where I see for the first time the "cotton aster," a vine by the wall of the station, having the deepest green leaves and the richest red berries in profusion. It is very rich and beautiful in appearance.

Going on, we arrive at 5.50 p. m. in ancient Stranrear, on Loch Ryan, where a line of sidewheel steamers run across the Irish Sea to Larne in the north of Ireland. A number of 'buses stood at the station and

I took the one going to Meikle's hotel. We passed along narrow and winding streets and saw at least one house thatched with straw. Arriving at the hotel which was a homelike, unpretending house, I was ushered into a clean, airy hallway where a number of neatly attired young women stood waiting or attending to various duties. They wore white lace caps with a black bow at the side. One said, "Come this way," and I passed into a pleasant, carpeted room where sat tables filled with eatables, side-boards, writing-desks, chairs and sofas. Another said, "Your number will be twelve, will you see your room?" I went up to a neat, little room next to the roof, and an apology was offered me that a party of noted people had taken nearly all their rooms and claimed their services. "Your bill will be two shillings six-pence for your room, two shillings for tea, two shillings for breakfast and six-pence each way for the 'bus. Breakfast at half-past six, you will be called at six."

The place seemed much like a home reception or donation party. I went down to the eating and waiting room and helped myself to cold meat, tongue, tea, toast, bread, scones, preserved strawberries, etc. After eating heartily I finished a letter to the *Telephone* and carried it to the post-office by a winding street which was wide at some places and narrow at others. The streets were dimly lighted and somewhat noisy with romping youths and I soon returned to the hotel. I retired at 9:45 and rested well.

September 22d, up at 6 a. m.; 6:25, waiting for breakfast—6:50 left Meikle's Hotel and now, 7 a. m., am on board a fine sidewheel steamer named Princess Beatrice. Near us at a pier is another steamer, the Princess Louisa, length two hundred and forty-five feet. Loch Ryan, a tidal lake, is ten miles long and is as "smooth as glass." The morning is cloudy. Yonder is Stranraer with a few spires and towers and a few high chimneys—about twenty boats and ships are lying idly; sea-birds quietly moving on water and in the air.

People come on board, men, women and children. The train, a half hour late, comes rushing right out on to the pier and soon there is a busy scene; more people, all ages, sexes and classes come on board. See the strange shaped trunks and boxes; made of tin, wood, willow, leather and canvas, black, white, brown, etc. The bell rings, the engine throbs, the wheels revolve and the air begins to freshen on deck. Our boat strikes out for the open sea and runs between long, high hills that are blue with the mist and smoke. On the hill yonder stands the monument to Sir Andrew Agnew; here to the right are the pleasant estates of Sir William Wallace.

Now, 10 a. m., the hills of Ireland are plainly seen through the haze and I stand by the great red funnel to keep warm, for our speed gives a smart breeze; but the sea is smooth as a lake in calm weather. A few ships are in sight, moving silently like spirits on eternity's ocean. On the trip I had noticed a bright, erect, elastic, red-cheeked, black-eyed woman in a plaid wool overdress, walking on deck, accompanied by a fair-complexioned young lady of a Swedish type of beauty. A gentleman said, "That is Mrs. Scott Siddons, the actress, and her maid." Indeed! She was the only person that fixed my attention on the voyage, and she no doubt has earned the fame she enjoys. She carried her satchel quite self-reliantly.

Now I have reached old Larne and set my feet on Ireland's soil for the first time.

# CHAPTER XXXII.

### IN IRELAND

INTERESTING COUNTRY — VELVET MEADOWS — CLEAR LAKES — PICTURESQUE MOUNTAINS — LEAVING LARNE — ENROUTE TO GIANT'S CAUSEWAY — PORT RUSH — DR. ADAM CLARKE'S MONUMENT — THE JAUNTING CAR — THE ELECTRIC CAR — THE MOWING MACHINE ON A CLIFF — DUNLUCE CASTLE — STRANGE IMAGES AND SHAPES — OCEAN WAVES MOANING IN CAVES — DINED NEAR THE GREAT FREAK OF NATURE.

Many readers have waited with patience to read what the writer thinks and says of Ireland, one of the most interesting portions of our world, politically and socially. My friends must remember that three days is far too short a time for an ordinary man to come to correct conclusions in regard to the financial, social, climatic and religious status of so large an island as Ireland, which covers an area of thirty-two thousand five hundred and twenty-one square miles, and contains five millions of people. Seventy-four per cent. of her territory is productive.

Great questions of law and religion, right and wrong, and government have agitated Ireland and claimed more or less of the world's attention for ages. It is exceedingly difficult for us to give up or divest ourselves of inherited property, vices or ideas. While many in Ireland and elsewhere doubt if it would be advantageous for her to be entirely divorced from British supervision, for my part I would be pleased to see her secure perfect freedom, in a manner just to all most concerned, for I am inclined to believe her condition would be improved thereby. Most likely then would hope take the place of despondency, and enterprise take the place of indifference, and national pride would move toward peace, order and beauty.

You have heard of the geographical beauty of Ireland, her emerald waters, her green meadows, her high, picturesque mountains and bright, romantic lakes and her handsome cities. I also add my assent to the beauty and charm of these things. I saw her meadows green with velvety grass, her fields white with bleaching linen and her mountains robed in white mist, but clouds of steam and smoke from factories and mines did not cover her valleys or mantle her hills. When you placed your ear close to this great human hive, the hum and buzz was not so pronounced nor assuring as that of England. The cities of Ireland were elegant enough, containing handsome buildings, fine parks and beautiful women, but the country, or farming portions were not nearly so well kept and tilled as was England. The difference was just the difference between a farm leased and a farm tilled by the owner.

I am now at Larne, on the north-eastern coast of Ireland. It is quite a busy little sea-port. A few ships lie in the harbor. We take the train going toward Belfast. I took a third-class car and found it like third-class in France, no cushions and not nearly so comfortable as third-class in England. Five good-looking and neatly-dressed women entered our compartment. The train runs out with the sea on one side and the cliffs on the other. Now we cross a long embankment which is thrown up across a wide sea marsh, and we see many sea-birds on the green islands and rocks, and here are great heaps of yellow seaweeds decaying on the shore. We pass a number of thatched houses. Now on the right are seen green mountains and nearer among trees, in a green vale is seen a handsome villa, probably the home of wealth and authority. Here is Ballygarry, a rural place, but we did not stop. We pass meadows, hills and trees, a country looking like Huntington, between Harveyville and Waterton. We pass Whitehead and arrive at Carrick-Fergus; pleasant little town; many thatched houses, one spire and one castle; green country, bay on one side, farms on the other; geese, ducks, hens and Guinea-fowls.

Now we reach Carrick-Fergus Junction, seven miles north of Belfast, in County Antrim, near Belfast Loch, and opposite are the green hills in County Down. Here we alight and wait for a train to Port Rush, which is in the north, near Giant's Causeway. The station-master, Thomas Bunting, was kind and attentive. Going on we come to Doagh, a small town. Some of the houses are white as lime, and thatched. Fine, green country sloping gently from the sands of the sea, away to high, green hills; turkeys, sheep, turnip and potato fields, hedges, fields and stacks. Here is Dunadry, where we see acres of linen on grass bleaching. There is a fine mansion in a beautiful park full of trees, knolls and ponds. Now we come to Antrim, surrounded by a fine, green country, and there among trees, we see a tall, round gray stone tower or castle.

We pass Cookstown Junction, Ballymena, Cullybackey, Killagan and come to Coleraine in County Derry. This a pleasant old town of considerable size. Ballymena was also quite a large, busy town. Going on I counted at least five stone houses in ruins. Here is Port Rush, a little sea-port in the north of Ireland and seven miles from the Giant's Causeway.

Here Dr. Adam Clarke was born, and within a few years a monument has been erected to his memory. It is about the size and form of the Wyoming monument, say sixty feet high and of gray granite. Here is where I first saw a real jaunting car, which is a two-wheeled vehicle drawn by one horse, with room for the driver and four passengers, two on one side and two on the other side, over the wheels, sitting back to back. The drivers urged us to go with them, saying we could go here and there, stopping where we pleased and returning when we pleased, but we nearly all chose to go to the Causeway by the electric railway.

Yes, it did seem to be somewhat remarkable that my first ride by electricity should be in the "Black

North" of Ireland  There an iron rail, about three feet from the ground, ran along by the track and our car put out her hands clad in steel gloves and the electric current was communicated and we ran quite rapidly, the metal hands sliding on the side rail near our car where we could often see the flashing of electricity.

As we approached the Causeway, one of Nature's great and curious works, we heard a familiar sound, and looking, saw a mowing machine cutting the second crop of clover on the cliff. Yonder is the blue sea with only a few silent sails in sight; the country is rugged, quiet and solemn-looking and not densely peopled. We ride along on the cliffs by the ruins of old Dunluce Castle and look down upon the sea and notice the singular and grotesque shapes in which the rocks and perpendicular face of the cliffs have been fashioned by the action of wind and waves and tides.

Many caves, caverns and deep pits abound where the solemn, restless waves of Old Ocean are always resounding; caves in which explorers may go in boats and look for strange shapes, places and things.

Yonder, two miles away, we see the farther point of the circular cliff which bounds the wonders of the Giant's Causeway. The cliff there is about four hundred feet above the level of the sea and it seems to be upheld by lofty columns standing on five receding plateaux, one above the other. Now we alight near the Causeway. About the only buildings are two or three good-sized and modern-looking hotels.

It is after 4 o'clock p. m., and, having little or nothing to eat since leaving Stranraer, in Scotland, I enter the finest looking hotel and have dinner before I walk out with Guide Stewart Dixon.

## CHAPTER XXXIII.

### IRELAND: FROM GIANT'S CAUSEWAY TO DUBLIN.

GIANT'S CAUSEWAY—A BEAUTIFUL AND WONDERFUL FREAK OF NATURE—FORTY THOUSAND COLUMNS OF STONE, CUT BY NATURE, ON THE SHORE OF THE SEA—"BLACK NORTH"—WAVE-CUT ROCKS—IN A CAVE—WALKING OVER PENTAGON AND HEXAGON COLUMNS—THE WISHING CHAIR—FINN M'CUE—FINGAL'S CAVE—FAMOUS NAMES—GOING TO BELFAST—FINE CITY—FOGGY MORNING—OFF FOR DUBLIN—INTERESTING PLACES SEEN—THE ROUND TOWERS—ARRIVE AT DUBLIN.

Probably all our readers have heard of the Giant's Causeway, in the north of Ireland, for it has been pictured and described in our geographies and histories for generations; yet, I will try to give a brief description of it as it appeared to me.

When the traveler reaches this famous locality he will not exclaim, "Sublime!" "Awful!" "Terrible!" "Grand!" No; it is not sublime and overpowering like Niagara; nor awful, like the Mammoth Cave; nor grand and majestic, like Yosemite, with her gay-colored walls of perpendicular rock towering into the clouds. Yet it is curious, interesting, beautiful and wonderful; a place where Nature appears to have tried her hand at rearing pillars of cut stone; where Nature, weary of working in rough rock, had resolved to set up myriads of chiseled columns on the floor of the sea and thus make a causeway from Ireland to Scotland.

This freak of nature is located on the northern shore of Ireland, where sea-waves always either roar or murmur, where billows are forever beating up and down the rocks; for Old Ocean is always attending to business and gives to a million brooks the power to "go on forever, forever." Industrious, restless Old Ocean, whose heaving tides cause Earth's heart to pulsate, and whose foaming, wind-tossed billows sweeten the breath of the world, what a pattern of healthful activity thou art! This region is locally known as the "Black North" of Ireland, a term as honorable there as the phrase "Black Republican" is respectable in the United States.

This curious work of Nature, as above mentioned, is on the shore of the sea where a cliff about four hundred feet high forms a semi-amphitheatre. Until you come to the brow of this cliff you see nothing remarkable. Standing at the edge of the cliff, you look down and see where dashing waves have carved the rocks into strange forms, that stand like monsters, animals and stacks in the water and on shore. The guide points out the stacks, the monkey rock, the giant's saddle, the organ, the loom, the gate, the giant's head, face and nose, the Scotchman's bonnet, the giant's grandmother climbing the hill, camel rock, etc. I went with the guide down a narrow and rugged path until we came near these objects and could trace at least a faint resemblance to the things named.

We entered a cave, which was forty-five feet high, three hundred and fifty feet deep and twenty feet wide and contained fourteen feet of water. It resounded with the dash of the waves as any cavern or mine does when agitated by sounds. The guide said there were twenty-seven of these caverns, many of them accessible by boat, but care must be observed to not let the tide come up and seal you in certain ones of of them. He also said, "We have only six feet rise and fall of tide here unless it is increased by a storm of wind." My guide's name was Stewart Dixon, a kind, honest man, looking much like many people I could find in Luzerne county. The man he made me think of most frequently is George White, of Lehman. I could scarcely refrain from calling him George. I think I did a time or two and then explained to him.

Now, we have come to the most wonderful part of the place—the Causeway. How shall I describe it? Your geographies give a good picture of it. The rock beneath our feet and on either hand resembles in form a great honey-comb. Imagine a pavement composed of forty thousand pillars of stone, set upright and extending along the shore and into the sea. At the edge of the water these pillars are even with the earth, but as we get away from the sea they begin to rise in irregular steps until in some places they are nearly forty feet high. These pillars vary in size, from nine to, say eighteen inches in diameter, and might average fourteen inches in diameter, and they have from three to nine sides and are set close together. They fit so well together that you could not put a fine knife-blade between them. They are chiefly pentagon, hexagon and heptagon, that is, five-sided, six-sided and seven-sided. I was shown one nonagon, nine-sided, one three-sided and one four-sided. There are no two alike. Their sides were straight, but of unequal length. It is not known how deep they sink into the earth. The longest one visible is sixty-three feet. These pillars of unequal size and angles fit water-tight and appear to prove how nature abhors a vacuum and delights in the union of apparently diverse objects or designs. These pillars have seams, points at which they easily unjoint, and my guide showed me the longest piece without a seam, and it was three feet four inches long. The guide said, "You must sit in the 'Wishing Chair' and make a wish." I sat where one of the columns had been broken out and left a circle standing on all sides but one. It was a solid, easy arm chair. What did I wish? Why, I wished to see Percy and all my friends again in health. At one place in the side of the cliff the columns stood and resembled a pipe organ. The guide said, "When that organ plays the whole place turns around three times!"

There are many legends told of the place, and some people appear to believe it is a work of man. The main legend is that Finn McCue, the Giant, lived here and attempted to build a bridge or causeway to Scotland. Some men think this singular structure of rock extends under the sea to Fingal's Cave in Scotland, where a similar formation is found. On the outside the stone is a yellowish brown, but when broken it is a dark slate color.

While some of our readers have seen these singular pillars of stone in their native place, others have seen good samples at the front gate of Mr. Richard Sharp's pleasant door-yard, on West River street, Wilkes-Barré, Pa. Mr. Sharp brought those pieces from there a few years ago. He has four pieces, each about a foot long, two pentagon and two hexagon.

I have given considerable time and space to this curious work of nature, but if even a few school-children receive clearer ideas of the Giant's Bridge or Causeway, I shall not regret the effort. That which has claimed the attention of scholars and travelers for ages may well claim our thought for a few minutes.

I am now ready to go to Dublin, via Belfast.

From this northern district of Ireland have gone many families to America who have made great fortunes and gained honorable names. Among these names are those of A. T. Stewart, George H. Stuart and the Greeleys; the Conynghams, McClintocks, Norrises, Steeles, Blacks, Johnsons and Browns, of Luzerne county, Pa., also hail from this part of Ireland. Our electric car, which was comfortably full of ladies and gentlemen, left the Causeway about 6 o'clock in the afternoon. The evening was clear and pleasant, and resembled an Indian summer day in America. As we reached Port Rush the red sun was setting, and it threw a beautiful glow upon the bay. Along the shore three miles of sandy beach stretches from

Port Rush toward the Causeway, making it a pleasant place for walking and bathing. Soon a train on the Belfast and Northern Counties Railway comes and we step aboard.

The Irish people are good company, as a rule, while traveling, for they talk with and chaff each other freely and are ready to respond to the inquiries of strangers. We traveled back over a good portion of the way we had come that day and arrived at Belfast about 9 o'clock p. m.

Belfast is a handsome, well-built city of about two hundred and twenty thousand inhabitants. I took a seat on top of a street-car and rode down a broad, well-lighted street, lined with good, substantial buildings of brick and stone, chiefly four or five stories high. I put up at the Royal Avenue Temperance Hotel and was kindly cared for. Belfast, as a manufacturing city, is noted for the production of fine linen goods.

Linen Hall is a large and handsome building. The postoffice is a neat and substantial building of gray granite. Not far from the Great Northern Railway station a large and handsome business building was being erected. It was of light-colored stone, with polished red stone columns supporting and ornamenting the several stories from the pavement to the roof. Its appearance was decidedly rich and substantial and evinced good taste and enterprise. I was sorry my time did not permit me to remain a day or two in this famous city in the north of Ireland.

I left Belfast at 7 o'clock in the morning. The morning was foggy, much like an autumn fog in the Wyoming valley, Pennsylvania. Now we are out in the green, park-like country, but it is so foggy we cannot see far. It is one hundred and thirteen miles from Belfast to Dublin, and we expect to reach Dublin about 11 o'clock.

Our train halts at Lisburn, and, going on, we pass through Moira, Lurgan, Portadown and Scarva. At 8:30 a. m. it is still foggy. Here is Goragh Wood, and we pass through some rugged scenery and find some pretty good farms and lots of stonewall. We saw quite a number of small stone houses in ruins. Now the fog begins to lift and we see fine mountains in the distance. There is a hamlet of thatched stone houses standing among trees and stonewalls, with blue smoke curling up. It is a pretty sight. Here are green meadows and large fields of potatoes.

Now we come to Dundalk, quite a pleasant town. My traveling companion, a young man from the potteries of Staffordshire, England, said: "Dundalk is the only town in the United Kingdom lighted wholly by electricity." We pass Castle Bellingham and Dunleer, small towns. Now we run through a region of bog and peat lands and see many cords of peat laid up to dry.

Now we run over the river Boyne on a high bridge and enter old Drogheda. A fellow-passenger said: "The battle of the Boyne was fought here." I saw about twenty-five ships and steamboats moored along the wharfs. I counted five or six tall spires and towers in the place and saw the Castle, a circular and picturesque structure. It is a pleasant place, and, as we move on, we see fine green fields with hedges slope gradually away into the sea or into the fog. Yonder are men with carts, on the broad sands by the sea, gathering sea-weeds for fertilizing purposes. I did not see many sheep in Ireland. September 23—many fields of oats are still out. I saw a good many cattle as we rode along.

Now we enter old Balbriggan, "where the Balbriggan hose originated." The sea murmurs on our left and hose factories click and rattle on our right. Here is a small harbor and a light-house.

Going on we saw a round tower of gray stone, say twenty-five feet in diameter and a hundred feet high, standing among the trees. A gentleman said, "There are many of these round towers, especially in the south of Ireland. It is not known who built them. The rock and cement are very hard. They will last forever. The walls are one and half yards thick." They are each about one hundred feet high and have pointed, conical tops or roofs of stone. I was much surprised to see these stone towers looking in such good order and to hear that history did not tell by whom they were built. I could hardly believe they had been built more than two thousand years.

Now we run over an embankment, for a mile or two, with sea water each side of us. Now we are amid beautiful park lands, trees and mansions and good roads. My companion, pointing to a fine mansion pleasantly located, said, "There is Guinness' place. You have heard of Guinness, the brewer?" Now we rush into the great stone railway station, but my companion would not leave me until he had escorted me into grand, broad, monumental Sackville street, in the heart of beautiful and far-famed Dublin, Queen of the Emerald Isle.

# CHAPTER XXXIV.

DUBLIN — PLACES OF INTEREST AND BEAUTY.

IRELAND'S CHIEF CITY — POSITION, COMMERCE, ETC. — POPULATION — THE BUILDINGS — SACKVILLE STREET — FINE MONUMENTS — GRAND EDIFICES — GLASNEVIN CEMETERY — MARBLE CROSSES AND MEMORIALS IN COLONNADES — THE CIRCULAR VAULTS — O'CONNELL'S LOFTY, ROUND MONUMENT — PHŒNIX PARK — CARPET OF RAINBOWS SPREAD BY ARTISTIC GODS — WELLINGTON'S SUBLIME MONUMENT — THE CORSICAN CORPORAL HEART-BROKEN — RED COATS — ALONG THE QUAY — BEAUTIFUL WOMEN — WHITE HAIR AND FRESH, PINK CHEEKS — CROWNED WITH THE GLOW OF AN INDIAN SUMMER SUNSET — PIES, CAKES, CREAMS, COFFEES AND CANDIES, ON SACKVILLE STREET — SERVED BY LADIES INCOG. — GOOD BYE — "GOOD BYE."

When we speak of Dublin it causes us to think of Ireland; her geographical position, her climate, commerce, learning, eloquence poetry and her beauty, for Dublin is the chief city of Ireland. Dublin is situated on the eastern shore of Ireland, nearly opposite Liverpool, England. The Irish Sea tosses her one hundred and twenty miles of white-crested billows between these famous cities.

A gentleman told me that Dublin contained a

population of three hundred and forty-five thousand, and if the suburbs, which apparently naturally belong to her, were taken in, she would number half a million people. The river Liffey runs through the city and empties into the bay of Dublin, which is noted for its beauty of outline and general surroundings. The buildings of Dublin are chiefly of brick, four or five stories high, while the public buildings and many others are of gray stone.

Sackville street, (many are calling this O'Connell street, wishing to give it the name of an Irishman instead of an Englishman's name; but I saw the name Sackville still painted on the buildings, and the papers too, spoke of it as Sackville street; so it is difficult to decide how the name will stand in future years) is the broadest, finest street in the city. It is probably two hundred feet wide and has four street-car tracks laid through it. In the centre of this street I noticed some fine monuments, one to Lord Nelson, one to Daniel O'Connell and one to Sir John Gray. Nelson's is a lofty column, say one hundred and fifty feet high with the statue of the great naval hero standing on the top of it, while the names of the victories he won are inscribed on the sides of the base. O'Connell's monument, though not lofty, is very elaborate and handsome. The statue of the patriot and statesman is surrounded by a number of life-size figures and a statue representing liberty holding a scroll, points all classes up to him, and below at the corners sit four large and beautiful marble angels.

I saw a goodly number of handsome, elegant and

extensive buildings here, built of gray stone and resplendent and impressive with forests of lofty and graceful columns, arches, domes, towers, battlements, minarets and spires, porticoes, courts, etc. Among these were the Custom House, the Four Courts, the Postoffice, St. Patrick's Cathedral, Trinity College, City Hall, Dublin Castle, Bank of Ireland, etc. These buildings are worthy of description, for any one of them would add interest to a city of importance. The river Liffey is about two hundred feet wide and is spanned by nine fine and substantial stone bridges. I mounted to the top of a street-car and rode up Sackville street and went to Glasnevin Cemetery.

This cemetery covers one hundred and twenty acres and is one of the most interesting burial-places on earth. Here are miles of gravelly walks lined with evergreens and trees, where marble, cross-surmounted, crowned, rosetted and inscribed, stands in long colonnades to perpetuate the names of departed loved ones. The features most interesting to me were the vaults, placed in circles. I will try to describe them. Let the reader imagine a ditch twelve feet wide and twelve feet deep dug in the form of a circle about two hundred feet in diameter. Stone steps lead down into this circular avenue, and in the sides of these walls are iron doors and bars through which we can look in and see the caskets containing the remains of the dead. Over these family vaults, on a level with the earth, are handsome and elaborate monuments, statues, etc.

In the centre of this circle (for the earth is not taken out of the centre) stands the magnificent round stone monument to Daniel O'Connell. This grand round tower is one hundred and seventy-five feet high and about twenty-five feet in diameter at the bottom, and tapers to say twenty feet at the top. A man working near said: "The man that put up the lightning-rod stood on the cross without holding on with his hands. He was an Englishman, a 'steeple-jack,' and has since fallen and been killed at Manchester, England." Looking through a door into one of the vaults (I counted seventy vaults in this circle), I saw the coffin containing the remains of O'Connell.

There is another of these circles full of vaults, larger than the one above mentioned, and at the centre, instead of being a lofty monument there is a large open place excavated and it contains also a number of vaults. The vaults or tombs each contain from two to six coffins. These circles resemble flower-crowned islands, surrounded by fine pillars and statues of marble and granite, reared by the loving children of genius, ambition, taste and wealth.

I found my way to Phœnix Park. This is a beautiful and extensive park, diversified by hills, dales, fountains, flower gardens, green fields, walks, drives, museums, monuments and the Zoological Garden. I was told that it is the largest park in Europe. Here is where Lord Cavendish and Burke were murdered, and in that locality I gathered up a small handful of gravel stones, that when I returned to America I might look at a small portion of the famous Phœnix Park. The features which I most plainly remember are the beds, banks, mounds and gardens of flowers. Colors, modest and brilliant, blended in the most pleasing forms. It looked as if an artistic god had plucked scores of rainbows from the heavens and cast them at the feet of white marble angels to form a carpet for water nymphs, fairies and queens.

Here also is the massive and lofty monument to Wellesley, the "Iron Duke," Wellington, who met Napoleon the Great on the plains of Waterloo, and forming his hosts into squares, waited encircled by men and horses and bellowing cannon and multiplied lines of bayonets; and as the thunder of battle increased he stood with closed teeth and clenched fists, within those walls of flesh and blood ribbed with iron and steel and belching fire and smoke, until the glittering banners of haughty France trembled and fell: then the brave men who had set new stars in the heavens, shouted, while the silk-clad followers of the Corsican Corporal gave a sorrowful wail and fled, leaving their great military genius dazed and heartbroken on the field where his more than kingly ambition and worshiped plans of his brilliant life lay in ruins amid the gory and ghastly fragments of cruel War. For size, solidity and plain, solemn grandeur this monument surpasses anything I have yet seen.

It stands on a green table-land, which I approached by forty granite steps and walked to its base. The first layer of granite is about one hundred and twenty feet square at the base. There are a number of these bases or granite plateaux and at the height of say fifty feet, the plain, tapering monument of granite rises one hundred and fifty feet higher — two hundred feet in all—like a solid obelisk of granite, say thirty-two feet square where it sits upon the lofty base. High on the dizzy sides of this stern-looking memorial, are the chiseled names of twenty-eight great battles that the chieftain won.

Though I rather have a monument in human hearts and books and in poetry, still, if I were obliged to have one of granite, I should choose one like this, for it seems so like a symbol of strength and eternity.

As I returned from the park I saw many red-coated soldiers drilling in a field, and others were seen coming and going on the street, some mounted and some on foot. Here and in other large towns I noticed many policemen in dark blue, pacing to and fro at railway stations and about public buildings. They belong to the Queen's constabulary forces. I saw nothing riotous, but in a town or two I heard discordant shouts as the train left the place.

I walked down along the quay with Daniel Duffy, a pleasant, sociable man, a boiler-maker, who was out of employment, but he had evidently earned and saved some property, and was not fretting over a few days of rest. He pointed out the bridges and some important buildings and was very willing to answer questions.

I again entered Sackville street, late in the afternoon, and saw handsome women walking and riding. Perhaps all European travelers have heard that Dublin is famous for her handsome women. Many of those I saw were certainly the equals of any I had seen anywhere. One was tall and not too slender, fair complexion, bright brown hair, modest, intelligent eyes, movements graceful and queenly, but not haughty; others with portly, generous forms, with faces, in which appeared the color of roses, lilies, pearl and jet. I cannot say they looked like Irish, Scotch, English or Welsh, but will say that if you met them anywhere in America you would pronounce them very beautiful women. However, there are handsome women in all places I visited; but just now I am thinking of Dublin, Liverpool, Manchester, Edinburgh and Paris. But, why do I mention this subject, one so little understood by me and so foreign to my nature, taste and culture? Why? because, I know many men and boys have expected me to say at least a few words on this line. I might also say that the very handsome young lady with gray hair lives in Dublin, for I saw her there. I also saw one at Whitby. Indeed, Nature pleased and astonished me much by draping such hair around faces so fresh and young. In London, near gray, monumental and magnificent St. Paul's, I saw a young lady move down the crowded street as I stood by a pillar and wrote. She glanced at me, and we both evidently wondered; she at the cool, meditative foreigner, writing on a stranger's door-step as four roaring streams of walking and riding humanity rolled by between granite palaces; and I at her queenly form, fair features and charming color of hair, eyes and cheeks. Her hair was long and abundant, light brown, tinged with gold, as if she wore a crown composed of an Indian summer sunset. Eyes dark blue, cheeks like fair peaches, teeth of pearl and lips shell color. I thought, what a libel to call so lovely a creature an angel. Oh, you need not smile, it was not a case of love at first sight, for I do not believe in such a love, and if I had time I think I could prove to you that love at first sight is impossible.

It is drawing toward the hour for me to begin to sail the Irish Sea, and I enter a confectionery, or bakery, or coffee or tea house, or eating house on Sackville street and find gentlemen, ladies and children eating and drinking, served by scores of handsome, modest and well-dressed girls, just such as you might see attending tables at fairs in America. They seemed to be born ladies incog. The cakes, pies, tarts, buns, scones, rolls sandwiches, meat-pies, candies, nuts, tea, chocolate, coffee, cream, milk, etc., were all attractive in appearance and taste. As I left the place I said, "Good bye," and pleasant voices repeated the words, "Good bye."

# CHAPTER XXXV.

### DUBLIN, AND VOYAGE TO LIVERPOOL.

DUBLIN—POETRY AND ROMANCE—STEPHEN'S GREEN—THE OLD SINGER—WEALTHY FAMILIES REMODEL GREAT CHURCHES—DRIVING TIMID, SAUCY AND WILD DROVES FROM FIELDS INTO SHIPS—ON A BLANKET AMONG TRUNKS—DARKNESS SITS ON THE SEA—RUDE, FURLOUGHED SOLDIERS SING AND DANCE—ROCKED ON THE SEA FAR FROM GREEN HILLS—HOLLY-HEAD—GREAT RAILWAY STATION AT MIDNIGHT—CARS FULL OF DROWSY PASSENGERS—ARRIVE AT LIVERPOOL—FINDING MY FRIEND'S HOTEL—MILES OF GLOOMY BUILDINGS—MEN SLEEPING ON STONE BEDS—I SLEEP ON A BENCH—THE BUSY MORNING.

Before leaving Dublin I am impelled to write a few lines more pertaining to the fair city.

Dublin is an old and beautiful city, where for hundreds of years poetry, romance, commerce and war have had their champions and their episodes. I remember, when a child, of hearing a sweet singer sing of "Stephen's Green" in "Dublin City," and when I at last saw these places the old love-song seemed dearer than ever. The tongue of the gallant, flute-like singer has long mouldered in dust, and I shall probably never hear such singing again.

As I have already mentioned, Dublin has some elegant and substantial buildings. The Custom House is grand, rich and spacious. The Four Courts is a handsome, solid and extensive building, surmounted by a broad dome upheld by many lofty and graceful columns. The Bank of Ireland is a large and magnificent building surrounded by many tall and massive pillars. This building was built for the Irish House of Parliament.

As I rode with a citizen upon the top of a street-car he said, pointing to a fine house and grounds: "The Guinnesses live here. They are celebrated brewers of stout, porter, etc., and they are worth six million pounds. Two generations made it. Yes, they are an Irish family; pretty fair people, and liberal." Sir B. L. Guinness, brewer, in 1860-3 restored St. Patrick's Cathedral at a cost of about seven hundred thousand dollars, and Henry Roe, a distiller, recently restored Christ Church at an expenditure of about five hundred thousand dollars. The quay walls for about two miles along the Liffey are solid and handsome.

On my way to the vessel in which I am to cross the Irish Sea I come where men and boys, with earnest activity and shouting and waving of shillalahs, are driving cattle, sheep and swine upon the steamers, which are that evening to sail for England. It takes the cattle from a thousand hills to feed old England with her great, rushing, roaring, smoking cities. The sheep are timid and do not like to walk the ominous gang-plank into the dark fold under deck—a fold that undulates on the heaving bosom of the sea—so the drovers seize a few of the front ones by the forelegs and drag them roughly in. They do not squeal and roar like the dirty and saucy hog, but hang back and protest with great, big, fearful and almost tearful eyes, for they seem to think they will find no sweeter home than the one they are leaving in the Green Isle. The cattle low and bellow, and one long-horned and wild-looking steer has escaped and goes galloping through the streets, followed by shouting men and boys. Yes, this shipping of farm animals has interest at least for "land-lubbers," and there are many to witness the scene.

I inquire for the steamer and am directed on board of one, and for a small sum a sailor gives me a place where I may rest for the night, or until we come to Holly Head. There are many men, women and children of nearly all classes on the ship, also quite a number of soldiers, who have furloughs and are going to see friends in England. As the ship sails out from land through the twilight into the darkness that sits on the sea it becomes too chilly on deck, and some of us go below. I find my blanket and lie on a seat between the side of the ship and a high pile of trunks, and as the sea is smooth I venture to try to sleep, believing the trunks will not tumble. .

Now, some Welshmen sing very sweetly, what appear to be hymns and patriotic songs; but the soldiers seem to tire of this and try their hands, or rather their voices at singing, and soon the Welsh voices cease, and then we have a number of very odd, droll, or rather coarse, love, comic, humorous and alleged patriotic songs. And later the soldiers begin to dance and are quite rude and boisterous, apparently determined that no one shall sleep until they see "Merry England." Now and then one would peer into my dark corner, and one ordered the sleeper, I mean the writer, to come forth. I lay still, resolved, if needs be, to let them know that I was an American. This was a new experience, for while I was neither sick nor frightened, I ever found myself in a respectful, attentive and at least thoughtful mood on the dark, pathless sea at night; for there we were in a strange ship, managed by strange men, (men who should have kept better order) in the middle of the Irish Sea, far from the solid, green hills and the teeming cities of earth. Explosions, collisions, etc., were possible if not probable. Still the thoughtless (perhaps I should say jubilant) soldiers danced and caroused, apparently saying, "We take care of you on land, and you must take care of us on the sea." Probably the quaint love songs and the pathetic home ditties had something to do in causing one to see the position in a strong light of contrast.

At length the lights began to glimmer along the shores of England, and about midnight our ship ran into a dock at Holly Head, and then for a time all is tumult and a hurrying to and fro, and we find ourselves in one of those great English railway stations seeking the right trains, for some wish to go north, some east and others south. I, with a number of drowsy men and women, enter a compartment of a car in a Liverpool-bound train. We rushed for hours through the country, hamlets, towns and cities, stopping but seldom, and about 4 o'clock we ran into Liverpool, the great sea-port of England. Presuming we were not far from Dutton street, where lives Thomas Puckey, circumstances seemed to challenge me to find Puckey's boarding house without calling a cab. I started off in the direction of the water side of the city and found the place dark, silent and lonely, with miles of streets full of tall, gloomy buildings, and policemen few and far between. I asked the direction and distance, and found I was a long way from my destination and it was now too late for cabs. I hurried on and felt uncomfortable when I met anyone except a policeman. Here are men lying on the pavement in a gloomy place; will they spring up as I pass? I moved steadily on and was not molested. It made me think of the night I was walking in the wide woods at the foot of North Mountain, in Pennsylvania, when the foxes barked in the thicket. At last a policeman said: "You keep this street until you pass that tower and come to a hall, and then turn to the right and go through the yard by the Court House and go under an archway, and you will then come to a thoroughfare which will lead you to Dutton street." This somewhat indefinite direction I was able to follow and at last came to the tall, gloomy building which I recognized as Thomas H. Puckey's Cornish Hotel. I knocked, but all was silent. I knocked again and received no answer. I knocked vigorously and then heard voices within and above; finally Mr. Puckey appeared and let me in. Of course, "the boy" was sleeping soundly on a bench in the room near the door. It was 5 o'clock and Mr. Puckey had retired later than midnight, and his house was crowded with emigrants. I lay on a bench till half-past six, when I awoke to find the house all astir, some going, some coming, some cooking and others eating. I could remember mornings when I had felt better, but I braced up and ate some ham and eggs and drank some tea and began to pack my trunks to be in readiness to contend with baggage men, steamship clerks, sailors, tenders, ships, stewards and the rude, rolling waves of the stormy Atlantic.

# CHAPTER XXXVI.

## MEN AND THINGS BEYOND THE SEA.

FRAGMENTS COLLECTED—COINS OF TWO NATIONS—ENGLISH PEOPLE; READING, DRESSING, EATING, DRINKING, MANNERS—COOL—NO FLIES—PLEASURES AND PALACES—ONLY ONE AMERICA—HER STARRY BANNERS WAVE BENEDICTIONS IN DISTANT LANDS—GREAT BRITAIN'S HEADQUARTERS—KINGDOM'S ADMIRED—ACKNOWLEDGING THE STARS AND STRIPES—LONDON'S CROWDS; ADVERTISERS, WORKERS AND THE POORHOUSE—WEDDED TO A GREAT CITY—THIRTY THOUSAND HOUSES A YEAR—DREAM LIFE—A FIRE IN WHEATLEY'S FOURTEEN-ACRE STORE—SEVEN HUNDRED DROWNED, BUT NOT MISSED—STRANGE SAYINGS—ENTERPRISING BARBER—PRICES OF VARIOUS THINGS—TWO SWIFT MONSTERS—ENGLAND'S CHAMPION HORSE—DIED THAT NIGHT—DOVER'S FAT MAN.

In former chapters I have at least partially promised to mention the prices of some things, and also other matters that came under my observation. This chapter, then, may be composed chiefly of fragments and things taken almost at random from my note-books and my memory. In giving prices I shall call two cents equal to an English penny. The smallest coin really current in England is the copper half-penny, which is about the size and worth of our old-fashioned large copper cent. The next is the copper penny, somewhat larger than our fifty-cent piece; then comes the three-penny silver piece, then the six-pence, and so on up to the gold five-pound piece, coined first last year, the jubilee year. My cousins and friends gave me some farthing pieces and also two, four and five-penny pieces in silver, but these I understand are not now being coined. They gave me coins up to the crown piece, which is worth about one dollar and twenty-five cents.

Our English friends have heard of the "Almighty Dollar." In fact, they know most of our pet and slang phrases and most of our jests. I presume this knowledge is gathered from the almost omnipotent and omnipresent newspaper, for I found the English, all classes, to be much given to reading papers, and books, too.

The great, powerful and good-everywhere British coin is the gold sovereign, or pound piece, worth nearly five dollars. I presume they are called sovereigns because they bear upon one side, the head of the reigning sovereign, king or queen, as the case may be, at the time of their coinage.

I found people in England, and indeed throughout the British Isles, to be very generally well-dressed, and when you saw a church filled with people you saw a company well and neatly clad. Nearly every man you meet, except those engaged in rough labor, has his shoes (they call them boots if they are not low shoes) nicely blacked, and I found that when I met women they almost instantly glanced to my shoes to see if I were a gentleman.

In the families of the middle and lower classes the women blacken the shoes every morning, and they do not thank their own people nor visitors for going out with soiled shoes. It was quite a cross for me to have women blacken my "boots," but I learned to submit. Now, in this brave, free land I can polish my own shoes or pay ten cents to a bootblack in the streets for making them "shine."

I found the fashions in eating and drinking much the same as in America. As to drinking, I may say that nearly all the houses you enter in Britain will soon offer you wine, beer, ale or whiskey, and also something to eat. Still you travel for days without seeing a drunken man. They seem to think a welcome must be acted, not merely spoken.

I did not see a mosquito while abroad and was not annoyed by flies nor anything in that line.

I have told you how cool and delightful I found the weather in England, although they said it was the warmest, dryest summer they had had in many years. It was a wonder to me how wheat, rye and barley could ripen at all, and generally they do not ripen until September.

I like England, Scotland, Wales and Ireland, and was somewhat pleased with fair, fickle, fun and wine-loving France, which are grand countries in which to travel, visit, learn and rest, for there you may travel amid "pleasures and palaces" for a life-time. But there is no place like home; I mean great, grand, broad, beautiful, picturesque, wealthy, enterprising, intelligent, free America.

Yes, it is grand to wander amid palaces, parks, museums, monuments, castles and cathedrals crowded with rare works of art, things old, curious and beautiful, but when you are set to work you come to yourself and say: "I will arise and go home to America," that great land stretching from the great sea in the east to the vast ocean in the west.

I found people who work in these lands beyond the sea rather better off than I expected. In this age of intelligence, cheap papers and cheap, rapid travel, and wonderful machinery for production and destruction, men are not willing to starve or serve for naught. I believe that America blesses the earth, and that hopes and benedictions fall from her flags as they wave and flap in all parts of our world. The overworked and under-paid in many climes say, as the starry banner shakes its fair folds in the sky: "There is a happy land, though far, far away, where 'a man's a man for a' that,' and if I am too much oppressed here I will go there."

It is said that when a child throws a pebble into the mighty Pacific a wave circles out which never ceases one instant until all the seas of earth have trembled and heaved their broad, sweet breasts a little nearer the bright, loving heavens; so the words and work, and life and death of quite an ordinary person may, and often does, "do good like a medicine" in far-off lands, where great cities roar with business and fields glisten with harvests and bright sails undulate on the great deep. Yes, it is possible for even a child to bless continents and comfort and counsel kings.

England is a fair and rather level country, full of great cities, farms, workshops and railroads. Of course, she has low mountains in some parts.

England is the headquarters, or office, where Great Britain plans, drafts and legislates for the control of her great and widely-scattered islands, kingdoms and empire.

In the British Isles, I noticed that when men met, I mean machanics, farmers and laborers, as well as others, they were more respectful and deferential in their greetings and salutations among each other, than we are in America. The modulated tones, for instance, in which Mr. Waddington would say, "Good morning, Mr. Nicholson," or "Good afternoon, Captain Pearson," coupled with the appearance of well-brushed hat and coat and blackened shoes, would all impress an American favorably, and make him think more highly of his neighbors.

Scotland is picturesque, mountainous and well watered; grand cities sit on her plains and hills, and old castles lend romance to many a vale and craig. Her hospitality is too well known to need repetition here.

Wales is mountainous and full of mines, and some good farms lie at the foot of her hills, while enterprising cities sit on her sea shore. Her people were also found to be kind, industrious and enterprising.

Ireland is green, meadowy and mountainous, poetic and pathetic, and some fine cities crown her tides and sparkle in her fair landscapes.

France is fair, rather level, with many farms and workshops, and a great, grand, proud city that mighty leaders have enriched with the sweat and silver of her millions. Her people love fun, fashion, wine, beauty and glory.

A poor boy in London blackened my shoes at the street corner, and when he had finished he said: "You are not a man of this country." "No, Tommy, I belong to a bigger country than this, to America; the daughter that has out-grown the mother. I'll not go back on the Stars and Stripes if I am in the heart of the British realms." He replied, saying that he had come from Canada.

In this mighty sea of London humanity there are many idle men as well as many busy men, but many of the idle men are quite willing to work, as the following instances will show: A business man advertised for a man for a certain place and so many came to answer the advertisement that policemen were called to keep order; in fact, I was told that this was not a rare instance. When the boys and young men find the places are filled they will sometimes hoot and cast dirt and pebbles.

A man advertised for a carpenter and a man seized a paper from the press and ran to the place, but the place was filled before six o'clock. All this seems to prove how rich and poor are wedded to a great city.

Think of a city so great that she builds thirty thousand houses a year! Equal to about six Wilkes-Barrés each year! One old carpenter, when he heard a young man say something about old men crowding out others, laid down his tools and went to the poorhouse to end his days after three-score years of work. My informant said he had been a very intemperate man.

There is such an awful rush, and whirl, and roar, and glitter, and enchantment in a great city that I think some people never come to themselves, but live a false or dream-life, willing to go with the multitude to glory or destruction.

While there, a fire occurred in Wheatley's, in London, and burned for a day or two. Henry said: "His stores cover fourteen acres and is the largest business in the world controlled by one man. He has 5,000 employés, and keeps 300 horses delivering goods. He sells anything called for, and once supplied a man with a wife. His loss was about $2,000,000, and $15,000 reward was offered to find out the incendiary. Four men were killed and a number wounded at the fire, and the streets were blocked for a mile around, and still London hardly knew the fire was going on. Capt. Shaw, chief of the fire department, is an able and popular man. One of Wheatley's secrets of success is that he has a promenade free to ladies, whether they buy or not, amid flowers, fountains, seats, birds, monkeys, etc."

One does, indeed, see vast and endless crowds of people in London. Without the great armies of visitors, it would require about a year for the citizens of London to pass a given point, on a slow walk, walking by daylight, in single file. Cousin John said, "A ship went down in the Thames, drowning 700 persons, but I did not miss one and saw no one who had lost a friend. They were not missed from the crowd."

Many droll and strange sayings originate in London. One man at a public house asks for "half pint of mahogany chips, two door-steps, thick, and a Billingsgate pheasant," and they handed him coffee, bread and a red herring.

D. & M., "What do those letters mean? I see them in many places, even the little shoeblacks have them on their boxes." "They signify Day & Martin, men who have become very wealthy making and selling shoe polish. Day was a poor barber, who gave a half-crown to a poor, lame soldier, and the soldier, to show his gratitude, gave Day a receipt for making shoe blacking. Day took it and made some, but there were many other makes in the market, so he hired soldiers to go to all the dealers and ask for Day's blacking, and soon it was in great demand, and now Day and Martin are a powerful and popular firm."

One of the first things I bought in Liverpool was a silk umbrella, which cost about four dollars and a half. Good shoes cost nearly as much in England as with us, and hats and clothing something over two-thirds what they are here. Laborers on railroads were paid about seventy-five cents a day, some places a few cents less; locomotive engineers from seven to twelve dollars a week; stokers, or firemen, from about five dollars to nearly six dollars a week; station masters, from seven to twenty dollars a week; farm hands, from three dollars and a half to five dollars per week; prints, five to thirteen cents per yard; good black dress goods, sixty-two cents a yard; dress goods, from six cents upward; hats, from two dollars and a half to five dollars; ladies' shoes, from two dollars and a half to five dollars and a half; flour, three and a half cents a pound; potatoes, from one to three cents a pound; apples, plums and other fruits, four cents per pound; currants, eight cents; raisins, eight cents; rice, six cents; sugar, from two and a half to five cents; milk, four to eight cents per quart; tea, twenty-five to sixty cents per pound; eggs, twenty-four cents per dozen; butter, twenty-five to thirty-five cents per pound; tomatoes, twenty cents per pound; peaches, eight cents apiece; green gages, fourteen cents a pound; cucumbers, six to twelve cents each; coal, in summer, in London, twenty-six cents for one hundred and twelve pounds; in winter the same for thirty-four cents; kindling wood, in London, five small bundles for four cents; hay, one cent a pound; fowls, fifty cents each; ducks, sixty-two cents each; geese, twenty cents per pound; turkeys, large, four dollars; cheese, twelve cents and upwards; bacon, fourteen to thirty-two cents; beef, twelve to twenty-two cents per pound; gas, one thousand feet, in London, sixty cents; water rent, in London, about twelve dollars per year.

After returning home, many friends and readers spoke to the author about the great steamship "Servia" and wondered at the amount of coal she consumed in making an ocean voyage, etc. They also manifested an interest and surprise at the account of the fine, large dray horses of Liverpool. While in England I was asked if I had seen the "big horse," which is stuffed and placed in the bar of a public house in Liverpool. The story told me was that the largest horse in England, weight about two thousand four hundred pounds, had drawn a load up hill, on a wager, that two other good horses could not do.

The "Umbria" and "Etruria," large and powerful sister ships belonging to the Cunard Company, are the fastest ocean steamers in the world and can make the distance between New York and Queenstown, Ireland, in six days and a few hours. Their engines have about fifteen thousand horse-power each. Wishing to know more certainly about these things, I wrote to Mr. T. H. Puckey, emigration agent of Liverpool, and among other items received from him are the following: "The Cunard steamers have most of their coals from South Wales and Lancashire. They fill up all the space they can in Liverpool and they have to take American coals to come to England, as they cannot carry enough to last both ways. The 'Umbria' and 'Etruria' each burn about three hundred and twenty tons in twenty-four hours."

About the great horse: "He died of inflammation through drinking lots of cold water after drawing the big load and winning the one hundred pounds ($500), as his master got drunk, they say, and did not attend to him that night. He was about one ton two hundred weight. He was open to be shown as the best wagon horse and to draw or back the most weight of any horse in England for one hundred pounds, and won, July 22d, 1857. He died July 22d, 1857. His skin is to be seen, stuffed, in the bar at Joseph Bryant's 'Grey Horse' wine and spirit vaults, 53 Lime street, Liverpool, England."

In a former chapter, when writing of Dover, I mentioned the "fat man" who lives there, but at that time I did not know his name. Mr. Alfred Martin, of Plymouth, kindly volunteered to write to his brother, a prison warden of Dover, England, and ascertain more definitely about England's largest man. Some of the facts written in answer to his letter are as follows: "John Longlay, of Dover, England, who keeps the Star Public House, back of St. Mary's Church, is forty years of age; six feet and one-half inch in height; weight five hundred and seventy-seven pounds. His flesh is not flabby, as you might suppose, but is very solid. The chair he sits in is three feet two inches wide. He enjoys excellent health. He began to get fat about ten years ago. His youngest daughter is thirteen years of age, and stands five feet three inches and weighs one hundred and ninety-six pounds. She is a fine girl."

## CHAPTER XXXVII.

### NORTH BURTON AND SCARBOROUGH, ENGLAND.

GREEN COUNTRY VILLAGE AND A SPLENDID WATERING PLACE—WYOMING COMPARED WITH OTHER VALLEYS—A SUNSET OF GLORY SEEN THROUGH "GATES AJAR"—THE AUTHOR'S FATHER AT NORTH BURTON—MEETS JUNIUS BRUTUS BOOTH — MARRIES — TRAVELING BY RAIL IN YORKSHIRE—AT HUNMANBY—NORTH BURTON—THE PUDSEYS—FATHER'S CHAIR—THE GYPSY—UNIQUE OLD CHURCH—SMUGGLING—GOOD LAND—SCARBOROUGH THE SPLENDID—IN STEAM-CARRIAGES ON THE CLIFFS—COLORED SAILS FLAP ON THE "PURPLE DEEP"—CHISELED BEAUTY BETWEEN HILLS BY THE SEA—CASTLE—SOLDIERS IN TENTS—HOTELS—SHIPS—FISH AND FISHERFOLK—ELEGANT BUILDINGS—FLOWERS AND LAKES UNDER IRON BRIDGES—MEN, WOMEN, CHILDREN AND HORSES ON THE SEA SANDS—THE AQUARIUM—POVERTY MIMICS PRIDE—GOING HOME—A DELIGHTFUL EVENING.

The indulgent and patient reader who has followed these letters for the past nine months, will probably be pleased to learn that a few letters more will bring the writer back across the Atlantic, to great, roaring New York city, on across New Jersey, through and over the mountains of Pennsylvania, until his feet once more press the flagstones in Wilkes-Barré, on the banks of the Susquehanna, in Wyoming valley: by travelers, said to be one of the most beautiful valleys on earth. There are thousands of fair valleys on earth and myraids of pleasing landscapes, and as long as the song truthfully says, "There's no place like home," so long will all these fair vales have admirers. And again, health, friends, love, peace and comfort, have very much to do with making our surrounding beautiful and pleasing, for nearly "every landscape pleases" him who has peace within and without. The reader knows how the toothache, or neuralgia, or an ill-fitting boot causes the fairest surroundings to appear insipid and displeasing, and so if the mind and heart are torn by pride, envy and jealousy or distorted with anger, nature may strive in vain to look gay. A lover is about certain to be happy at home or abroad. I mean a lover of nature— a lover of everything that is beautiful, curious, valuable, true, lasting and great. To be candid I dare not say that Wyoming is the most beautiful vale on earth, for stern, iron-handed Business has come from various quarters of this great land of ours and torn great chasms into the dark foundations of our hills and strewn black debris in many places, while hissing and smoking monsters rush along dusty highways of clanging iron and flying cinders. Let the reader imagine a valley as large as ours, with mountains ten times as high, whose brows are always white with snow and whose feet rest in flowery meadows by bright waters; bright, still waters where brilliant-hued boats, enveloped in sunshine and music, convey happy people to places of beauty, peace and pleasure. Where the cold, glittering avalanche leaves its cloud-capped home and rushes with an awful roar toward the genial and attractive vale. Where rushing, foaming cataracts leap from giddy heights, and where rivers rush through mighty cañons, apparently hurrying on to join the dress parade of waters in the pleasant valley. This is a faint reference to some valleys in our own broad land and those in portions of Europe.

However, I can scarcely wish to see anything more lovely than the sunsets I have witnessed standing on the river bank at Wilkes-Barré, Pa. The green willows and meadows beyond, and, farther off, the dark green mountain full of strength and beauty, and the winding river faithfully copying the glories of the sky, making the heavens look so near; yes, there appeared to be two heavens, one above and one below. The gates were left ajar—gates of pearl, crystal, amber and jasper, and gates sprinkled with crimson. They move; they fold and unfold, and Fancy sees angels draped in many delicate hues, moving with grace superhuman, their fair banners turning this way and that, as if signaling to beings above and below, saying: "All is well;" "Peace on earth, good will to men;" "Rest sweetly, mortals, for ye shall see the sun again."

I told you in a former letter that my father was born at Whitby, a picturesque and interesting town in England, on the north-eastern coast, where the tides of the German ocean are always murmuring or roaring up and down the sands. When I was a boy he wished me some time to go and see the land of his birth. I had the pleasure of sleeping a number of nights near where he was born and where I could hear the hoarse waves roar and dash all night. Indeed, it was the sound of many waters, so well calculated to drown the voice of human beings who might be calling for help. Fifty-eight years ago last May my father, John Linskill, left his native land and sailed to America, being thirty days on the sea.

When he was a boy he was apprenticed to Stephen Pudsey, a tailor at North Burton, which is about forty miles from Whitby and a few miles from the sea. He served seven years to master the trade. For a while he was attached to a theatrical company as tailor and traveled with them through the north of England. While in this position he met the star actor, Junius Brutus Booth, father of the infamous John Wilkes Booth, who murdered President Lincoln in April, 1865.

Here, at North Burton, he married his first wife, the widow Rebecca Wharram, *née* Major, in 1824. From here he emigrated to America, leaving Hull on the 3d of May, 1830, and landed at New York June 2d.

Being anxious to see also the place where he spent his youth, and early manhood, and was married, I began at Whitby to inquire for North Burton, but as the place is now mostly called Burton Flemming, it was not so easy to learn which way to go, but my dear friend, G. W. Waddington, of Whitby, and my cousin John, station-master at Sleights, equipped me with maps, guides and railway tickets, and soon I was on the way there.

I went up the valley of the Esk and saw the high moorlands clad with purple heather, where the grouse and the plover abound, and passed old Pickering, on by Thorntondale, Wilton, Snainton, Sawdon, Wykeham, Forge Valley, Seamer Junction, Clayton, Christhorpe, and arrive at Hunmanby.

At this old village, which is three miles from North Burton, I took dinner at the White Swan, an old-fashioned hotel, which probably looked almost exactly the same as when father saw it, seventy years ago. As I entered the place I heard a noise, and looking, saw men threshing out stacks of grain near a barn, and the threshing-machine was run by steam power.

Near the village I noticed a lofty and massive stone archway and gate, through which a driveway led up through a grove. The following sign was displayed: "This desirable residence to let for a term of years, with or without 6,000 acres of shooting."

I asked, "Are there any Wharrams in this place?" "No, sir." "Any Majors?" "No, sir." "Any Pudseys?" "No, sir; but a Stephen Pudsey lives at North Burton, three miles away." "Any Linskills?" "Yes, sir; one family, Thomas Linskill, a farm laborer." I called on the family, but we could not trace the relationship, if any.

I went up over the hill and walked along a good, smooth turnpike, which was about fifty feet wide and lined on both sides by good thorn hedges. Now I look off over, say 5,000 acres of good farm land, in large fields, some of which are green, and others are yellow with harvests. A grove is seen on a hill, and in a hollow here and there, but scarcely a house or barn is seen. I found the houses later at North Burton, surrounded by trees, and stacks of grain and hay.

Yes, here is North Burton, a farming hamlet, looking almost exactly as it did sixty years ago. The houses are brick and stone, and nearly all plastered over and painted white, and most of them without dooryards. Perhaps there are fifty buildings all told. I here found Stephen Pudsey and his sister, Mrs. Nixon and her family. They were son and daughter of the Stephen Pudsey with whom my father learned his trade. They would not listen to my going away before morning. They had good, clear recollections of my father, and told me many characteristic anecdotes of his youth and early manhood. Mr. Pudsey, (he was a hardy, well-preserved bachelor of about seventy-one years), accompanied me about the place and showed me where father lived when first married, and pointed out the old chapel where he attended services.

Here is the Gypsy, or rather here it is sometimes, but the channel, (about four feet deep and eight feet wide), is dry now. Sometimes it runs full to overflowing with clear water for weeks, and again for weeks or months it will be dry, so it is called the Gypsy, for it comes and goes. This is the only stream I saw (or rather, did not see) in this broad, fertile valley. The soil being gravelly under, the water is thus absorbed.

Mr. Pudsey said: "Yonder is the wind-mill that the Majors owned before going to America, and this large farm is where old Mr. Major lived." Here is the old and unique church near the centre of the village, surrounded by the yard which contains graves, and on the headstones I read these names: Francis Wardell, William Major, John Appleby, Robert Artley, Thomas Wharram Major, Temple, Pudsey, Ireland, etc.

Men are at work cutting holes in the stone tower to put in a clock. I met Matthew Hodgson and James Mallery at work here. One said: "No one can tell how old the church is." I entered the church, which was indeed unique and antique. I saw the high pews, the old oak rafters and beams inscribed with Scripture texts, the pipe organ, the pulpit, etc.

Mrs. Nixon and daughter Fannie prepared a very pleasant tea, in which fine white bread, fresh butter and honey formed an agreeable portion. The kind people said: "The chair in which you sit was your father's chair." It was a well-preserved and easy arm chair. Mrs. Nixon said: "In this room your father worked with my father, and he sat near that window and sewed many a day. Yes, this is the same brick floor as it was then, and these shelves to hold the goods are the same as then."

After a pleasant night's rest and breakfast, I bid good bye to the Nixons and leave North Burton accompanied by Mr. Pudsey, who walked with me until we came to an eminence from which we could look off and see the white sails on the great and beautiful blue sea. Mr. Pudsey said, "Your father was a great reader of newspapers; then there were but two or three taken in the place and he would go and read them. In the grove on the hill away yonder is where your father found seventy tubs of smuggled goods, tobacco and tea. He and my father watched all night there and informed the officers. Yes, they were rewarded."

"Yes, beautiful land; wheat averages forty bushels to the acre; one man, near Driffield, had sixty-four bushels of wheat to the acre. Oats yield eighty and more bushels to the acre." Mr. Pudsey said, "I do not like the entailment of property. It prevents improvements of the farms in scraping up money and means for the younger ones. We will have to do away with the system, for we are getting the franchise down."

We shake hands and take feeling adieu, one walking back to North Burton and the other going toward the sea. Turning about I saw the kind-hearted and sturdy, little bachelor plodding steadily homeward.

One pleasant morning in August, aunt and I took the train at West Cliff, bound for Scarborough, which is about twenty-one miles south of Whitby, on the eastern coast of England. Scarborough is one of the most pleasant and most fashionable watering places on the north-eastern coast of England, and has long been called the "queen of English watering places," and more recently she has been named "Scarborough the Splendid."

The route from Whitby to Scarborough lies along the high, irregular cliffs which overlook the cool, blue

German ocean. From the car windows, as our train curves to the right or left and runs down into shady ravines, and again climbs along the side of high, green, cultivated hills and rushes through a tunnel or cut at the top of the hills, we can look off on the rolling sea where ships with white, black and brown sails are seen, and farther out where great coal, lumber and passenger steamers pass, going up and down, keeping the trade and travel of England at an equilibrium. The breath of the laboring steamers look like great streaks of soot on a blue curtain. On the other hand we look out upon broad fields, hills, groves and hamlets. Now, away below us, between high cliffs, terraced above the restless tides of the sea, is seen the ancient and picturesque village called Robin Hood's Bay, where the steep roofs of red brick tiles are conspicuous. This is one of the places where the famous smuggler and outlaw, Robin Hood, is said to have done some of his most daring feats of robbery and romance.

Yonder is Scarborough, a chiseled beauty between high hills, the bright waves of the sea foaming and murmuring on the broad white sands in front, and in the rear are vales and farm lands through which railways enter the place. As we enter, on the right is seen Oliver's Mount, with fields on its side and a grove at the top. On the left is a high, bold eminence where yet stand the ruins of Scarborough Castle and walls. Between these eminences run fine, broad streets full of stately buildings. The place is in the form of a semi-amphitheatre and the bay is said to resemble the bay of Naples. There are some handsome terraces and crescents here. I saw some elegant stores, among which I remember those of William Rowntree and Marshall & Snellgrove, of London.

The chief hotels are the Grand, the Royal, and the Crown. The Grand hotel stands by the sea, and is tall and extensive; from the sands where the sea almost washes its pavements, to the top of its tower, appeared to be sixteen stories high.

The tall cliff to the south of the city is terraced and ornamented with walks, trees, flowers, pleasant seats, music stands, inclined plane, and a large ornamental building, called the Spa Saloon, which overlooks the white sands and the sea, and where good music is almost continuously discoursed.

On the broad, clean beach are hundreds of ladies and children, dressed in many bright colors, sitting and walking, while young men in gay costumes canter over the sands on jockey-clipped and kept horses. Here are donkeys for the children to ride, and along the clean thoroughfares people ride in various vehicles drawn by horses ridden by postillions in coats, hats and breeches of many gay colors.

Over there, at the foot of the abrupt castle hill, is the harbor, full of ships and fishing-boats. I walk out on the pier and see tons of nearly all kinds of fish. I see strange men, strange women, strange sailors, and hear strange words and strange languages. Here in ships and on shore we see nearly all kinds of fishing paraphernalia. We see men and women "fat, ragged and saucy," laughing at each other's wit and double-meaning remarks.

It is a novel, yet somewhat unpleasant experience, so I went back and joined aunt, and we walked to the top of the castle hill, going up through passages walled or cut in rock, through heavy gateways, and under arches, and arrive at the top and look down upon the city, the sea and the shipping. On the top of this bold, fresh promontory, we found seven hundred soldiers enjoying their annual vacation, or camping-out days. They kindly showed us around, and let us look through the tents, and also examine the long row of cannon that opened their black mouths over the sea.

Returning we went down into an enchanting and shady park in a ravine in the lowest part of the city, where drives and lakes and fountains and flowers, and easy seats abound, while lofty and graceful bridges leap across the vale, far over our heads. Slanting drives go up terraced ways where stand elegant mansions among trees and shrubbery.

Nearer the sea and underground is the aquarium, where rolling wheels and human feet move and flowers bloom above it. A crystal goblet or a metal tank may be called an aquarium, but this one covers nearly an acre and is placed under the ground to be handy to the sea and its waters. You might imagine as you walk under the arches and through the colonnades of columns and by the walls resplendent with colors and pictures and great glass reservoirs of sea water, that you were in a mine from which had been chiseled much marble of many rich colors. Here are fishes great and small to be seen through crystal walls on either hand, while birds sing, monkeys chatter and beg for candies and nuts, and "Music with its voluptuous swell," sets hearts and feet to keeping time. Here also are play houses, bazaars, refreshment rooms, grottoes, fine panoramic views of the wide world's beautiful and famous places.

Britain is great on land and sea, on earth and under the earth; great in war, peace and pleasure; great in learning, wealth and buildings; possessing great pride and much poverty.

Wealth comes to these great watering places, apparently seeking a nepenthe, and pride and poverty come to admire and mimic. If the wealth of the world were not woefully and wickedly misapplied there would be little or no poverty.

Our journey homeward in the evening along the sea was a delight, closing a day long to be remembered. The sun set in a region of glory, and "the white sails flapped on the purple deep." As we emerged from the tunnel near the peak a vast amphitheater of green fields encircle Robin Hood's Bay in a semicircle of nearly six miles, where millions might sit and gaze down into the sea. Our steam-driven carriages cease their rushing and roaring on West Cliff, and a short walk brings us again to old Whitby, where homes and friends and relatives await us.

# CHAPTER XXXVIII.

## LEAMINGTON, WARWICK, STRATFORD, ETC.

GRAND WARWICKSHIRE — LEAMINGTON — GARDENS — DRIVES—MEDICINAL WATERS—WARWICK CASTLE—AN OLD GLORY SURROUNDED BY BEAUTIES OF NATURE AND ART—PEACOCKS AND CEDARS OF LEBANON—THE DUNGEON, DARK AND DREADFUL—STRATFORD-UPON-AVON — SHAKESPEARE'S BIRTHPLACE — THE ROOM WHERE THE GREAT POET WAS BORN—NO FIRE ALLOWED—STEALING A PLACE TO WRITE A NAME—RELIC HUNTERS—SHAKESPEARE'S CURSE—A DELIGHTFUL RIDE ON THE AVON—COVENTRY—OLD CHURCHES WITH TALL SPIRES—ST. MARY'S HALL—LADY GODIVA RIDES NAKED THROUGH THE CITY—"PEEPING TOM" IS NOW BLIND TOM—LEAVING FAIR LEAMINGTON.

On my way to London I stopped at Leamington, in Warwickshire, where I remained a few days with cousins, and with whom I visited Warwick, Guy's Cliff, Coventry and Stratford-upon-Avon.

Warwickshire is one of the midland counties of England, and is also one of the fairest and most interesting portions of this beautiful island. Warwickshire is a green and level county, abounding with meadows, groves, small rivers, canals, fine trees and gardens, and some rock-founded eminences where stand massive and ancient castles, palaces, ruins and churches.

Leamington, one of the most beautiful places I saw in England, sits on both sides of the river Leam, and contains about twenty-five thousand inhabitants. The place is not ancient, and its streets are broad, smooth and quite regular; still some of its avenues wind gracefully along the river, or through gardens and groves, among the churches and handsome mansions which are spacious, commodious and sufficiently secluded by shrubbery and ornamental trees. There are medicinal springs here, which, for many years, have been in favor with the Royal family, and the place is named "Royal Leamington Spa." There are springs here which are termed generally, Saline, and Sulphurretted Saline. One, at least, of these springs is free. I tasted the water and found it to be exceedingly unpleasant. The churches are quite fine. Fine gardens and walks, full of rare plants and trees abound, which make the place seem like a city of gardens, or a city in a garden.

In fact, the whole county, which contains Kenilworth, Coventry, and Shakespeare's birthplace, and other places famous in poetry, romance and war, would make a great park. Yes, these midland counties are magnificent with meadows and still waters, while grand trees stand in nearly all the fields, as if saying, "Let us have shade and beauty if crops are somewhat shortened thereby." In all my journey I saw no other place where beauty, comfort, agriculture and wealth, were so harmoniously blended as in these midland counties.

Warwick is two miles from Leamington and is a very old and interesting place. The chief place of interest is Warwick Castle, which stands on a small eminence by the river Avon. This castle, I was told, is the residence of the Earl of Warwick for nine months in the year. In going into the castle grounds, which enclose about one thousand acres, we go in under massive arches and go along a broad, deep and winding road cut in rock, both sides being ivy-grown and covered at the top by a cool thicket, while great trees throw out their branches above our heads. This is altogether a most romantic place. See the great gray castle with arches, columns, porticoes, windows, battlements, towers, turrets, etc., surrounded by green lawns, flower gardens, lakelets, thickets, lofty towers and walls, where proud peacocks sit idly smoothing and re-arranging their bright plumage, while white swans with curved necks move gracefully through bright waters. We went through this lordly palace and saw things of great age, worth and beauty; things historic, antique, curious, war-like, and artistic; furniture costly, and rare portraits and paintings of kings, queens, lords and ladies, and of battle-fields fierce, crimson and decisive. We gaze from windows upon the beautiful Avon as it winds through a landscape of rare beauty, and there are the old and gloomy "Cedars of Lebanon," planted by the Crusaders in the days of Knight Errantry, when to successfully woo for a fair hand the gallant knight must first bathe in the blood of infidels in a land beyond the great sea. We ascended a lofty tower up many winding steps of stone and gazed from the giddy height upon castle, and park, and city, and a wide, lovely landscape. We went down dark passages and stairways cut in rock, and gazed with horror into a dungeon where the sun can never enter. The opening at our feet is one foot square, and is the only door or window of ingress or egress the dungeon has. If a poor, unfortunate, ill-guided patriot or criminal passed through that opening he would never come out until his lifeless body was dragged out by the hirelings of justice, cruelty, ambition or envy. It is used no more, fortunately; and, besides, some of the prisoners of state confined there may have been worthy of death —a speedy, painless death—but I would let an awful, blasting, withering, smoking, earth-rending curse fall on and around the man, or the woman, or the nation that wilfully tortures the body and mind of a fellow human being of any color or in any clime. The spirit of the Great One must be exercised if we would conquer human nature—Him who, as He passed along, gave sight to the blind, strength to the lame, food to the hungry, and, when His mild eye rested upon the poor, torn, cut and raving maniac of sin, he was soon afterward seen sitting clothed and in his right mind. Water turned to strengthening wine at his bidding, and foaming, angry billows sank into sleep at His command. At last, when He was nailed up on a hill in the centre of earth and His rich blood dripped down to heal the wounds of His enemies, He stretched out His hands, saying: "Come unto Me, all ye that labor and are heavy laden, and I will give you rest." Yes, love is the most mighty force known. It is stronger than mountains of rock, and the vast, inconceivable force of attractive gravity is one of its offsprings.

I had the pleasure of passing about two hours at the birthplace of the great Shakespeare, one of the greatest writers that has ever walked our earth. Some of our readers may possibly know who William Shakespeare was. He was the greatest writer of dramatic plays that the human race has produced. He put so much of human nature in his plays that it seemed as if he knew all that men then knew or could think and feel placed in any condition in life. He was born here in 1564, of humble parents. I entered the quaint, old-fashioned house and the upper room where he was born. I saw the old, open fire-places, the black, oak beams and rafters that have stood here more than three hundred years. The cottage is two stories high, and on the outside you see the old oak beams and braces, filled in between with concrete. No fire or light is ever permitted in the house. Mr. I. E. Baker was the polite attendant below and his lady attended above. Of course no one is permitted to write or cut his name here, yet I saw no place on the walls, posts, mantels or window frames where there was room for another name. I may here say that I did not write my name once, on my tour, in a public, famous or conspicuous place. It is a forlorn, sentimental habit, productive of no good.. If one's name is worth preserving it will be preserved, and "don't you forget it;" I beg to be excused. No, I will not cross out that sentence, for a good name will be remembered somewhere. If not on marble and in books and hearts here, it will "shine forth as the sun" in that "far country" "when the books are opened."

Relic hunters are watched closely here, and as I walked over the stone floor, I noticed a small piece of stone broken off, and in presence of the guide I put it in my pocket; then he opened a drawer and handed me some flowers and stems, saying, "These are from Shakespeare's garden, and I brought them home. We went to the place where he lived and died. The house is gone, all but a portion of the foundation. We drank out of his well and ate a few mulberries off a tree of his planting, they say. We saw the church where his dust reposes, and thus far proud, intelligent, glory-worshiping England has not dared to move his bones to Westminster Abbey, (where they should be,) on account of these lines on his tomb, which some people think he wrote, viz:

> " Good friend, for Jesus sake forbeare,
> To digg the dust encloased heare;
> Bleste be the man who spares thes stones,
> And curst be he that moves my bones."

We saw the spacious and modern new Shakespeare theatre on the banks of Avon, and were pointed to the handsome Shakespeare fountain that Mr. Childs, of Philadelphia, was erecting. We took a boat ride on the green, willow-banked Avon, and floated amid meadows and mansions, swans and shadows, and passed other oarsmen in gay dress, accompanied by fair ones in bright attire. Altogether it was a day to be remembered.

We went to Coventry on another day and looked about the unique old place. We stood on the bridge and saw "the three tall spires," or rather, we saw two tall spires, for one was being rebuilt. The spires are of stone, and are said to pierce the heavens more than three hundred freet from the earth. They are needle-like and graceful, and belong to three old churches that stand not far apart. The names of these churches are as follows: St. Michael's, Trinity, and Christ Church. The churches are very old, and very beautiful inside. One might spend days admiring and studying the beautiful scriptural and historical pictures which serve as the stained glass windows. We looked through St. Mary's Hall, which was erected in A. D. 1340. This is very ancient and curious within, and contains a very handsome statue of Lady Godiva, and also fine paintings. St. John's Baptist Church is also a fine building. Bablake Hospital and Ford's Hospital are also ornamental structures. A guide-book says: "Coventry has for centuries been an important manufacturing centre. Watch-making and its kindred trades still flourish here, and the town is famous for its bicycles, sewing-machines, art metal work, and frilling is another manufacture of recent introduction." Anyone at all acquainted with Coventry always speaks of "Peeping Tom." To those who do not know of "Peeping Tom," I will say the legend runs this way: A thousand years ago the Earl laid a tax on the people of the town, and they came with their wives and babies to have the tax taken off, saying: "If we pay it we starve." His wife, Lady Godiva, interceded for the poor people, and the proud, cruel Earl told her she would not weary her little finger to save them. She said she would even die for them. The Earl replied: "If you will ride, at noon, naked through the streets I will let them go free." Then Godiva consented to ride on horseback naked through the town. She ordered everybody to shut themselves in their houses and she shook down her long hair and disrobed, and mounted her horse and galloped through the streets, and returned as the clocks in the towers were pealing midday. One man, Tom, peeped out of a small upper window, and as she rode by his eyes shriveled and he was struck stone-blind, and the traveler may yet look up to a niche and see the image of "Peeping Tom," now Blind Tom. I often wonder how these strange legends originated, but presume there was generally something to found them upon. This story may all be true, except the part pertaining to Tom's miraculous blindness, and still the mean and doubtless jealous old Earl may have caused Tom's eyes to be put out.

Towards evening we return to fair Leamington, and the following day I bade farewell to my kind cousins, and departed from this most delightful portion of old England.

## CHAPTER XXXIX.

### FROM ENGLAND TO WYOMING VALLEY.

IN ENGLAND'S BUSY SEA-PORT—GOING TO THE SHIP—MISS OLIVER—THOUSANDS OF PEOPLE SAILING OUT INTO THE FOG TO LANDS BEYOND THE SEA—LIVERPOOL FADES INTO SMOKE AND FOG—SUNSET SMILES ON THE SEA—MOONLIT HIGHWAY—ROCKETS BURSTING ABOVE THE WAVES—WEEPING AND DANCING—A SUNDAY FAIR ON A GREAT SHIP—"LOVELY APPLES"—CANES—CAPS—PIPES—BOG OAK, ETC.—IRELAND SINKS INTO THE SEA—SEA ROUGH—THE SNORER—THE WINDS LIFT UP DARK WAVES—MANY ILL—SEA GRAND—ALLEGHENIES OF WATER—CHINAWARE CRASHES AND LIGHTS GO OUT—TOSSED IN BED—THE DECK LIKE A BARN-ROOF—NOT AFRAID, BUT SATISFIED—COMRADES RECOVERING—MR. G—— ILL.

After nine weeks of journeying through the British Isles and France, I arrived at four o'clock in the morning, in the great, solid, busy and wealthy city, Liverpool. It took me about an hour to find my way from the station through this great forest of tall buildings to the public house of T. H. Puckey, where my trunks were awaiting me. I lay and slept for an hour and a half on a bench in a waiting room, and when I awoke the house and the city were astir and aroar, for thousands that day were to sail in ships large and small, from Liverpool to various parts of the earth. I did not feel greatly pleased at the thought of leaving Old England; for had I not had a pleasant time, seeing friends, and things new, old, great and beautiful?

After an early breakfast the hurly-burly begins. Emigrants from various portions of England are packing their trunks and boxes and securing them with straps, ropes, etc., while others are procuring mattresses, pillows, tin dishes, etc., of Mr. Puckey. Now the boxes and baggage are being loaded upon carts and taken to the dock. Now, at 9:50, am on the wharf with Mr. Puckey and Miss Oliver. Now we are on board of the tender waiting to be conveyed to the "Servia."

Miss Oliver is near. Mr. Puckey placed her partially in my care. She is a Cornish young woman, going to Iron Mountain, Michigan, to meet a brother, a brother-in-law and her lover, whom she will probably marry.

Great black steamships with red, yellow, white and ringed funnels are coming and going, and others are moored to the floating wharf taking on or putting off passengers and luggage. Some tons of mail matter is being carried aboard our tender. Thousands of people have come and gone, but there are still hundreds on the wharf. There comes a large double-decked tender from the "Etruria" with a thousand or two of passengers right from America.

Now we move off; handkerchiefs wave, tears fall, and the masts, spires, walls, domes, chimneys and warehouses disappear in the smoke and fog. We have arrived at the "Servia," the great steamship anchored in deep water, the same ship I went over on. Now we let loose from the great floating buoy and the mighty engines begin to propel us into the Irish sea. The afternoon is fine; it is the 24th of September and I feel just a little anxious when I remember we have not had the equinoctial storm yet. Land has disappeared and we are fairly on our way to America. At 5:30 o'clock the sea is so smooth we hardly know the ship moves until we look over her prow and see the white waters roll back to make way for us.

Looking towards the setting sun, the warm, hazy sky, the color of yellowish silver, is reflected on the water, and it is nearly impossible to discern the line between the sky and sea, except one is burnished somewhat more than the other. The supper-bell rings; all are well and have good appetites, and I wait for the second table. After supper took a walk with Miss Oliver on deck. Saw the moonlight on the waters make a silvery path toward the New World. Passed a great steamer and she saluted us with rockets, and we returned the salute in a similar manner.

At 7:40 am in my state-room writing. Hearing music on deck I went up and found a man fluting, and sailors and passengers dancing. I was amused to find one woman dancing gaily, who was crying in the morning because she lost a ten-shilling piece, and had nothing to pay the carter for bringing her luggage to the wharf, so I lent her three-shillings and she asked me to take a gold ring in security. Toward evening she sent me two-shillings and I sent her ring back, but she did not expect it until all was paid; so in the evening, with her mother and child among the spectators, she laughed and danced on the great, grand, glittering sea. She was going to her husband in America, the land that lies so solid and green beyond the broad Atlantic.

September 25th, Sunday morning, anchored off Queenstown, near the shores of fair Ireland, waiting for later mails from London and the British Isles. I will copy from my note-book. "Irish men, women and girls come on board with apples, oranges, lemons, caps, mufflers, handkerchiefs, canes, pipes, etc., for sale. 'Have some apples, sir? beautiful, lovely, loveliest apples you ever eat, splendid, sir. Lovely apples, grandest you ever eat, a bird pecked that, sir. Only eighteen-pence for the cap, sir; never no wool nor trouble spared on that cap. It is just now I came, sir, got no money yet, sir.' 'But you will get some before you leave the ship.' 'Yes, God is good, sir. I paid eighteen-pence for the boat to bring me here.' 'You should sell cheap, you have no shop.' 'Yes, but I pay rent, sir.' 'Yes, he might evict you.' 'If I had a shillalah I'd fix him, sure. Nice muffler; you will be tired washing it. I am washing one this six months for my little boy.' Second woman—'Hand-made cap, sir; you might buy this cap, sir, and take it home from old Ireland and make a present of it, sir. Three ounces of wool in it. Handkerchiefs, blue, pink and cream, silk and linen, sir; six-pence each. Have a black-thorn cane? Take a bog-oak pipe?'" Thus we lay that bright Sunday from 7 a. m. to 1 p. m. waiting for the mails, and the fair went on; ladies and gentlemen walking the deck, while many were reading and writing. My friend, Miss Oliver, was found on the forecastle deck reading a religious book. "Hundreds of sea-birds, white and gray, the size of crows, ducks and geese, flying just above the water, or sitting on the water and occasionally dipping down as if catching a crust of bread from the water. They caw and twitter and squeal somewhat like crows and ducklings. 7:30 p. m., after tea; now in dining-room; people reading and talking around. Have had a fine day and quite uneventful, but not passed as a Sabbath should be passed."

My last letter ended at about 7:30 o'clock p. m., Sunday, Sept 25th, on board the steamship "Servia," on the Atlantic, just west of Ireland. We had been in sight of Ireland all the day long and could see her green hills, and light-houses and white towns along the edge of the water. It is a pleasing sight to look from the sea to a fair, green land, even if you have not been long upon the sea. Perhaps I had better copy from my note-book; it will be easier for the writer and may be as acceptable to the reader. "Retired at 9 o'clock; dark, windy; sea quite rough; the aspect threatening; many quite fearful. Was annoyed by a snoring man. Oh, the snorer! what a mysterious arrangement that he is given a place in animate nature, I mean a place where nervous and sensitive mortals are expected to sleep. This snorer was a perpetual, sonorous, spasmodic and explosive snorer. I thought, as I listened to his loud solo at midnight and in the dark, sounding and solemn fourth watch of the night, of dogs snarling, hogs grunting, bellowing bulls and demons defiant. I sympathized with the poor palate, for the lungs seemed to have it all their own way. I was so glad that he was not a Rip Van Winkle that I must watch for twenty years. Now the bell strikes one, and I know it is half-past four, and as the ship rolls and pitches the watchmen above call out, 'All is well!' I say to myself, 'It is not all right here. Oh, that it were morning!' As the lady wrote, 'I have had tender thoughts, etc.,' but my thoughts were not that kind. I thought of the man beheaded in Paris, of the one hanged in London and the one who suicided in Middlesborough. I wished for hand grenades and was glad the ship rolled from side to side so he might get seasick. Yes, have all the seasickness of the ship. I wished he had been an American Indian, then his father or mother would have closed his mouth when he slept, and if they could not have taught him common sense, they would have turned him on his side and all gone quietly to sleep; but he was a white man, and a big one, and he probably snored in Irish, English, Welsh, French and German, and I do not know which was the most execrable. If I had a patent on slang, I would say 'he was a regular rip snorter.' I got up and slammed the door, but the interval of peace was very brief. I dreamed of donkeys, horse-fiddles, hand organs, bagpipes, woodpeckers, brand new brass bands and amateur pianists. At half past five a sailor begins to pound with an axe or sledge on deck above us.

Surely, now we must all awake, but no, he snored right on, not like one of the seven sleepers, but like all of them.

"Morning once more; we arise and go upon deck. 'The stormy winds do blow;' great waves dash upon deck, and white hills roll from the bow of our monster ship as she pitches or bows her head to a great billow which dashes with a roar on her forecastle deck.

"Just finished dinner; the waiter said, 'I was one out of eleven that came to dinner.' Many are now ill, weak, pale, limp and vomiting. The sights and sound on the ship are very unpleasant, but off on the sea the scene is one of indescribable grandeur. A few miles away, the sun, shining between dark clouds, kisses the dark waters into broad fields of silver.

"What could be grander than sitting in this porthole and rocking up and down in a great steel ship with a thousand other souls? As the forward part of the ship falls into the dark, blue waters, they turn milk-white and a light blue and dash away like a foaming Niagara, up hill, so to speak, on both sides, while the great ship rolls along in a great white, foaming valley of water. The ocean now looks like a rolling prairie of water, or should I say an Allegheny of waters? To me the motion is easy and pleasant and it seems like rocking in a vast cradle that sinks down into feathers. I often think of King David's poetry, where he wrote, 'They that go down to the sea in ships, that do business in great waters; these see the works of the Lord, and his wonders in the deep. For He commendeth, and raiseth the stormy wind, which lifteth up the waves thereof. They mount up to heaven, they go down again to the depths; their soul is melted because of trouble. They reel to and fro, and stagger like a drunken man, and are at their wits' end. Then they cry unto the Lord in their trouble, and He bringeth them out of their distresses. He maketh the storm a calm, so that the waves thereof are still. Then are they glad because they be quiet; so He bringeth them unto their desired heaven.'

"Retired about 9:30. The ship rolls much. The waves roar hoarsely, sailors shout, the boatswain's shrill whistle is heard as the wind roars and screeches through the lofty rigging of the ship. China and glassware rattle and crash into fragments on the floor; trunks, satchels, boots, canes, etc., go scraping and banging across the floors of the state-rooms; and, as the ship plunges, the mighty screw-wheel, in a grasp stronger than ten thousand horses, revolves with rapidity partially in air and sends a shudder through the ship. Amid other noises come the sounds from poor, suffering people ill of sea-sickness. Now, as the ship gives another fearful plunge, which nearly throws us out of bed, there comes an awful crash of broken crockery, and Steward Kennedy shouts to his lieutenants to make all secure, and the electric lights flash out and all is dark. What has happened? Nothing; at 11 o'clock every night the electric light is cut off. Now the ship pitches, and, as she bows her head, a great wave of clear salt water baptizes her with tons of water, which roars like a small Niagara as it rolls from the forecastle deck down upon the main deck. It is difficult to undress and hang up one's clothes, and impossible to lie still in bed.

"Sept. 27th. Arose about 7 a. m. Ship still 'rolling and pitching,' difficult to wash and dress. Ate heartily of good bread and butter, mutton-chop and coffee. Went on deck and gazed on the rolling and roaring sea. About as difficult to walk the watery deck as to walk the roof of a barn in a thunder storm: rain and salt spray sweeping the deck! now a wave goes over me and I am wet through, but there is none on deck to laugh: I go to my room and change my clothes. Now, 9:30 a. m., writing, while many are ill and lying in their beds. 5:30 p. m., the day has been rough and nearly all are sick. I have been writing 'Here and There,' and would walk out for rest now and then, and cheer my comrades up somewhat. I left my friend, Miss Oliver, in care of Mr. G——, and Miss Walker, and Mr. Hackett and Miss Schwinn. She is quite a favorite. She has been sea-sick to-day and finds it nearly impossible to smile. They tell me if I do not keep in the open air, and write less, I will get sick; but I tell them, banteringly, the Atlantic can not roll and roar high enough, and loud enough, to make me sick. 'Would you like to see it rougher?' 'Yes, I would, but for your sakes I will say I am satisfied." 8 p. m., the night is dark and wild; I fear we shall not sleep very well.

"Sept. 28th. Arose about 6:30; rested quite well. Fresh atmosphere; sea is calmer, sky clearer, writing and waiting for breakfast. Many passengers coming around again and reporting for meals. In afternoon; pleasant day. People getting well; they not only begin to eat but continue to eat. My friend, Mr. G——, a carriage blacksmith, of Rochester, N. Y., a very clever, kind-hearted man, is ill, and I have been nursing him and administering medicine, and I hope he is now sleeping. I am now nearly ready to retire. Have had a pleasant day—some sunshine and the sea is not very rough."

## CHAPTER XL.

### FROM ENGLAND TO WYOMING VALLEY—CONTINUED.

MISS OLIVER WOUNDED — MR. G—— PREPARING TO BE BURIED IN THE SEA—TOOK HOT RUM AND QUININE—"GET OUT"—MISS OLIVER WORSE—THE SURGEON ASSISTS—STEAMERS RACING THROUGH WHITE-CRESTED BILLOWS—OFFICERS KIND—THE MAGICAL SEA—SHIPS LIKE BUTTERFLIES ON CRYSTAL VASES—SINGERS CHEER MISS OLIVER IN DARKNESS—SANDY HOOK—ANCHOR CHAINS RATTLE—A GREAT CITY'S CRYSTAL GATE—SHIPS, FORTS, HILLS, MANSIONS, MONUMENTS, CHURCHES, BRIDGES—ON THE WINGS OF THE MORNING—THE SEA'S BIRTHS LIKE A RESURRECTION—LETTERS FROM DISTANT KINGDOMS—CUSTOM HOUSE—ROUGH AND DUSTY—OFFICIALS SEEM UNFEELING—TAKE AWAY MY WATCH—TELL WHO I AM—WATCH RETURNED—MISS OLIVER'S BROTHER—SHAKE HANDS AMID TEARS, GOOD-BYES AND PARTINGS.

Sept. 29th. Up at 5 o'clock; windy and rough for an hour or two; many passengers are still ill. Mr. G——, my good-natured friend, is quite ill and keeps his bed. Now, after dinner, we are in a dense fog, and the hoarse steam fog-horn sounds at frequent intervals. Writing most of the day.

Took a walk on deck, found Miss Oliver with

handkerchief wrapped around her left hand, and she showed me a small pink mark in the palm of the hand which had been caused by the rusty blade of a penknife, while she was cutting a lozenge to divide with her friends. It is somewhat swelled and painful. I gave her some Eclectic Oil to apply and also applied a piece of bacon. Her friends were somewhat amused at my anxiety. The reader will remember that this is the young lady who is on her way to Iron Mountain, Michigan, to meet and marry her lover, Fred. Ennis. She is from Cornwall, England, aged 22 years, tall, good-looking and an unsophisticated, candid Christian girl.

In the evening Mr. G—— sends for me, says he is worse; has fever and pain, and fears inflammation of the bowels. Thinks he will not live to see America, and his wife and son and daughter in Rochester, N. Y. I was quite surprised at his quiet, good nature and resignation. He had been on a visit to England to see his parents and sisters and was now going back to work and duty. He said, "I will leave my family in comfortable circumstances, and I am worth as much to them dead as living. I will probably not live to see morning. I have about sixty dollars with me. I want you to see that Miss Oliver gets five dollars for her kindness to me this afternoon, in bringing me tea, toast, etc. I like the girl; she is a good girl." His voice trembled, and a red handkerchief shaded his eyes from the electric light, as he continued: "I want to go down right. You will find two black suits in my trunk; put the best suit on me, and after all is paid, send the balance of the money and things to my wife." I said, "Ebenezer, we will not let them bury you in the sea." "Oh, you can't help it." "Yes I will." I went and called the ship Surgeon, and he said it was fever and ague and rheumatism, and he directed me to give him some rum, hot water and sugar and follow with quinine every two hours for awhile. I remember, though he seemed willing to die, he was also willing to take the hot rum; still I must say he also took the quinine just as he took everything else, good-naturedly, for he was fat and jolly, and although he said droll things, he did not laugh much. He wished to see Miss Oliver, and I called her and he gave her his blessing and bade her good-night. Her hand was in a sling and pained her greatly, but she cooled his brow with her left hand. I retired rather late.

Sept. 30. Up at 6:30; took a walk on deck; fresh air; cloudy; good day for time of year. Some sun, not much wind; a sprinkle of rain. Passengers generally getting better. Miss Oliver's hand worse; much swelled, and the Doctor is afraid to cut or open the wound, as I wished him to do. Mr. G—— did not sleep and is still suffering in bed. Doctor came and said, "You must get up and move around or you will die," He said, "Well, I'll try." I was surprised, but in less than an hour I found him and Miss Oliver on deck surrounded by some comrades, trying to talk and be cheerful. In short, he slowly recovered, while the young lady grew worse, and when I was alarmed and feared lockjaw, Miss Walker gave me almost angry looks and words. But I always contend that if people know the full danger they are more apt to get out of it than if they do not see the danger. Her hand and arm were swelled to her shoulder and very painful—she could not take food. The Doctor applied cotton and oil silk and anodynes.

Evening—I have written "Here and There" nearly all day. We passed a number of sailing ships to-day—one very near, trim-built, full sail, black hull, also sailing west. The First Mate said, "Yes, we passed the Arizona last night ten or more miles to the south." The Arizona had left Queenstown a few hours ahead of us, and nearly all the time, day and night, we had been "racing" towards the New World, over dark, tossing billows-Atlantic. In the daytime she seemed a black speck on the horizon and at night a faint glimmer of lights. After the reader has seen the world of waters that always roar and toss white-crested billows to the sky between Europe and America, he will have more respect for the noble Columbus of four centuries past.

The night is very dark, windy and threatening. There is music and dancing on deck by the sailors and steerage passengers. Many men and women have passed the day playing at cards. Chief Steward Lyle and Assistant Kennedy, and Chief Cook Hoy were kind and helpful to me. The Chief Steward said: "If there is anything you want let me know and you shall have it." So I asked only for oranges, apples, figs, raisins and prunes.

Oct. 1st. Up at 6; clear, fine, breezy. People generally well. Saw a number of ships, three of them being steamers. Delightful weather: the clouds begin to look like home. Yes, John Howard Payne is right, the skies above one's home look different from other or foreign skies. We have three hundred and sixty-eight cabin passengers, eighty-two intermediate, and one hundred and sixty-eight steerage passengers, and an army of sailors, cooks and waiters. We have passengers from Japan, Sweden, France, Germany, Italy, Ireland, England, Wales, Scotland, etc.

Saturday afternoon; how fine it is! The sea is calm and glossy, the color of the sky. Cooks in white caps, and aprons, and linen coats, going to and fro. Boys peep in at the door as if wishing for oranges, raisins, nuts, apples, or the brown wing of fowl which is roasting. Ladies, some invalid, some sewing, knitting, reading, talking, and others walking the deck. Our Swedish friend gazes through his glass far out on the sea.

Oh, look! there, where a few minutes ago we saw only bright water, is now a beautiful ship under full sail. Did it come out of the sea, or did it drop from the sky? Yes, the world is round, and the ship sits there as beautiful as a butterfly on the crystal home of the gold-fish. The manifold glories and beauties of earth are indescribable.

Oct. 2d.—Sunday. Arose at 6:30; took walk on deck. Made good breakfast on bacon, bread and butter, oatmeal and coffee. Miss Oliver's hand is bad; I fear lockjaw and blood-poisoning. The day is damp, foggy, rainy. Attended religious services in the saloon. They were remarkably formal, dry and brief. I think the young M. D. officiated. The fog-horn sounded for an hour or two. Now, 12:15, I, with others, are waiting for dinner. Nearly all well; fog gone; mild, but no sun; people rejoicing because they are nearing New York. Two steamers and five sailing-ships in sight.

In the evening a number of ladies and gentlemen gathered on deck to sing gospel hymns. They sat around Miss Oliver, and her weak voice was heard among the others, and her white face shone in the darkness like phosphorus. We could not see all the singers, and angels seemed to be lending their voices and presence. The occasion was as solemn as a funeral, and I think many considered the poor girl fatally wounded.

Monday, Oct. 3d. Waked about 2:30 in the morning by the awful rattle and roar of the great anchor chains dropping through the iron nostrils of the ship into the great deep. Looking out at the window we find we are at anchor near Sandy Hook. At a distance is anchored another great steamer, which proves to be the Arizona. The lights hanging to her masts look like stars above a distant village. Yonder are lighthouses on the hills of New Jersey.

Daylight is coming and people are getting up, and I hear walking, and talking, and laughing, on the deck above me. I arise and go on deck; the sun is rising; the sea smiles in silver and earth's emerald bosom heaves above bright waters, and the heavens show the sign of the cross. Now we see many ships, large and small. Yes, we are at the beautiful water-gate of one of earth's great cities. A few hours ago we were in darkness, tossing on billows, far from our native hills, and out of reach of the great, busy hemispheres; many hoping and wondering if we should ever again walk the dry lands of earth. Now we see a new day and a new world: oblivion seems to have given birth to these great ships, with their thousands of passengers, and we are all borne in through the Narrows on the wings of the morning.

What wonderful and beautiful things have birth amid darkness, danger, doubt, and apparent oblivion! The beautiful ships coming in out of darkness and billows from unseen lands, made me think of a resurrection.

When I finished the above paragraph we were entering New York's beautiful gateway from the great sea. We stood for a short time at quarantine, until the doctor came aboard of our ship and asked our officers a few questions, and when he found we were generally well and free from contagious diseases, we steamed on up toward the great metropolis of the western hemisphere. We saw the islands and green shores of our dear native land, embellished with fortresses, groves, light-houses, mansions and churches. The lofty and colossal statue of Liberty Enlightening the World was an interesting and very conspicuous feature of the scene, especially for those who were seeing it for the first time.

Now we see New York surrounded by her sister

cities. There, swinging in strength and grandeur above the water, from great city to great city, is seen the most wonderful bridge on earth, while nations cross it, and the ships of all lands sail beneath it. The waters on all sides of us are full of boats, ships and steamers, of many sizes, shapes, colors and nations. Some rock idly on the waves; some spread their white wings as if to reach distant ports; others, with steady breath and pulsation, move forward with passengers and mails from foreign shores, much as to say, "You will make way for me, for I am engaged in a great work upon great waters. I have news and messages from men and nations from beyond the deep blue sea." Others, like floating islands or hotels, with great wheels churning the water into foam, and every now and then lifting up their loud voices, as if hoarse, with excitement and excess, saying, "Ho, there! we come; make room! my people are in a hurry to reach the strand where gay banners of pleasure, fashion, ease, wine and love float above palaces, groves and halls, dedicated to feasting and dancing." Now we see plainly many of the spires, domes, and most lofty buildings of New York. We pass up by Castle Garden and land at "Pier No. 40," where we had waved a "good-bye" to home and friends, that very hot afternoon, nearly three months before.

Soon as our ship was safely moored, the passengers began to descend the portable steps into the Custom House, where we gathered in sections designated by the letters representing our respective names, to wait the coming of our baggage, which must be inspected by government officials before we could depart with it. The hurry, and noise, and jostling, and apparent confusion, and lack of considerate feeling in a Custom House are things to be dreaded by the average man and woman. Here were people of both sexes, and nearly all ages and conditions in life, waiting by their trunks and boxes for an inspecting officer to come and examine the contents of said packages, and if they found things on which they should pay duty, they were charged accordingly. One lady (?) had asked the Stewards on the ship to use her fine cutlery so she could tell the officer it had been in use and thus avoid the duty. The steerage, or emigrant passengers, were taken to "Castle Garden," where so many millions of our foreign brethren have been born, as it were, into this great country. I found my friend, Mr. G——, now nearly well, good-natured as ever. He said: "I had to pay five dollars on the few things I brought over."

Not far off is Miss Oliver, pale, weak, suffering, walking about among trunks, boxes, etc., in too much pain to sit and hardly strength to walk. At last a woman came to examine her luggage At length I learn that I must go to the far end of the building to ask an inspector to come and examine my trunks. I opened my trunks—it was a novel sight to see the wide floor of a dusty rough-looking building strewn with everything near and dear to a traveler. Those trunks revealed great and curious things—things worn and unworn—things necessary, things useful, things ornamental, things common, rich and rare; things literally from land and sea; things present, and things future or memorial.

The officer asked: "Have you anything which should be taxed?" I replied, "I hardly know; you can look; here are some inexpensive jet ornaments, which cousins gave me for my relatives, and a few toys, cheap pictures and books." "Would the jet jewelry come to five dollars?" I said, "probably not." "Well, I think I will pass you. What is in that box?" "My old watch; this one I am wearing is a present to my son." "All right, you may pass free." I began to pack my trunks again, and for safety I took the little box containing my watch from the floor and put it in my pocket. When nearly done packing, I took the box from my side coat-pocket and put it in the trunk, when a man tapped me on the shoulder and said, "I'll take that box." I gave him a surprised look and said, "I guess not" I thought he was a fraud of some kind, but with his thumb he pulled out one of his suspenders from the armhole of his vest, and I saw he was a detective officer in the employ of the government. I was chagrined and annoyed at being suspected and protested mildly and clearly that it had been seen and properly passed by the other officer. Not believing me, he took the box and said, "I will send it to the office at Castle Garden, and you may get it to-morrow there." He also sent for the inspector, and the poor man, pale and nervous, came and also tried to explain. The detective said, "You have got this man, the inspector, into trouble, and he will probably loose his place." I said with much effort to control my varied feelings of pity, anxiety, mortification and, at least a little, resentment at being misbelieved, "I would rather throw the watch into the sea than cause this poor man any trouble." The detective went off with my watch. After a long time I went to look for him, and Mr. G—— came and found me and said, "They want you over where your trunk is." There were several officers consulting and finally one old man in the crowd asked, "Where was the watch made?" They looked and found it was an American watch; the new one, though bought in London, was also an American-made watch. One said, "They are free then." The detective wavered and hesitated, and finally said, "I think I will keep the watch; you may perhaps get it free at headquarters to-morrow." Finally some one asked, "What is your name?" Then I remembered that I had a name and hailed from a great inland city in the Keystone State, and I told them so with some spirit, and began at once to prove it by drawing from my inner coat-pocket, a large envelope from which I took my United States passport, and letters from the Governor, from Congressmen, Senators, Generals, Judges, Capitalists and others, and very soon the detective said, "I think it will be all right to let you take the watch," and as I took the little blue box from his hand I fancied he was much pleased to be rid of it. In all my journeys abroad I had not been annoyed by any kind of Government officials. But this is a free country, and of course it costs a good deal to keep it free. Yes, freedom is like gold, hard to get and hard to hold.

The shipmates were mostly scattered and gone. There, by their baggage, sat M. Fujisawa and his sister, from Japan, little, inoffensive, quiet people, who were on a tour around the world. I stopped to bid them "good-bye." I wondered how Miss Oliver would travel to her lover and brother in far-away Michigan, for some had said, "Remain in a hospital in New York until better," and others said, "Go on to your friends." Knowing the worth of loving relatives in time of disaster, I concluded to see her and her baggage safely on a westward-bound train. While considering what was best to do, a tall and well-dressed young man was seen with Miss Oliver coming toward me. I rejoiced, for I said to myself, "Her lover has come, and my responsibility is removed." Coming nearer she said, "My brother, from Connecticut, Mr. L——." She told him of my humble services, and as he asked Heaven's blessing upon me, tears of pity, suffering and gratitude flowed freely. Shaking hands, we parted, probably to meet no more on earth.

# CHAPTER XLI.

FROM ENGLAND TO WYOMING VALLEY—CONCLUDED.

IN NEW YORK CITY—FIVE HUNDRED THOUSAND PEOPLE IN CARS ON STILTS—CROSSING NORTH RIVER—THE GIANTS RACE THROUGH AUTUMN-CROWNED NEW JERSEY—BRIGHT MOUNTAINS AND FLAMING FURNACES IN PENNSYLVANIA—OH, THE SUNSET!—GAZING, WITH THE FULL MOON, DOWN UPON WYOMING VALLEY—MEET FRIENDS ON WARM HEARTHSTONES—THE WOUNDED GIRL TELLS HER OWN STORY; CROSSES WIDE STATES WHILE SUFFERING, AND FINDS LOVER AND BROTHER; GETS MARRIED—BETTER, BUT NOT WELL—MY TRIP AND ITS HISTORY TERMINATES—A PANORAMA OF GREAT GLORY, FULL OF MUSIC, LOVE AND UNDYING BEAUTY—KIND READER, ADIEU.

After bidding good-bye to shipmates at the Custom House, and ordering my baggage taken to the Pennsylvania railway station, I went to Fordham, in the north of the city, to see relatives. The following day I returned; on my way looking into the great and beautiful Central Park. Think of it! this Park, once rugged farm and woodland, miles above the city, but now with its rocks, and hills, and trees, its fountains, lawns, and lakes, its drives, walks, museums, and monuments, covering two and a-half miles in length by half a mile in width, is literally in the centre of the city, and the great metropolis, with its restless tide of busy humanity, roars and flashes on all sides of it.

I again go upon and over the Brooklyn bridge, endeavoring, if possible, to grasp its magnitude and indelibly photograph its form, beauty and size on my memory.

I came down into the heart of the great city on an elevated railway, a railway lifted up, out of and above the street, and held aloft by a great forest of mighty, iron pillars. A gentleman said, "There are eighteen thousand people at this moment rushing up and down through this city on these elevated railroads. And each day they carry five hundred thousand passengers."

At about 1 p. m. I find my way to the Pennsylvania railroad ferry, and with a crowd of people, am soon on a great ferry-boat plowing the north river toward Jersey City. On the boat I met Mr. R. Scott, of Plymouth, Pa., looking sunbrowned and hearty, also on his way home from England and the British Isles, where he had had a grand and profitable tour. He was the only person I met during the voyage that I had known before. Now we enter the train bound for Wilkes-Barré, and if all is well when the mantle of evening again falls upon the earth, we can look forth from the mountain-top and see the lights gleam in Wyoming valley along the Susquehanna.

Our engine breathes heavily and stretches himself and appears to roll up his sleeves and gird himself for the race. Now he hisses and snorts and roars and rushes along by the sea marsh, by cornfields, through groves, and into and through towns and cities; screeching and thundering; not only demanding the right of way, but commanding that the way be free and unobstructed.

The artist, Frost, has been at work, and we see some of the glories that Autumn throws over the American forest; banners crimson, purple, yellow, golden and glorious float along the hillsides beyond green fields. See the beauty of vine-draped trees in low places! See how the maples blush at the rude kiss of the frost! Other trees, seeing the sign of death, turn pale. See, a thing of beauty! the Stars and Stripes flying over "Menlow Park." Behold the beauty of that hill, crowned with cone-shaped evergreens! See the rustic saw-mill! So different from anything in England! See! yonder are the mountains; the stately steppings of Autumn have made them a camp-ground for angels. Here are girls gathering hickory nuts; beautiful villas among trees; herds of cows in meadows; blue mountains, still and dreamy in the distance. Yonder is a white spire to add charm to the landscape. Now we "race" with the train on the Central Railroad of New Jersey. For a long way we rush side by side, shoulder to shoulder, waving hands and handkerchiefs from train to train.

Yes, this is a great country; room to race in; room to win and room to loose; and if we do not get there we may rest assured that there are enough of our American cousins there to have a good time without us.

Yes, this is "home," for I see peach orchards, turkeys, pumpkins, buckwheat and corn. Now, I hear the free, off-hand salutations of Americans: "How are you, Mr. Hare? quite a stranger! How are your folks?"

Wonderful age! A man hands me a paper and I read: "Telegraph messages can be sent from this train while in motion." I expect to see Americans within a few years traveling ten miles a minute, and when for a trifling sum you may see and hear all that is going on in this world of ours, when Edison and others have learned to drive a four-in-hand, composed of water, air, gravity and electricity.

Here are Phillipsburg and Easton, and the mountains of dear old Pennsylvania. Now we rush up along the Lehigh, through iron-working towns. See the furnaces and foundries brilliant with streams and fountains of liquid iron! See that saw revolving in the centre of a shower of red-hot iron! The ease with which the saw cuts the red-hot iron proves the the value of improving opportunities. See what a glorious amber sunset! beyond the green isles and gappy hills, which seem to uphold banners of many colors. Ah, there is Slatington. The brakeman calls out, "Slatingtin!" I said to myself, "That is a bad pronunciation for a place that has slate for sale. He should have said Slatingdone. Here is Mauch Chunk. Yes, Mauch Chunk, modest little Chunk, you can beat great, roaring London in one thing—that is mountains.

We pass Penn Haven Junction, Hickory Run, Tannery, White Haven, Moosehead, Glen Summit and Fairview, and as the glorious full moon rose over bold Penobscot, I gazed once more into Wyoming valley, and saw her many lights of oil, gas and electricity.

At about 8:30 p. m. I stood on the pavements of Wilkes-Barré, and an hour later greeted my sister and family in Kingston, and for some days the time was pleasantly passed in seeing and meeting kind friends and familiar scenes.

Naturally the reader will ask what became of Miss Oliver, the young lady with the wounded hand. The following letters will explain:

> Iron Mountain, Michigan,
> October 14, 1887.

Mr. L——: Dear Friend:—Just a few lines in answer to your kind letter, which we got yesterday. I was glad to hear you got home all right. I got here on Thursday about 10 a. m. I should have been here on Wednesday, but after I parted from my brother at New York, I had the company of that young man called Hackett, you remember him, he is from Ohio, but when I got to where he had to get out, he would make me get out with him, as my hand was so bad, and I had a doctor there. He gave me something to paint my arm, as it was swollen so, and poulticed it, so I started again the same night and got to Chicago the next day about 11 a. m., and I had to stop there until 9 p. m. I was so ill when I got there I did not know

what to do, and I did not know anyone; but I got one
of the girls, that keep the waiting-room clean, to get
me a cup of tea, and I lay on the lounge until it was
time for me to start again. But there was a nice young
gentleman and lady going the same way as me, so
they were very good to me, and did all they could for
me. They came as far as where I had to change cars, so
when I got out to change, Fred was there to meet me;
but they were all surprised to see my hand and arm. My
arm was as large as three. They got two doctors and
they took all the skin off of the middle of my hand, and
then he scraped it and lanced it. You would be surprised to see it. I cannot tell you one-half I have suffered since I saw you. I should have wrote to you but I
only had one hand, and I hope you will be able to read
it, as I cannot use a pen very well, and Fred is at work
and I cannot get him to write. Dear friend, I hope in
a few days my hand will be better, as I cannot do anything yet. But they are all very kind to me, and I have
had three different doctors. My brother, that you
saw, did not think it was half so bad, as I did not show
it to him. He is troubled very much about it, but I
hope, by God's help, it will soon get better. I thank
you very much for your prayers for me, and I hope
God will bless you for your kindness to me, and all the
other friends I found, as I can never pay them. Mrs.
Hackett was so good to me when I went to her house
with her son. I must thank you very much for the
paper. I have read some of it. I hope you will forgive this scribble, as I have only one hand, and my
brother is busy. I hope to be able to let you know

that my hand is well, soon. Many thanks for your kindness to me. May God bless you.

I remain yours,
K. OLIVER.

IRON MOUNTAIN, Michigan,<br>November 14th, 1887.

Mr. L——: DEAR FRIEND:—After a long time I now answer your most welcome letter and was glad to hear by it that you was well. I must thank you for the papers you have sent me; I received one yesterday. I hope you will forgive me for not writing to you before, but I have been rather busy and had too many to write to since my hand has been better. It is a good deal better, but not quite well. I can't do much yet. My fingers are still stiff. I cannot close my hand. I hope it will get all right again after awhile, but sometimes I think I shall never have the full use of it like I had before, but I am living in hopes that after some time it may come all right again. Dear friend, I must tell you now that I am married. I was married a week ago Saturday, and it is much more comfortable in my own house than in other people's. I cannot do much house-work, but with Fred's help we have managed pretty well so far. My poor, dear mother is in a dreadful way about my hand, but I think it will relieve her when she hears it is much better. I have got nice company, as my brother comes to see me very often, and my sister's husband and Fred's brother, so there is some one to speak to from home, and I had a young man come to see me last week; he just come from England, and he was from the same place as me. I was very glad to see him. He is a Bible Christian preacher. You remember my brother that met me at New York? He has gone to a place called Cornwall. He has got a shop of his own, so I hope now he has started a business of his own, he will get on all right. He was out of work some time. I hope you will forgive me for not writing before. I had a letter from Mrs. Hackett. She is anxious to know how my hand is. I have got a nice little house and am very happy in it. I have just sent a letter to Miss Walker. I hope you may forgive this scribble, and may God bless you. I remain yours, sincerely,

K. ENNES.

P. S.—I must thank you again for all your kindness to me. I wonder how Mr. Grimble is getting on. I often think of you all. K. E.

IRON MOUNTAIN, Michigan, }
August 20th, 1888 }

MR. LINSKILL: DEAR FRIEND:—I am almost ashamed to write you after keeping you waiting so long for a letter. You must not think that I have forgotten you, and all your kindness to me. If I neglect writing I often think of you. I was somewhat surprised when Fred came home and brought me so many papers, but more so when I saw my name in them. I have read most of them. I must thank you for taking so much trouble to send them up to me. It is more than I deserve. I suppose you are thinking me very unkind in not letting you know how my hand was getting on. I am thankful to say it is getting on good so far, but I don't think I shall ever be able to use it as well as my other. I feel it pain if I lift anything with it, and I have not got any strength in two of my fingers. I can not close them more than with my other hand, and then I have not strength to keep them closed. But, I am thankful it is so well as it is. I hope this will find you enjoying good health; as for myself, I have been very sick, but am glad to say I am much better. Fred is well. My brother is gone from here, and also Fred's and my brother-in-law. I feel the want of them. I have not had any answer from the letter I sent Mrs. Hackett. I hope they are well. I hear from Miss Walker sometimes. She was quite well when I last heard from her. I was just thinking, it is nearly twelve months since I left home. The time goes by quickly. I think it don't seem so long as that since we were on board ship together. I shall be glad to hear from you when you can spare time. Hoping this will find you well, with my best wishes and respects, I remain your true friend,

KATE ENNIS.

The reader will see that the above letters tell the story more clearly than I would have told it.

My travels in lands beyond the sea came to a safe and pleasant termination, and as this volume nears its finish, my trip passes before me like a grand panorama, and I again see the broad, green meadows, the fields of golden wheat and barley, the wide, high moorlands covered with blooming heather that looked like purple snow; the green mountains of England, Wales and Ireland, and the dark, conical, lofty and jagged mountains of Scotland. I seem again to dash for miles through the dark, resounding foundations of mountains, and under cities where stand mighty buildings of granite, and vast crowds of human beings walk and talk and do business over our heads. Again the tireless horse of steam leaps with us over rivers and canals, across wide valleys, where old and stately cities sit apparently guarding gray and solemn cathedrals, massive castles and lofty monuments, and parks full of fountains, flowers and statues; places where kings had been born, crowned beheaded and buried; over fields where great battles have been fought, and through fields that have been plowed and reaped for two thousand years. We run through deep, ivy-grown cuts in rock and gazed to where mansions and palaces stood decked in green, fragrant with flowers, and where gray ruins stand among lordly trees; over high bridges where hamlets lay at our feet, while quite near, the restless bosom of the sea heaves foamy waves on the white sands and shakes a thousand sails along the shores. I walk and ride by miles of columned buildings and others with spires, domes and towers, and gaze upon many thousands of fine paintings and see exhibitions where the pride, wealth, art, beauty and enterprise of a great nation seemed at stake to please and instruct the world; where shining fountains of water and fire play to show the glories of gilded lawns, lakes and fairy-like structures; where thousands of lovely women and brave, handsome men gathered to see handsome things; where plaided and bonneted Highlanders, with bagpipes and drums and flutes, marched up highways cut in rock, while their ravishing music echoed above the battlements of ancient castles and fluttered down over grand, proud cities: again I see the tally-ho coach drawn by four white horses, with its score of gaily-dressed young ladies and gentlemen, and as they roll through a street in queenly Manchester, their long silver horns, graceful as the neck of a crane, sound forth sweet, cheering notes of music: again I walk where great guns, ships and engines are being made, and again sail over waters green, blue, purple and white, and see tall cliffs of chalk, light-houses and flocks of white sea-birds. Once more I walk where soldiers encamp, and where ladies and chilren in gay costumes walk, sit or play on the broad, white strand of the sounding sea. I remember the moonlight night when fair cities slept and the river gleamed and long rows of tall poplars stood in beauty as our train thundered through a populous and peaceful realm; and finally, the many kind friends and dear relatives, who treated me with such marked respect, hospitality and affection; but I must now bid them and you, kind reader, adieu.

www.ingramcontent.com/pod-product-compliance
Lightning Source LLC
Chambersburg PA
CBHW030602300426
44111CB00009B/1080